Becoming a Team
Achieving a Goal

New - 131 $
Used - 126 $ -
48 $ - 27 $

THOMSON

SOUTH-WESTERN

Australia · Canada · Mexico · Singapore · Spain · United Kingdom · United States

THOMSON

SOUTH-WESTERN

Becoming a Team, Achieving a Goal
Roy C. Herrenkohl

VP/Editorial Director:
Jack W. Calhoun

VP/Editor-in-Chief:
Michael P. Roche

Sr. Publisher:
Melissa Acuña

Executive Editor:
John Szilagyi

Developmental Editor:
Vicki Hunter Ross

Marketing Manager:
Jacquelyn Carrillo

Production Editor:
Amy McGuire

Media Developmental Editor:
Kristen Meere

Media Production Editor:
Karen Schaffer

Manufacturing Coordinator:
Rhonda Utley

Production House:
Argosy

Printer:
West Publishing
Eagan, MN

Design Project Manager:
Bethany Casey

Internal Designer:
Bethany Casey

Cover Designer:
Bethany Casey

Cover Images:
© SolusImages

COPYRIGHT © 2004
by South-Western, part of the
Thomson Corporation.
South-Western, Thomson,
and the Thomson logo are
trademarks used herein under
license.

Printed in the United States
of America
1 2 3 4 5 06 05 04 03

ISBN: 0-324-17788-7

Library of Congress Control
Number:
2003105219

For permission to use material
from this text or product,
contact us by
Tel (800) 730-2214
Fax (800) 730-2215
http://www.thomsonrights.com

For more information
contact South-Western,
5191 Natorp Boulevard,
Mason, Ohio 45040.
Or you can visit our Internet
site at:
http://www.swlearning.com

To Ellen,

with whom I have learned much about working together to achieve a goal

Brief Contents

Contents

Preface

It's hard to miss the fact that the interest in teams and in teamwork is growing. A recent *Wall Street Journal*/Harris Interactive survey[1] on qualities in business graduates sought by corporate recruiters ranked teamwork and interpersonal skills high on the list. Academic institutions that encourage students to develop these qualities were likewise given high marks. Look around. Corporate America has made its position on teamwork known in countless op-eds and in countless above-the-fold stories in the business press that stress the very, very collaborative correlations between people, productivity, and profits. But when Jim Simms, CEO of well-known high technology consulting firm Cambridge Technology Partners, addressed faculty and students at Lehigh University and reported that out of every ten technically qualified individuals interviewed for a position by his company, only one had the social skills needed to qualify for this team,[2] we decided to act. We couldn't ignore that 10-to-1 ratio any longer.

Team-based management places enormous responsibility in the hands of a myriad body of teams, all charged with the mission of pursuing product quality in the interest of increased customer satisfaction. This poses a challenge to many young, technically qualified individuals who find that working in and with teams seldom unfolds as planned.[3] The challenge that arises from being required to coordinate one's work with the work of others and to have one's own performance inextricably tied to the performances of others, as Jim Simms pointedly remarked, is a losing proposition for most.

Hiring workers for both their technical and social competencies contrasts with earlier recruiting standards, when firms primarily sought technical skills, such as those related to accounting, engineering, architectural design, biological research, or software design. Possessing relevant skills and, it was hoped, innovativeness in using them, a worker could expect to be told *what* his or her specific job was. The job was then performed with supervisory guidance and with a minimum of interaction with others. Completely consistent with this view, our educational system paralleled this way of working, in that teachers told students *what* to do and student levels of proficiency were judged by how well they did it.

What we demanded of workers began to change in the 1980s. Under the impetus of management strategies such as *reengineering, quality improvement,* and *lean production,* layers of managers who had once provided one-to-one supervision of workers' activities were greatly reduced. Increased responsibility for performance was transferred to teams and *team-based* management was born. The unit of production is no longer the individual but, rather, "the team." This perspective presupposes that there are multiple paths by which a team can reach a goal. But beyond merely reaching a goal, a team is to find—given its goal, its resources, and its environment—the most efficient path to that goal.

This change of direction from direct supervision toward team-based management continues into the present decade and has generalized to many fields of endeavor. Several results have occurred; some more obvious than others. First, there is the demand by business and industry, as described above, for social competence. College graduates who lack the relevant skills required to work in teams are not as desirable as others who, through course work and other experience, are so prepared. A second implication centers on academic institutions. To teach teamwork skills, academic disciplines, especially business disciplinary areas, are shifting as well. This means that students are learning about accounting, architecture, engineering, journalism, and human services as members of teams rather than as individuals. In this new mode of teaching, however, students are often placed in teams without addressing either how successful teams perform or how to correct problems when a team is not performing well. Too often the assumption is that students know instinctively how to work as a team, that teamwork is already a built-in skill. Participation in athletics is often cited as evidence. If students cannot work in a team, it is commonly thought that there is something wrong with that particular team or with those team members. This assumption fails to consider that almost all of a student's prior education emphasized individual performance. It also fails to consider the differences between athletic teams and nonathletic teams—the amount of coaching and practice that is part of performing as an effective athletic team being but one example. Consequently, students commonly become anxious and frustrated when placed in team contexts. They may fully recognize that their team is performing poorly, but they do not know what to do about it. Not infrequently, they fall back on what they do know—doing the tasks by themselves. The better students get team tasks done, but not without considerable residual anger.

There is a better way.

TOOLS FOR A NEW WAY OF WORKING

Much as they are expected to learn mathematics skills, English composition skills, accounting skills, or engineering skills, students should be expected to develop teamwork skills and be given an appropriate level of coaching throughout the teamwork process. *Becoming a Team, Achieving a Goal* addresses this mandate and represents the end of a journey that began when a colleague, Tom Judson, asked me to consult with Computing Devices, International, on developing a procedure for assessing *employee empowerment*. We developed an assessment procedure, and in the process, I realized that empowerment makes little difference for a poorly functioning team.

Related to this experience, as a university administrator, I was continually hearing from business executives that students who graduated from Lehigh were having difficulties, in spite of their technical excellence, working in teams. I was also experiencing difficulties working with my fellow administrators to define a goal, plan a strategy to achieve the goal, and then implement it. Therefore, when I returned to full-time teaching, I decided to teach a course on teamwork. Keith Gardiner, director of Lehigh's Manufacturing Systems Engineering Center, encouraged me. Out of discussions with Keith and others, a series of visits was arranged by William D'Arcy, at Ford Electronics Division (now Visteon) in Lansdale, Pennsylvania; by Russell Erath, at Lockheed Martin in Binghamton, New York; by Alan Prichard, at several Boeing Commercial

Aircraft Divisions in the Seattle, Washington area; by Rhonda White, at Harley-Davidson in York, Pennsylvania; by Ross Born, at Just Born Candy Co., Bethlehem, Pennsylvania; and by H. A. Wagner, at Air Products and Chemicals in Trexlertown, Pennsylvania. I also participated in a week-long workshop, "Building and Sustaining High-Performance Work Teams," conducted by David Miller & Associates, Orlando, Florida.

As I began to teach this new course, I looked for text material that beginners to the subject could manage. Although much literature exists going back several decades on group dynamics—and more recently, on teamwork—most of it addresses specific, often technical, issues. Failing to find an accessible text on the topic, I decided to write *Becoming a Team, Achieving a Goal*. A proposal for the book was submitted to South-Western/Thomson Learning, and after discussions, John Szilagyi and Vicki Ross became the very supportive editors for the book.

BECOMING A TEAM—An Accessible and Applied Plan

A team's work is achieving its goal. A team is effective when its functioning supports its goal achievement process. To achieve its goal, a team's members, as a group, need both the requisite technical skills and the relevant social and organizational skills. A team can be effective if its members understand how a team functions, know how to coordinate the features of this functioning, and can identify and remove barriers to goal achievement. The premise of *Becoming a Team* is that these capabilities can be learned, but to do so requires *thought, experimentation,* and *practice*.

Thought

Becoming a Team takes it as a given that students are relatively new to group processes and experiential learning, so this four-part text begins by building up a common language for understanding teamwork. "Introducing Teamwork" defines teams and teamwork and presents a broad systems perspective on how teams function, including the "input, throughput, output" model of systems theory. "Initiating Teamwork" examines the "input" aspect of teamwork. It considers creating a team, team goals, and member skills and behavior styles. "The Teamwork Process" examines team "throughput." It begins by examining team planning, then considers team leadership, team task performance, coordination of member activities, satisfaction of member motivation, a team's relationship to its environment, and team evaluation and feedback. The final section examines three results, or "outputs," under the heading "The Products of Teamwork." The first is the result of a team's reaching its goal, its product. This is followed by an analysis of team development and learning. Finally, the meaning of team effectiveness is considered. At the conclusion of *Becoming a Team*, there is a brief summary overview of the text.

Experimentation

Without the chance to actively experiment as teams, any course in teamwork would be a dull business. *Becoming a Team* provides lots of opportunities to try out productive behaviors, take risks, voice opinions, delegate tasks, and take teamwork beyond the merely conceptual. Each chapter opens with specific real-world challenges that help students structure team roles, resolve conflict, provide feedback, and engage in a variety of high-impact "roles and routines" assessments. Assessments and evaluations are also part of *Becoming a Team*'s mix of materials (see Appendix 1), further integrating the importance of self-observation into the course and facilitating the recognition and reward of group performance.

Practice

Hands-on exercises are included in every chapter to illustrate major concepts. As part of permanent or ad hoc teams, students take skills inventories, identify barriers to team functioning, take part in formal "dialogues," and explore a model of team effectiveness. All exercises have been designed to help students develop a repertoire of skills needed for effective collaboration. The exercises require that students be formed into teams, preferably teams of five members. In my experience, using teams composed of the same members to perform the exercises enables team members to experience the process of team development over the sessions of the course.

ANCILLARY SUPPORT

For Instructors

Instructor's Manual

The Instructor's Manual for *Becoming a Team* furnishes aids that provide strong support for a collective learning experience. The manual includes suggestions for generating team involvement in discussing and learning text material, assessment procedures to elicit discussion of issues that are difficult to identify or address, and suggestions for gaining and sustaining involvement in the exercises. The Instructor's Manual also includes a section describing variations in class team development that instructors can expect.

For Instructors and Students

Website

A companion website (http://herrenkohl.swlearning.com) includes the Instructor's Manual (downloadable), "Management News" (updated regularly), and a link to "TextChoice." TextChoice is the home of Thomson Learning's online digital content that provides a fast, easy way for instructors to create their own learning materials.

ACKNOWLEDGMENTS

The book's preparation has benefited immeasurably from the reactions and feedback of students in my courses during the last five years. More recently, Christopher Cunningham, while doing his own research on team collective efficacy, reviewed and commented on several chapters. Many other reviewers read and offered insightful suggestions that helped shape the manuscript. I am grateful for their comments:

Bud Baker, Wright State University

Melissa Baucus, Xavier University

Wendy S. Becker, University at Albany

Ronda Callister, Utah State University

Jack D. Cichy, Davenport University

Max E. Douglas, Indiana State University

Joe Downing, Southern Methodist University

Sonia Goltz, Michigan Technological University

Willie E. Hopkins, Colorado State University

Fred Kiesner, Loyola Marymount University

Giuseppe Labianca, Emory University

Joseph T. Martelli, The University of Findlay

Mark A. Mone, University of Wisconsin–Milwaukee

Edwin Mosher, Laramie County Community College

Cliff Olson, Southern Adventist University

Bruce N. Peterson, Sonoma State University

John E. Sawyer, University of Delaware

Louise Sellaro, Youngstown State University

Diane Withrow Sinkinson, Cape Fear Community College

William L. Sparks, Queens University

Thomas Li-Ping Tang, Middle Tennessee State University

S. Stephen Vitucci, Tarleton State University

Mary J. Waller, University of Illinois

J. L. Waltman, Eastern Michigan University

Timothy Wiedman, Thomas Nelson Community College

Vincent Zocco, Regis University

Finally, members of my family—my sons, Eric, Todd, and Joshua, and their partners, Kelly, Leslie, and Joy—have helped immensely by suggesting relevant material and examples and by reading portions of the text. Ellen Herrenkohl, especially, encouraged my doing the project, read and discussed chapters, and endured my times of stress. Without her support, the book would not have happened.

To all who have helped, supported, and encouraged, please accept my sincere gratitude.

NOTES

1. R. Alsop (2001, April 30), Top Business Schools (A Special Report)—Why They Won: A Close-up Look at the Top-rated Schools, *The Wall Street Journal*, New York: Dow Jones and Company, and National Public Radio, *Morning Edition*, Burrell Information Services, Livingston, NJ.

2. Speech at Lehigh University by Jim Simms, CEO of Cambridge Technology Partners.

3. Interviews conducted by the author in several manufacturing companies.

About the Author

Roy C. Herrenkohl is distinguished university service professor in the Department of Sociology and Anthropology at Lehigh University. He joined Lehigh's faculty in 1966 after completing a Ph.D. in social psychology at New York University. Prior to that, he had attended Washington and Lee University where he received a BA, Reading University (England) where he studied philosophy and sociology, and Union Theological Seminary in New York City. He was employed with the W. T. Grant Foundation, initially as a research assistant and later as associate secretary. At Lehigh, Dr. Herrenkohl directed the Center for Social Research (1974–1990) and was Vice-Provost for Research and Dean of Graduate Studies (1990–1996). He returned to full-time teaching in 1996 and began his research on teamwork and team functioning. He also conducts research on family (another type of team) dynamics and child-rearing practices.

The Challenge
Introducing Teamwork

Performing as a team differs from individual performance. Team members work together as a unit and are rewarded for their joint effort. In the case of individual performance, individuals work "on their own" and are rewarded individually. To work effectively, a team becomes a dynamic system of interrelated parts performing in an environment that provides the team resources to be used to pursue its goal. When a team achieves its goal, the product of that achievement is returned to the environment in return for its support. Effective teams carry out this process efficiently and ineffective teams do not. Members of effective teams experience satisfaction in their team's achievement even though becoming a team requires change.

chapter 1

Introducing Teamwork

In 1953, a team led by Sir Edmund Hillary reached the peak of Mt. Everest.[1] In 1967, a surgical team led by Dr. Michael DeBakey was the first to conduct a heart bypass operation using an artificial heart pump.[2] In 1970, after an explosion in space, a team of engineers developed a strategy for repairing Apollo XIII sufficiently to enable it to return to earth safely.[3] In July 1994 the Prineville (Oregon) Hot Shots, an elite team of forest firefighters, completed fighting a major fire in Oregon and were complimented on "a job well done."[4] In each of these accomplishments, the term **team** or a synonym is prominent.

Teams are used to address complex, often dangerous, problems that require multiple skills to be coordinated in order to reach a goal. One person may take the lead, but teamwork is considered essential to the overall accomplishment. An assumption is that capability is added when individuals are organized as a team. A team coordinates diverse skills, knowledge, and perspectives in an effort to achieve its goal. The interest of business and industry in teamwork is in part due to a team's potential to address complex and unusual situations on the spot with constructive decisions and timely implementation of the decisions so as to achieve a goal.

> *"A team coordinates diverse skills, knowledge, and perspectives in an effort to achieve its goal."*

Teams, however, are not always successful. Other Everest expeditions have resulted in disaster and death.[5] One explanation for the 1986 *Challenger* space shuttle disaster was the failure of an engineering team to interpret correctly and communicate adequately data indicating the vulnerability of the *Challenger* rocket motor gaskets to low temperatures.[6] Teams of specialists are working to determine what went wrong with the latest shuttle disaster. Medical teams, such as those involved in experimental gene transplant therapy, have experienced failure.[7] The Prineville Hot Shots had a tragic failure late in July 1994 after their Oregon success. They were called to Colorado to help fight the Storm King Mountain fire, and nine members were trapped in a flare-up and killed.[8]

Failure occurs for various reasons. For example, the challenges posed by a team's environment might be too difficult. A team's goal might be poorly defined or a team might be diverted from its goal. Communication, among team members or between the team and its environment, might be inadequate. A team might have been assigned a goal better suited to individual performance. A team might lack the skill and knowledge needed to reach its goal or fail to plan and coordinate its activities. A team might fail to keep track of where it is on the path to its goal, or its goal may result in a product of poor quality that is rejected.

What are the ingredients that give a team its presumed advantage in achieving a goal? How does a team fail to realize that advantage? How does teamwork that transcends individual capability come about? To begin an examination of these questions, which is the focus of this book, consider first *what* teams are, what they *do*, and *how* they do it.

TYPES OF TEAMS

Many activities are associated with teams.[9] *Athletic teams* consist of specialists who coordinate their activities according to a set of rules and seek to score points or to prevent an opposing team from scoring points. *Musical ensembles* consist of instrumentalists who coordinate their activities to perform a piece of music in an aesthetically pleasing manner. *Surgical teams* are comprised of medical specialists who perform complex medical procedures aimed at improving health. *Human service teams* are made up of specialists who coordinate services to satisfy individual or societal needs. *Software development teams* involve computer scientists who design systems to solve problems or to store and retrieve information. *Manufacturing teams* include technically skilled individuals who coordinate their activities to produce an artifact.

Most of us feel that we know what teamwork is. We see it in athletics and on TV when a team is assigned to deal with an emergency of some type; we hear it discussed by businesspeople, and we experience it in the classroom. Of course we know what teamwork is. But do we? Is the teamwork we observe in a college basketball game the same as the teamwork of a surgical team or of a business management team? Are the dynamics operating in a team that has worked or played together for many months the same as the dynamics of a team whose members have known each other for only an hour?

Consider the difference between an athletic team and a management team. An athletic team has a goal of scoring points in order to win. It can be high performing, often because its members possess talent, but always because the team has a set of strategies (often called "plays") that are practiced until the team can execute them precisely. A management team also has a goal, for example, increasing the company's market share. It is high-performing because it can take a rather undefined situation, create a plan, and then implement it. Both types of teams use strategies; however, these strategies differ considerably in how they are developed and applied.

These illustrations suggest that different teams can do quite different things, but the performance issues are, to some degree, similar. What are these performance issues? To answer this question, we begin with a more precise definition of teamwork.

DEFINING TEAMWORK

What is teamwork? In the simplest terms a team is a group of interacting individuals with skills, sometimes quite specialized, who coordinate their activities to achieve a mutually agreed-on goal.[10] Analyzing this in more detail, a team consists of **interacting individuals**. Central to this interaction is **communication**, often over a span of time. If this were all that were involved, individuals sitting in a lounge, talking would be considered a team. However, members of a team have a **mutual goal**. They interact for a purpose and consider the interaction meaningful because of their purpose. Psychologically, they are a team because they are aware of themselves as cooperatively pursuing their goal. From this mutual awareness develops their **perception of membership**. Members have a collective perception of their unity and seek to act in a unitary manner toward the environment in which their team functions. Furthermore, as members they have impressions of each other that are distinct enough for them to react to each other as individuals.

"members of a team have a mutual goal"

Team members, cooperatively interacting in the interests of achieving a goal, are aware of their **interdependence**. This means that they recognize that an action by one member affects other members, and events that affect one, affect all. They share a common fate. Interdependence also fosters **mutual influence**. This means that members interact with one another in such a manner that each member influences and is influenced by every other member. Relationships among team members are also **structured**. To facilitate its goal seeking, a team has its members assume one or more roles, such as leader. It also develops a set of standards or norms that regulate team and member behavior, at least in matters of consequence to the team. Individuals also join a team to *satisfy personal needs* through their joint association. Satisfaction of individuals' needs depends in large measure on the *nature of the relationships* among a team's members.

"Individuals also join a team to satisfy personal needs through their joint association."

Change characterizes a team's pursuit of its goal. A team's functioning changes as the team becomes better organized and practiced in its actions or as it becomes more disorganized and less adept in its actions. It does not remain static. As a team performs, members' ability to perform as team members changes as do their perceptions of the team's goal, of each other, of the team, and of the team's environment. Team member relationships also change as they become more or less relaxed and coordinated. A team's environment changes, requiring the team to make adjustments. Effective teamwork possesses a fluidity that makes improved performance possible but also makes deterioration possible as well. A team is a "system" of interdependent features that is always in the process of becoming.

TEAMS AS SYSTEMS

Teams are frequently viewed as systems.[11] This means several things. First, a team is a total social organization that is capable of acting as a singular entity in pursuing a goal. For example, an athletic team, a design team, or a musical ensemble each acts as a unit to achieve its goal. Second, a team performs in an environment, interacts with its environment, and must periodically adjust to its environment. For example, an athletic team plays before spectators on a field with referees. A design team works in a business organization and reports to a supervisor or manager who represents the organization. A musical ensemble plays before an audience in a concert hall with a conductor who directs the flow of music. Third, a team is comprised of interrelated parts referred to as "subsystems" that are the means by which it moves toward its goal. For example, an athletic team consists of different "positions" that perform different tasks in a game. A design team has members with different design-related skills, all of which are equally necessary to the development of a new design. Similarly, a musical ensemble is made up of musicians who play different instruments required to perform a piece of music. Fourth, a team takes resources (inputs) from its environment, uses them to proceed through a series of activities to its goal, and finally achieves its goal (produces a product). A team's *product* represents the achievement of its goal. Its product can be a manufactured item, a report, a completed theatrical performance, or a medical service.[12]

A team is *dynamic* in three senses: in pursuing its goal, in relating to its environment, and in its subparts or subsystems relating to each other. To understand how a team system does its work, these three aspects of teamwork are considered next.

A Team and Its Goal

A team system's direction is established and maintained by its members' attending to their team's purpose, that is, its goal. Examples of team goals are to win a game, to prepare a report, or to manufacture a product. Teams that achieve their goal are in one sense successful. Teams that lose their direction and do not achieve their goal are not successful. Closely related to a team's achieving its goal is its vision of the significance of the achievement. This vision is, for example, a team's expectations for its report's quality and the impact the report will have on the organization. To actualize a challenging, engaging vision for its product, a team must reach its goal, that is, produce a product, but do so in a manner that realizes its vision for the product and satisfies its customer (the recipient of the product) at the same time. Figure 1.1 depicts this process.

Human systems, including teams, have *multiple paths* by which to reach their goals. There is no one best strategy.[13] One challenge for a team is to find the path to its goal that is both most efficient and most satisfying to its members. Addressing this challenge requires planning. A team's plan is a mutual agreement about how to proceed and how to keep its goal clearly in focus. One reason that work teams are viewed favorably by business is the belief that those working as a team are better suited than individual supervisors alone to identify an efficient, satisfying path to a goal.

> *"Teams that lose their direction and do not achieve their goal are not successful."*

A Team and Its Environment

Systems can be either open or closed to their environment. **Open systems**, in contrast to closed systems, interact with and are dependent on their environment. They can also have an effect on their environment. Human systems are open. For example, humans are open to the air, to being rained on, and to being affected in other ways by their environment. To control the effects of their environment, humans build houses and carry on activities in quasi-sheltered settings. Teams are also open systems that must work out a relationship with their environments.[14] Figure 1.2 depicts the teamwork environment.

Distinct advantages accrue when a system is open to its environment. Resource *inputs*, such as people, equipment, and information, are available. These inputs enable a team to perform its work. For example, a team charged with implementing new computer software, but lacking relevant skills among its members, can seek training from outside the team. This adds to the team's resources. Information inputs are also accessible to an open system. For example, a team, working on a project, receives an unexpected call from a superior saying that part of the team's project is needed two days earlier than previously expected. The team revises its work plan to meet the deadline. In making this adjustment, the usefulness of the team's product increases with positive results for the team such as rewards and added resources.

FIGURE 1.1
The Teamwork Process

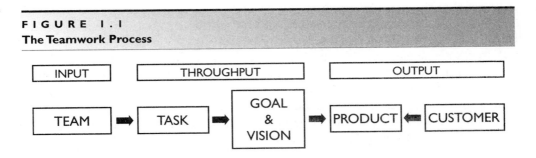

FIGURE 1.2
The Teamwork Environment

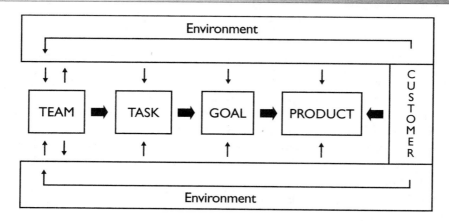

> *"Complete openness to the environment can destabilize a team's activities and divert the team's attention from its goal."*

There is a need, however, for a team to control openness to its environment. A team must protect its activities and preserve the relationships among its members. Complete openness to the environment can destabilize a team's activities and divert the team's attention from its goal. For example, a team that chooses a public location in which to prepare a report may find that distractions divert the group's attention and slow progress. Working in a more secluded location allows the team to be more productive. A team is responsible for balancing its need to shelter its activities from diversions and its need to be open to its environment for both resources and feedback.

A Team and Its Subsystems

A team system proceeds along its chosen path toward its goal and the realization of its vision by means of its **throughput processes**. These are depicted in Figure 1.3. These involve the functioning of each subsystem and relationships among the subsystems. Examples are members who cooperate in performing different subtasks that when effectively coordinated comprise the team's overall task performance process. Coordination of these subtasks is facilitated by members' cooperation. A team's leadership facilitates its throughput processes by assisting in the development of an effective plan, by facilitating implementation of the plan, by encouraging evaluation of each aspect of the process, and by negotiating with the environment about resources, about the team's product, and about rewards and subsequent resources for the team.[15]

Interdependence characterizes the relationship between system subparts or features. Interdependence occurs when a team's members mutually accept their team's goal and agree on a path to that goal. Their individual commitment to the team's goal engenders interdependent relationships among subsystem features. Interdependence means that what happens in or to one subsystem feature affects other features. These features can be considered from two perspectives. One is the

F I G U R E 1 . 3
Team System Throughput Processes

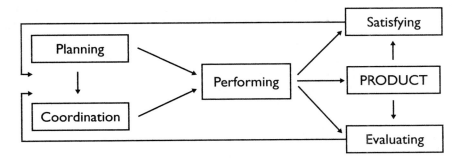

team members themselves. When interdependence exists, the actions of one member can affect the actions of other members. For example, a team member who is upset or dissatisfied by another member's actions can affect other members and their performance. A second feature is subprocesses of the throughput process. For example, failure to monitor coordination among team member activities can result in undetected, often negative, changes and, as a result, performance declines.[16]

A team system tends to become disorganized unless effort is exerted to enhance its organization. For example, product defects occur if quality is not attended to. Member dissatisfaction arises if members' needs and concerns are not addressed. Interpersonal conflict occurs if ways are not found to maintain cooperation and remove sources of conflict. Overall effectiveness decreases if subprocesses are not monitored and appropriate adjustments made to improve effectiveness. The tendency to disorganization and ineffectiveness can only be reversed by increasing emphasis on the goal and by added effort to improve the goal achievement process. Broadly, this means improving efficiency through enhancing interdependence.

Structure in social interactions aids coordination. For example, team members may be observed to speak to each other frequently, occasionally, or not at all. If, over time, member A speaks frequently with member C and only occasionally with member B, and A speaks only with D, who does not speak with any of the other members, a communication structure can be said to exist in the group. This structure has A at the center of the interactions and, as will be shown later, in a position of power. B and C are somewhat less central in the structure. One implication of such a structure for a team is that, for example, a team leader who is at the center of the team's communication network is in the best position to facilitate a team's activities.[17]

Information inputs, sometimes called *feedback,* help a team to maintain its direction and improve its functioning. These are signals about reactions from a team's environment or from the team system about its functioning. **Positive**

> *"Interdependence occurs when a team's members mutually accept their team's goal and agree on a path to that goal."*

> *"A team system tends to become disorganized unless effort is exerted to enhance its organization."*

> *"Without feed-*
> *back a system*
> *can expend*
> *resources and*
> *not make*
> *progress."*

feedback tells a team that it is proceeding in the correct direction and at an acceptable level of quality. For example, a customer who is pleased with a team's product provides feedback that confirms the team's direction. **Negative feedback** tells a team that something is wrong. It enables a system to identify and correct inadequacies. Without feedback a system can expend resources and not make progress. For example, a team that is informed that a customer has cancelled its contract might begin to make changes in an effort to win the contract back. A direct question to the customer, however, could show that the problem was timeliness of delivery. Knowing this, a more focused and energy efficient remedy can be developed.[18] Chapter 9 discusses at greater length feedback and its importance for effective teamwork.

Open systems both change and remain relatively constant in character. In general, any threat that could disrupt the system's character is countered by forces aimed at restoring the system to its original state. A challenge for a team is to achieve and maintain stability without limiting its flexibility to improve its performance. For example, a team that has previously had efficient planning meetings begins to have meetings that are longer and longer with relatively little being accomplished. Some members want to establish rules about how long meetings should be. Other members want to discuss why the meetings have lengthened. The discussion reveals that fewer members are preparing for the meetings. Knowing this, members agree to come to meetings better prepared. To introduce a set of rules might limit the team's flexibility, but improving an area of deficiency avoids further increasing rigidity while achieving improvement.

> *"The challenge*
> *for a team is to*
> *focus the growth*
> *process on*
> *improving*
> *quality of*
> *performance."*

A qualification to the tendency for a system to maintain its original character is a system's tendency to grow. The most common growth pattern is to increase quantity, generally by adding resources, rather than to increase quality of performance. The challenge for a team is to focus the growth process on improving quality of performance. For example, a team, fearful of being overwhelmed by its responsibility to produce a long-range plan in a short period of time, may be tempted to ask for additional team members to assist in the planning process. Adding members will, however, increase coordination problems. A more effective strategy is to identify more efficient ways to reach its goal, that is, to produce its long-range plan without adding resources.

As a system develops, its activities tend to become more specialized. As this happens, the system becomes more efficient but, eventually, less flexible. Greater efficiency arises from increasing expertise in performing an activity, but decreasing flexibility results from the team's becoming dependent on one or a few members to perform each activity. When members are placed on a team to perform a specific role they are likely to be satisfied with increased specialization. When, however, members are self-selected or initially there are no specialized roles, this trend may be contrary to some members' wishes to perform a variety of roles. For them the experience can be less interesting and satisfying. For example, a team is formed to develop and present sales strategies for a company's products. The team has several members who wish to develop their presentation skills. Initially, presentation responsibilities are shared. Eventually, one member, who is especially effective, assumes most of these responsibilities. The members who desired the experience may then become dissatisfied and less involved.[19]

The negative effect of tending toward greater member specialization can be countered by unifying functioning. In social systems there are two paths to such unification, *coordination* and *integration*. Coordination involves finding strategies and control devices that lead to more coherent functioning. For example, periodic team planning meetings enable team members to harmonize member activities and interests. Integration achieves unification through shared norms and values. For example, when a team establishes its operating principles for guiding member interactions, an integrating effect results. These operating principles are shared norms and values that become points of reference for member behavior. Once they are understood and accepted, each member knows how to apply them in specific situations. Establishing and learning how to apply norms and values can require extended discussion. The effect, however, is an increased sense of sharing in the performance of each other's activities.[20]

> *"Coordination involves finding strategies and control devices that lead to more coherent functioning."*

Effective Team Functioning

Table 1.1 summarizes several principles of effective team system functioning. Stating the principles is easy; making them a reality is not. Organizations that implement team-based management do so with the expectation that these principles can become a reality. Often they do not anticipate the difficulties. Some difficulties encountered when implementing team-based management are described in the next section.[21]

TABLE 1.1
Effective Team System Functioning

A team system maintains its integrity by pursuing its goal.

A team system pursues its goal by using resources provided by its environment.

A team system returns to its environment the results of reaching its goal, that is, its product.

A team system chooses from among multiple paths to its goal, the most efficient and satisfying path.

A team system's pursuit of its goal is characterized by interdependence among all of its features.

A team system's interdependence results in changes in one feature affecting every other feature.

A team system's features are structured to reduce effort and to enhance performance quality.

A team system's structure involves subdividing tasks, assigning roles, and setting standards.

A team system seeks feedback on the quality of its performance.

A team system uses feedback to improve the quality of its performance.

A team system's effectiveness involves improving its product and increasing member satisfaction.

A team system becomes more effective because every feature becomes more proficient.

A team system's environment continues its support based on the quality of the team's product.

TEAMS IN ORGANIZATIONS

Seeking to address a variety of issues that reduced worker productivity, business and industry in the1970s and 1980s faced a choice between technological and social solutions. Characterizing the technological solution was the statement that ". . . efforts to automate the production process must be re-doubled so that production can be made goof proof and fail safe. 'Peopleless' factories are the goal; machines don't take coffee breaks and over-stay them."[22] This same sentiment was expressed in an interview with an electronics manufacturing plant manager who voiced a longing to have machines that would do most of the tasks now done by workers who make mistakes that result in defective products. The plant manager noted, however, that the high cost of such equipment made clear the advantages of workers' improving their performance.[23]

Enabling workers to accomplish a more "social" solution involved reorienting management practice. At the time of making the choice, companies had removed layers in their management hierarchies and placed responsibility for identifying and correcting defects on line workers. *Reengineering* emphasized the importance of reviewing production and management processes to remove unnecessary, or *non—value adding*, steps. This made possible further workforce reductions.[24] Lean production reduced costs further by minimizing inventory and the associated warehouse personnel.[25] Each of these strategies, when introduced, had several implications for manufacturing. One was a significant reduction in the number of workers required for jobs and greater responsibility placed on those who remained. A second implication was reconsideration of how work was to be organized. Where each employee was the unit of work, large numbers of supervisors were needed. With a radically reduced supervisory staff, how was work to be organized so that productivity was not just maintained, but improved?

"A team of workers is considered to be in a better position than a supervisory or management group to identify performance problems and to solve them immediately."

The answer many companies have chosen is team-based management. As one manager said: "We have adjusted our business systems, improved our technology, and the only other area in which we can improve productivity is personnel performance."[26] A team of workers is considered to be in a better position than a supervisory or management group to identify performance problems and to solve them immediately. In some organizations, management sets performance goals in consultation with work teams. Teams take responsibility for decisions about how to perform the tasks required to achieve those goals. This perspective is reflected in an emphasis on team *empowerment*.[27]

The increasing complexity of equipment and processes also suggests that those closest to the work should take responsibility for its performance. Individual managers often lack the level and variety of specialized skills needed to identify and correct complex, technical equipment problems. In contrast, a team with members who operate the equipment has many of the competencies needed to address problems that arise. To add to the skills of team members, so that they can take responsibility for an even wider range of performance-related issues, organizations invest considerable resources in training for team-related activities.

A further feature of team-based management is acknowledgement of the presence of informal groups among workers and their significance for workers' satisfaction. By being allowed, even encouraged, to consult among themselves, teams can provide members social support and enable them to experience more satisfaction in their accomplishment. *Cross-training* enables team members to learn each other's jobs and to help each other as the need arises. Cross-training also extends workers' competencies, expands their awareness of the work of other team members, and helps to reduce boredom that may develop from doing the same limited task repetitively.

As a consequence of these and related considerations, team-based management was introduced. Early on, a few large companies, such as Procter & Gamble, turned to teams as part of their business strategy and for some time kept their practices and experience relatively secret.[28] More recently, other companies, like Harley-Davidson, have been more public in turning to teams.[29] The latter worked in close collaboration with their employees' union to develop teaming as did Ford's electronics division (now Visteon).[30]

Some companies continue to struggle with the implementation of teams. One reason is that implementation is never complete. One human resources manager, in a company that has successfully adopted teams in its workplace, indicated that introducing teams and teamwork is a continuing process. When a company begins to believe that it has completed the process, it is, she noted, in trouble.[31]

Another implementation difficulty is the change in management strategy that is required. The traditional, highly directive management strategy was designed for workers who often had little education and who were assumed to need close supervision. Today's workers have more education, and companies are providing even more so that employees can take on more responsibility for their jobs. Managers, by contrast, are being asked to give up some responsibility. For some managers this can be particularly difficult. Having grown up in a society oriented to individual performance in which the image of the "boss" is one of telling workers what to do, it can be difficult for a manager to reorient to teams of workers taking increasing responsibility for their own work.

An example is a young engineer who was a team manager in an electronics assembly facility.[32] In describing his work, he used dramatic terms, "It is a lot like death, but you learn a lot!" When asked what was so difficult, he described a team of machine operators who made electronic controllers for trucks. The operators were older women who were experts in running their equipment and managing their part of the manufacturing process. Some could read at roughly a sixth-grade level. Although the young engineer was supposedly the technical expert, in reality the operators were teaching him how to operate their sophisticated equipment. His image of his skills, his status, his perception of himself was being transformed in the process of learning to work with others in pursuit of a goal.

> *"Cross-training enables team members to learn each other's jobs and to help each other as the need arises."*

In almost any discussion of teams in industry, the statement will be made that it is difficult to change the *culture*. In using this word the speaker is noting that how we work together involves how we have *learned* to work and how we have become comfortable working. Changing the culture means initiating new ways of behaving that are unfamiliar and less comfortable. Also, the change requires rethinking how work is evaluated and rewarded. This process can be as fundamental as learning to speak a second language. It is not only difficult to learn that language but it takes a while for a person to become comfortable using it. With practice and a supportive environment, it can be done.

The Challenge Revisited
Introducing Teamwork

1. Effective teamwork requires commitment to the view that *we* can reach the goal.
2. Under stress, some members may more readily trust their own ability to reach the goal. This ambivalence undercuts support for and confidence in a team's capabilities.
3. For a team to perform effectively, its members must desire to achieve an important goal, must be committed to working as a performing unit, must understand how teams perform effectively, and must know how to apply their understanding.
4. A team's ability to achieve its goal is always *becoming.*

EXERCISE 1.1 • *Effective and Ineffective Teams*

1. Working in teams of five or six, have each member write a brief description of the most *effective* team and the most *ineffective* team he or she has ever participated on or observed.
2. Share your descriptions with the team. Then develop two lists of the characteristics or behaviors that appear to be common to your descriptions of each team type.
3. Next, ask yourselves this question: What principles about effectiveness and ineffectiveness can be derived from the two lists?
4. Develop a formal set of principles that would encourage or support effectiveness and a set of principles that would discourage ineffectiveness.
5. As a team prepare and present to the class a report of your team findings. Discuss how a team might become effective or ineffective over time.

EXERCISE 1.2 • *Developing Coordination*

1. Form the members of the entire class (or, if the class is large, into groups of 20–25) in a circle with members holding hands. Separate one pair of

hands and hang a hoola hoop over the arm of one participant who again joins hands with the person next to him.

2. Without breaking the circle, pass the hoola hoop around the entire circle. When the hoola hoop returns to its starting point, ask yourselves:

   a. What actions moved the hoola hoop around the circle faster? Slower? More slowly?

   b. What does this exercise tell us about coordination? How is coordination achieved?

3. Repeat the process as above, except introduce a second hoola hoop on the side opposite the first. Start the two hoops in opposite directions. When each hoop returns to its starting point, ask yourselves:

   a. How was it possible for the hoola hoops to pass each other?

   b. What coordinated actions helped the team overcome this obstacle?

   c. What does this exercise, with its increased level of difficulty, tell us about coordination?

QUESTIONS FOR REVIEW AND DISCUSSION

1. What is a team? What types of activities do teams perform? Why do they succeed? Why do they fail?

2. Why is a team considered a *system*? What are the primary characteristics of a team system?

3. What is meant by the term *interdependence*? What is the effect of interdependence?

4. What is meant by the term *open system*? What are the implications for a team of being an open system?

5. What is the team system process? What is the objective of this process?

6. What is meant by the phrase *subsystem processes*? What are a team's subsystem processes?

7. How does each subsystem process work? Why do they tend to become disorganized?

8. What is the function of information feedback for team performance? What is negative feedback? What is positive feedback?

NOTES

1. The Southeast Spur of Mount Everest was first climbed in 1953 by Nepalese Tenzing Norgay and New Zealander Sir Edmund Hillary.

2. In 1967, M. DeBakey was the first to use an artificial heart pump successfully with a patient; *Encyclopedia Americana,* Vol. 8 (1996), Danbury, CT: Grolier, p. 573.

3. J. J. Trento (1987), *Prescription for Disaster,* New York: Crown Press.

4. J. N. Maclean (1999), *Fire on the Mountain,* New York: William Morrow.

5. Jon Krakauer (1997), *Into Thin Air: A Personal Account of the Mount Everest Disaster,* New York: Villard.

6. F. F. Lightall (1991, February), Launching the space shuttle *Challenger:* Disciplinary deficiencies in the analyses of engineering data, *IEEE Transactions on Engineering Management,* 38, 63–74.

7. Suit filed over death on gene therapy test, *New York Times,* September 19, 2000.

8. Maclean, op. cit.

9. A variety of team types are described in J. R. Hackman (1987), *Groups that Work (and Those that Don't): Creating a Foundation for Effective Teamwork,* San Francisco: Jossey-Bass.

10. This summary of definitional perspectives on teamwork is abstracted from D. W. Johnson & F. P. Johnson (1987), *Joining Together: Group Theory and Group Skills,* Englewood Cliffs, NJ: Prentice Hall, pp. 4–7.

11. This perspective has been suggested by social scientists over several decades. For example, Stodgill (1959), *Individual Behavior and Group Achievement,* New York: Oxford University Press, p. 18, defined a group as ". . . an open interaction system in which actions determine the structure of the system and successive interactions exert co-equal effects upon the identity of the system." Cited in Johnson & Johnson, op. cit., p. 5. See also D. Katz & R. Kahn (1966), *The Social Psychology of Organizations,* New York: Wiley. More recently, systems theory has provided the underpinnings for theoretical perspectives on group behavior; see M. von Cranach (1996), Toward a theory of the acting group, in E. Witte & J. Davis (Eds.), *Understanding Group Behavior,* Vol 2, Mahwah, NJ: Erlbaum, pp. 147–187; H. Arrow, J. McGrath, & J. Berdahl (2000), *Small Groups as Complex Systems,* Thousand Oaks, CA: Sage; and D. E. Yeatts & C. Hyten (1998), *High Performing Self-Managed Work Teams,* Thousand Oaks, CA: Sage.

12. A team's output, that is, what a team accomplishes when it achieves its goal, is referred to throughout this book as its *product.*

13. Team-based management differs significantly from "scientific management" as presented by F. W. Taylor (*Scientific Management,* 1911). The latter sought the "one best way" to perform a task and reach a goal. A team is considered to have multiple paths to its goal (Arrow, et al., op. cit., p. 80) and a team is to select the best path, given the circumstances. See also C. Gresor & R. Drazin (1997), Equifinality: Functional equivalents in organizational design, *Academy of Management Review,* 22, 403–428.

14. Teams and their organizational environments are considered in a number of sources. See, for example, E. Salas, C. Bowers, & E. Edens (2001), *Improving Teamwork in Organizations,* Mahwah, NJ: Erlbaum.

15. Leadership is a subprocess of teamwork. See, for example, Yeatts & Hyten, op. cit., pp. 302–308.

16. On interdependence see R. Wageman (2001), The meaning of interdependence, in M. E. Turner (Ed.), *Groups at Work*, Mahwah, NJ: Erlbaum, pp. 197–217; and E. Sundstrom, M. McIntyre, T. Halfhill, & H. Richards (2000), Work groups: From the Hawthorne studies to work teams of the 1990s and beyond, *Group Dynamics*, 4, 44–67.

17. Structural features such as norms are examined in Yeatts & Hyten, op. cit.

18. Feedback is discussed in E. Salas, T. Dickinson, S. Converse, & S. Tannenbaum (1992), Toward an understanding of team performance and training, in R. W. Swezey & E. Salas (Eds.), *Teams: Their Training and Performance*, Norwood, NJ: Ablex.

19. System subprocesses are considered in Yeatts & Hyten, op. cit.

20. See Arrow, et al., op. cit.

21. See D. L. Gladstein (1984), Groups in context: A model of task group effectiveness, *Administrative Science Quarterly*, 29, 499–517. See also Sundstrom, et al., op. cit., pp. 44–67.

22. L. D. Ketchum & E. Trist (1992), *All Teams Are Not Created Equal: How Employee Empowerment Really Works*, Newbury Park, CA: Sage, p. 5.

23. Author's interview with Dudley Wass at Ford Electronics (now Visteon), 1996.

24. M. Hammer & J. Champy (1993), *Re-engineering the Corporation*, New York: HarperCollins.

25. J. P. Womack, D. T. Jones, & D. Roos (1991), *The Machine that Changed the World: The Story of Lean Production*, New York: Harper.

26. Personal communication from G. T. Judson, 1995.

27. R. C. Herrenkohl, G. T. Judson, & J. A. Heffner (1999), Defining and measuring employee empowerment, *Journal of Applied Behavioral Science*, 35, 373–389.

28. J. Hoerr, M. Pollock, & D. Whiteside (1986, September), Management discovers the human side of automation, *Business Week*, pp. 70–76. Cited in Ketchum & Trist, op. cit., p. 21.

29. Author's interview with Rhonda White, Harley-Davidson, York, PA, 1997.

30. Author's interview with Rhonda White, Harley-Davidson, 1997, and interviews with several employees at Ford Electronics (now Visteon, 1996).

31. Author's interview with Rhonda White, Harley-Davidson, 1997.

32. Author's interview with employee at Ford Electronics (now Visteon), 1996.

Initiating Teamwork

section one

Forming a team involves several considerations. Initially, a team's members should consider how knowledgeable they are about team functioning and how experienced they are in applying that knowledge to achieving a goal. Questions to ask include these: What is the team to accomplish? Who will its members be? How must its members work together to reach its goal? What can be expected to help or hinder its performance? Members must be clear about and agree on their team's goal. A clear goal gives direction to and motivates members. To perform effectively, a team's members must reach agreement on a single team goal. They must also take time to identify each member's skills and knowledge and agree on how these can contribute to pursuit of their team's goals. Members must also recognize that each has a style of performing that reflects his or her individuality and provides to the team different perspectives on its functioning. These must be understood and coordinated in ways that enhance rather than detract from team performance. The importance of this preliminary process for effective team functioning should not be underestimated.

The Challenge
Creating a Team

A team is created by specifying a goal and by designating as members those who have or who are willing to develop the capabilities needed to achieve the goal. Relevant capabilities are both those required to perform the team's tasks and those that enable members to work together effectively. Members use these capabilities to choose a path to the goal and to proceed along the path. Establishing interpersonal interdependence, that is, seeking ways to assist each other's contributions, utilizes an important asset available to a team. Along the way, as the team encounters barriers to achieving its goal, its problem-solving capabilities can resolve the barriers and maintain effective performance.

chapter 2

Creating a Team

A team often eagerly begins work, having given little consideration to planning how most effectively to perform the activities intended to achieve its goal. Such eagerness may reflect a commitment to "get the job done," but it can often result in significant difficulties. Without adequate planning, these difficulties can surface and have a negative effect on team performance and generate member dissatisfaction.

Before beginning its work, a team should address several questions. First, where is the team headed and what must it do to get there? This means defining the team's goal, verifying that all members see the goal in the same way, and identifying tasks required to achieve the goal. Second, who are the team's members? This means identifying members' skills and experience and determining whether these will enable the team to reach its goal. Adjustments, such as additional training, must be made if these are inadequate. Third, how will the team do its work? This requires establishing principles about how members are to work together to achieve the goal. These principles derive from the concept of interdependence and contrast with member independence. Fourth, what enhances the team's performance? This addresses how factors that facilitate high performance are identified and supported, and how factors that lower performance are avoided. The following discussion introduces these issues.

WHERE IS THE TEAM HEADED?

"Where is the team headed?" means "What is the team's goal?" For example, an athletic team has the goal of scoring points, a manufacturing team has the goal of producing a product, a musical ensemble has the goal of performing a piece of music. A closely related question concerns the level of quality a team expects its product to possess. For example, is an athletic team aiming to score 7 points, 70, or just enough to win over the other team? Does a manufacturing team aim to produce 1, 20, or 200 units of its product? Does it expect a quality level of 20 defects per 1000, 10 defects per 1000, or none? Does the musical ensemble seek to perform a piece of music without considering quality, at an average level, or better than they have ever performed the piece before? These latter questions concern what a team's achievement will "look like" when it reaches its goal. It is the team's vision for its achievement. This is what captivates a team's members and keeps them engaged throughout the process.[1] These are the most fundamental questions for a team, for its activities, and for the quality of members' experiences. Although this may seem obvious, it is often not addressed. Team members often think the goal is clear, that everyone perceives it the same way, and so they proceed without discussion. A team given a clearly defined goal can still have some members misunderstand it. A team given an unclear goal can have all members misunderstand and not realize it. When there is confusion about its goal, a team can begin to perform inefficient tasks that take members along a path away from the team's goal. A team must be clear about its goal. It is also important for a team's members to recognize that a goal can be achieved at different levels of quality: poor, average, or superior. A team must decide what level it aspires to achieve. This decision determines both the challenge members experience and the pride members will feel when the goal is achieved. These issues are examined more fully in Chapter 3.

"A team must be clear about its goal."

A related issue is the path along which a team proceeds to its goal. This may not at first seem important. When a team faces its deadline, however, the issue becomes quite important. A team generally has available multiple paths to its goal. Finding the best path to the goal can be a challenge even for a team that is given a clearly specified assignment. *Best,* as used here, has several meanings: most efficient, most satisfying for members, best suited to members' skills and experience, and/or most likely to achieve the team's vision. An important difference between a team in the workplace and an athletic team is that the latter often has preplanned paths to its goal, called "plays," while a workplace team is challenged to find its own "best" path to its goal. This means that nonathletic teams will need to spend time identifying and planning a path to their goals.[2]

WHO ARE THE TEAM'S MEMBERS?

Creating a team is a two-part process. The first part occurs when individual members become a performing unit, a team. The second happens when the team begins to pursue its goal. To accomplish both involves two broad types of skills.[3] The first type is **technical skills**. These skills are needed to perform the specific tasks that enable a team to achieve its goal. For example, an athletic team, say, a soccer team, requires members with offensive skills and defensive skills. A manufacturing team, say, one producing electronic controllers, needs members with the skills required to run the machines that attach the components that make up the control unit. A musical ensemble requires members with the skills required to play the different instruments in a manner specified by a particular musical piece.

The second type of skill is **social skills**. These skills enable members to interact in ways that facilitate task performance and progress toward the team's goal. These are much the same for different types of teams. Members of athletic teams, manufacturing teams, and musical ensembles must be able to discuss among themselves what skills they have to contribute, how best to coordinate their activities, and how best to resolve differences in points of view. For a soccer team this discussion may concern how and when to pass the ball as the team moves toward the opponent's goal. For a manufacturing team this may involve discussions about how to reduce defects. For a musical ensemble it may involve discussing the timing of different instruments' entry into a passage of music, or the dynamics of expression for different sections of a piece. A variety of social skills is relevant to a team's functioning. These include decision-making, problem-solving, negotiating, bargaining, planning, and communication skills and skills in running productive meetings. These skills are discussed in Chapters 4 and 5.

"Experience may or may not prove useful to a new team depending on what each member has learned."

In addition to skills, members either have or lack experience working as members of a particular type of team. Experience may or may not prove useful to a new team depending on what each member has learned. Prior positive experience can help individuals to understand how effective teams work. Members with this type of experience can help get a team started. Previous team-related experience can also be negative because the experience involved dissatisfaction and even failure. If the experience demonstrated pitfalls to avoid, this can be useful to a new team. If, however, the experience soured the person on being a member of a team, this can be detrimental and should be addressed before a team proceeds. There is also the issue of the degree to which experience on one type of team is transferable to performing on a different type of team. Because not all experience is relevant, how useful it is depends on what the person learns and how well it generalizes to a new situation.

HOW WILL A TEAM DO ITS WORK?

A team's path to its goal involves members performing tasks that move the team toward the goal. A team's work is generally characterized by some degree of

interdependence.[4] This means that the way one team member acts affects other members and vice versa. For example, two persons shooting "hoops" with one basketball are interdependent in that only one person at a time can take a shot at the goal. The problem is resolved by taking turns. This establishes interdependence. Interdependence breaks down if one person insists on taking all of the shots. Coincidentally, in such a situation the interest of the excluded player is likely to wane. Interest is regained by renewing taking turns. Independence in this setting contrasts with interdependence. Independence involves working on one's own without reference to others, that is, having two balls and two baskets such that neither player needs to consider the other while playing.

> *"Interdependence is at the heart of teamwork."*

Interdependence is at the heart of teamwork. It is what gives teamwork its potential superiority over the same number of persons working (or acting) independently. However, efficient interdependence among team members can be difficult to achieve and to maintain. The following three scenarios illustrate different possibilities. They depict working independently, working with efficient interdependence, and working with inefficient interdependence.

Scenario 1. A team of five members is expected to prepare a report on five competing products manufactured by five different companies. The team's achievement is judged by three criteria: completion of the report, quality of the completed report, and timeliness, that is, the time required to complete the report. Team members meet and decide that each member will analyze one company and its competing product. Two members are slower than the others in finishing. One has difficulty obtaining relevant information. The other has to make an important business trip in the middle of preparing the report. When each one has completed his or her analysis, prepared a report on his or her company, and prepared a presentation of findings, the five reports are bound in a single volume. At the meeting with the company CEO, each member presents his or her report in the order that the information is presented in the larger report. Using a scale of 0–10, with 0 meaning nothing achieved and 10 meaning completely achieved, the team received 10 for completing the report, 5 for quality, and 4 for timeliness.

Scenario 2. As in scenario 1, each member is assigned one company. Before beginning, the team chooses a leader who suggests that the completion of the report, its quality, and completion date are the responsibility of the entire team. She further notes that the team should follow two guidelines. One is to cooperate in any way possible to help each other achieve the highest quality in the shortest time. The other is for members with special skills and experience to make those skills and experience available to other members as needed. The **collective responsibility** guideline aims for members to have a feeling of mutual responsibility for achieving the team's goal. Rule 1 aims to have members, as they do their own research, watch for information relevant to others' analyses. Members also share insights and ideas. Rule 2 aims for two members, one with experience developing benchmarking analyses and the other with an accounting background, to make suggestions to other members about information to look for, important financial features to consider, and how to proceed most efficiently. This approach helps the member who has difficulty finding relevant information. The member who must travel is kept informed about team deliberations by means of a conference call and new information relevant to his analysis is e-mailed to him while he is away. For the report and the presentation to the company's CEO, the team prepares an executive summary that highlights those findings that provide the greatest potential for their company increasing its market share. Using the same 0–10 rating scale, the team received a 10 for completing the report, an 8 for quality, and a 9 for timeliness.

Scenario 3.   As in scenario 2, each member is assigned a company, and a leader is chosen who outlines the previously noted guidelines for proceeding. There are several differences among the members, however. First, the member who has previously worked on a benchmarking team feels that he should be team leader. His resentment at not being chosen leads him to resist sharing with other team members the benefits of his experience. A second member is simultaneously assigned to another company team that requires as much time and effort as the benchmarking team. This person feels that the second team is more important for his career advancement. These two members are less available to the benchmarking team. This in turn reduces assistance to the member with the more demanding assignment and to the member who has to travel. The team leader tries to compensate for the deficiencies but begins to resent the poor participation. The result is reduced effort and increased frustration. Because the report is behind schedule, minimal joint effort is given to developing the presentation. The report is completed and presented to the CEO. It is rated 10 for completion, 3 for quality, and 2 for timeliness.

> *"A hidden agenda is a covert goal that a member has for him- or herself that is not a goal for the team."*

These three scenarios demonstrate how working interdependently when resentments are not at issue and there are no hidden agendas (scenario 2) can produce a superior outcome. They also show how working independently (scenario 1) can surpass outcomes from working interdependently when resentments and interpersonal issues are not addressed (scenario 3). In this latter scenario there are two barriers to high performance. One is a "hidden agenda" and the other is "reduced member involvement". A **hidden agenda** (the member who feels he should be leader) is a covert goal that a member has for him- or herself that is not a goal for the team. It can have negative consequences for team performance as indicated in scenario 3.[5] Reduced member involvement, or what is sometimes referred to as **social loafing**, can have serious implications for team performance. It can occur for various reasons.[6] Both issues are described later in this chapter.

How can interdependence be established and maintained as a positive influence on team performance? To answer this question, consider two broad types of interdependence and the way they are created.[7] One is **structural interdependence.** This refers to how a team's task(s) or task-related activities are organized to encourage interdependence. The second type, **behavioral interdependence,** refers to how much interdependent behavior actually occurs regardless of the way the tasks or activities are organized. That these are considered distinguishable underscores the fact that even when a situation exerts pressure toward interdependence, it may not occur and that when there is no pressure toward interdependence it still may occur.

Structural interdependence among team members can be generated by several strategies involving how a team performs its tasks. First, equipment can create interdependence. For example, on a children's playground a teeter-totter is designed in a way that makes two children interdependent. Resistance to the interdependence stops the activity. Similarly, a two-person bobsled creates interdependence. One person steers, the other handles the brakes. By contrast, when playing golf each player has his or her own set of clubs and golf balls. There is no interdependence except in the order in which shots are taken, per the rules of the game.

A second task-related strategy for creating interdependence is to assign to all members responsibility for achieving the team's goal. This is collective responsibility. For example, if a coach tells an athletic team that if every member does not achieve a given standard in practice, the whole team must run laps, then that team is confronted with collective responsibility. This contrasts with situations where individuals are responsible only for performing their own tasks. Failure by one has no implications for others.

A third strategy involves rules that establish interdependence. For example, instructions can specify the necessity of sharing resources, helping each other, taking turns, selecting the best answer from among all the answers team members can think of, among others. In the earlier "shooting hoops" example, when there is one basketball goal and one ball, taking turns is a strongly implied rule that makes players interdependent.

Finally, rules about how differentially distributed resources are to be used by team members can establish interdependence. If each team member has only a portion of the skills needed to complete a task, interdependence among members is essential to completing the task. Members must help each other. Such rules often need to be made explicit. For example, a soccer team needs players with offensive skills and players with defensive skills, each assisting the other. A high level of interdependence among players with the two types of skills is needed to play effectively. By contrast, if each team member has all of the skills needed to perform a task, then interdependence is not required. In golf, there is no interdependence because each player must have all the requisite skills to perform well.

> *"If each team member has only a portion of the skills needed to complete a task, interdependence among members is essential to completing the task."*

A second type of structural interdependence concerns whether performance outcomes are assigned to the team as a whole or to individual team members. When *outcome measurement* reflects team performance as a whole, rather than individual members' performance, interdependence is encouraged. For example, in soccer, performance is measured as a collective output. Even though some members have no opportunity to score, the score is a team score representing the efforts of all members. This fosters interdependence. By contrast, in singles tennis, a score reflects an individual's performance. This fosters independence.

Reward assignment for the team as a whole also encourages interdependence. For example, a winning football team that gets to have a celebration dinner for all members is being given a collective reward that fosters interdependence. Reward independence is created when rewards are given to individual members. If a celebration dinner were promised to each football team member who scored one or more points, the effect would be to create independence. In the latter case, the effect on the motivation of members who could not score points, in contrast to those who could, is likely to be quite different.

> *"A challenge for such teams is to establish their own rules to encourage interdependence."*

The preceding examples describe rules drawn from sports because sports are played according to more explicit rules. Similar rules can apply to teams in business and industry or other types of organizations, although relevant rules in such settings may be less explicit and sometimes unspecified altogether. A challenge for such teams is to establish their own rules to encourage interdependence. These rules can become standards or *norms* that govern members' activities. The assumption is that such rules support effective performance.[8]

The following example illustrates interdependence in a business setting: A product design team is aware of the implicit upper management expectation that the group is collectively responsible for the "product" of their deliberations, rather than just the team's leader. Based on this understanding the team develops several rules. One is that members are to help each other by critiquing each other's verbal and written contributions. Also, recognizing that each member of the team possesses different skills, the team decides that each member is to offer his or her expertise to others as needed. Furthermore, members are to feel free to ask each other for assistance specific to the expertise the member possesses. A second rule is that each team member is to consult with employees in his or her division and share the results of these consultations in their team discussion. Finally, the design and associated report, resulting from the team's efforts, are to be considered and presented as a team product. If a bonus is given for the work, it will be to the team as a whole, rather than to the team members judged to be most deserving. These decisions and rules support interdependence and have a positive effect on team performance.

> *"Although task structure and outcome structure may exert pressure to behave interdependently, individuals can vary in how much they actually do so."*

This preceding approach contrasts with an approach in which each team member does his or her assigned tasks while avoiding discussion of interdependence issues. This allows members who are so inclined to avoid involvement in other members' activities. Consequently, opportunities for performance improvement that can result from interdependent activity are lost. It also allows members to establish their own individual levels of effort and quality since these are not linked to the level of effort and quality of other members. Table 2.1 summarizes different strategies intended to engender team member interdependence.

Finally, there is *behavioral interdependence*. This focuses on how much interdependence actually occurs relative to each of the issues described earlier. It also indicates that behavioral interdependence can be unrelated to how tasks or performance outcomes are structured. Although task structure and outcome structure may exert pressure to behave interdependently, individuals can vary in how much they actually do so. For

TABLE 2.1
Sources of Interdependence

	Athletics	Organizational
STRUCTURAL—Task Related		
Equipment design requires interdependence	Teeter-totter Bobsled Eight-person rowing skull	Hook and ladder truck Pilot/copilot
Assign collective responsibility for achieving goal	All responsible for winning	All responsible for completing report
	All responsible for errors	All responsible for defects
	All responsible for member satisfaction	All responsible for customer satisfaction
Rules specify interdependence	Take turns	Teach other members relevant skills
	Block for runner Pass basketball	Share relevant information
Members' differential resources require interdependence	Players coordinate activities	Coordinate members' varied skills
		Use own skills to assist other members
STRUCTURAL—Outcome Related		
Performance measured for team as a whole	Score is for entire team	Rate of defects for entire team
		Production rate for entire team
Reward to team as a whole	Celebration for entire team World Series rings for team	Bonus to entire team Wage increase for entire team Recognition for entire team
OBSERVED BEHAVIOR		
Observation of behavior	How much cooperation	How much interworker assistance
	How much interplayer assistance	How much cooperative learning
		How much shared information

example, even though a planning task is designed to elicit optimum interdependence, one or more members may resist and take independent action. Conversely, in situations structured for independent behavior, individuals may act interdependently. Consequently, actually assessing the amount of interdependent or independent behavior is important.[9]

WHAT HELPS OR HINDERS TEAM PERFORMANCE?

Member involvement is essential to any effective team performance, especially when members are interdependent. One member who is not involved can disrupt the entire goal-oriented process. His or her lack of involvement not only loses for the team the uninvolved member's contribution to achieving the team's goal, it also generates resentment in other team members, often resulting in an overall reduction in effort. Involvement is based on actual or anticipated satisfaction. Reduced involvement occurs because of actual or anticipated dissatisfaction.

> *"Team members need to voice their expectations so that other members become aware of them."*

Satisfaction or dissatisfaction can derive from one or a combination of sources. First, there are each team member's expectations on joining a team. Initially, there may be as many different expectations as there are team members. One member expects to enjoy working with other team members. Another expects to enjoy the experience of producing a product or of providing a service. Another does not expect to enjoy the experience at all since his or her previous experience on a team was unpleasant. Such anticipated dissatisfaction is likely to inhibit involvement. Team members need to voice their expectations so that other members become aware of them. Some expectations can be fulfilled, for example, satisfactions from working with others, while others may need to be adjusted. For example, what was dissatisfying about a previous experience should be voiced and ways sought to provide a more satisfying experience.

Second, once under way, members can experience satisfactions and/or dissatisfactions. Satisfactions can come from using one's skills to promote the team's progress toward its goal, from learning new skills, or from improving existing ones. The social experience can also provide satisfaction. For example, team members who help one another to learn new skills or to improve existing ones can experience a satisfying sense of social support. As team members plan and execute their tasks and experience the satisfaction of accomplishment, a sense of social cohesion can develop. When disagreements and conflicts arise, addressing and resolving them can also be satisfying.

A third consideration is the experience of members' acknowledging and recognizing each other's contributions to the team's accomplishments. Team members are on a team because each has something to contribute to the team's achieving its goal. While "just doing their job" might seem like reward enough, in fact, it is not. Membership requires, to some degree, submerging one's individuality in the group's activities in order to perform interdependently. This should not mean losing the individuality or innovativeness that members bring to team activities. Rather than no longer needing to have one's contributions recognized by one's teammates, need for recognition becomes greater. A junior member of a product design team, whose primary function is to check patents on design features, needs to hear from the more senior members that the patent searches have helped the team to clarify and to reach its goal. The senior members also need to hear from each other that their contributions are respected and appreciated.

A fourth major source of satisfaction arises when a team's goal is achieved at or above the desired level of quality. The challenge is for all team members to experience a shared sense of accomplishment. If members have recognized each other's accomplishments and contributions as work progressed, then the foundation for a sense of shared accomplishment is already available. If recognition was not part of the members' interaction, then members may need more time to recognize each member's contribution to their team's accomplishment. Sources of member satisfaction and dissatisfaction are discussed at greater length in Chapter 9.

"The challenge is for all team members to experience a shared sense of accomplishment."

Member diversity characterizes teams. Members are chosen because implicitly or explicitly they are different. They have different skills, different perspectives on problems, different personalities, and different backgrounds. Whereas diversity is a source of team strength, it also poses challenges. Differences in interpretations of a team's goal must be identified and a single, shared perspective developed. Different activities relevant to a team's reaching its goal must be identified and coordinated in ways that facilitate goal achievement. Differences that are irrelevant to goal achievement must be disregarded, unless they become sources of resentment and conflict. When conflict develops over such differences and affects team performance, it must be addressed.[10]

Consider two examples. The starting five members of a women's varsity basketball team include a point guard who is excellent at making long (three-point) shots. She is on the team for this reason. She also tends to shoot every time she gets the ball, a tendency that aids the opposing team because knowing that she will shoot whenever she gets the ball, she can be more closely guarded. This is a source of resentment and conflict because other team members are denied a sense of accomplishment. A parallel example from business is a team formed to plan the development of a new product line. One member of the team was chosen because of her design skills. She also tends to assume the leadership role immediately after the team first convenes and before the team considers how to address the leadership issue. This engenders considerable resentment in other team members. In both instances, a team member chosen for one skill brings with her other characteristics that affect team performance. This requires attention by the team. How are these sources of dissatisfaction to be addressed?

In the illustrations of the point guard who shoots too frequently and of the designer who too quickly assumes the leadership role, there are several pitfalls to avoid in addressing the problems their behavior poses. The first is for a team to avoid blaming. Instead the issue should be raised in the context of improving performance. The second is for the team member being asked to change to focus on improving team performance and reaching the goal rather than on personal hurt. A third is for other team members to focus on improving performance and attaining the goal rather than on expressing any personal frustration. Finally, it is important for team members to congratulate the member who is asked to change, when change, which may be slow in coming, actually occurs.

Member communication is at the heart of effective team performance. Effective communication enables a team to address

"Member communication is at the heart of effective team performance."

issues that are barriers to coordination of members' activities. It is the means by which members cooperate in support of each other's performance. It is how conflicts and dissatisfactions are addressed in a positive manner. It is how members give recognition to each other for their team's progress.

Member interactions are characterized by communication. If the interactions are task-oriented, discussion will be about the activities required to achieve the team's goal and about which members will conduct each activity. In other words, the team initiates a planning process. If members are not very task-oriented, they may discuss any of a variety of topics. In either case, observation of the communication interactions, that is, who speaks to whom and how frequently, will reveal a pattern of interactions. Such a hypothetical pattern is depicted in Figure 2.1. In this figure, arrows represent the direction of communication. Heavy lines represent frequent communication. Light lines represent infrequent communication. No line represents an absence of communication. Member D's lack of interaction signals a lack of involvement that needs to be addressed by the team.

A pattern of communication can readily become consistent for a specific team. Some members speak more often, others less; some are spoken to more often, others less. If this process is monitored for a period of time, it can be seen that one or two members become the focus of much of the team's communication. There is, in other words, a *structure* to the team's communication. The significance of this structure is that those who are central in the structure (that is, those who speak and are spoken to more frequently) tend to become the team leaders.[11]

Structured communication among team members is to be expected. Variation in frequency of sending and receiving messages is not detrimental to team performance as long as the differential in amount of speaking is not too great. When the differential becomes too great, that is, when some members speak and are spoken to frequently and others speak and are spoken to infrequently or in the extreme, not at all, team performance is likely to be negatively affected. The reason is that those who interact infrequently or not at all are much less likely to contribute their skills and insights, are less likely to have or

---

F I G U R E   2 . 1
Communication Network Structure

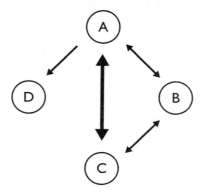

to develop a sense of involvement, are more likely to experience dissatisfaction, and, in the extreme, are more likely to be viewed as "outsiders" by team members who are more actively involved.[12] Communication is considered more fully in Chapter 5.

Team size can influence team performance either directly or indirectly through several processes including member level of participation, difficulty of reaching consensus, and challenges for leadership. Broadly speaking, as team size increases, resources available to a team increase. Increased resources can mean a larger pool of skills, knowledge, and experience from which to draw. Concurrently, the complexity of interactions also increases because of the greater number of potential exchanges among members. This complexity arises because more members can mean more communication difficulties, more complex coordination of activities, and potentially increased performance times. Another drawback of a larger team size can be the reduction in the average amount of member participation. Whereas some members of a larger team will have a high level of participation, other members will be less inclined to participate. Broadly, this means that larger teams require a level of leadership skill that smaller teams may not need.[13] Team size is examined more fully in Chapter 7.

A team's *environment* is also influential. A team performs in an environment, generally a larger organization, that usually has an investment in the team's achieving its goal. The environment can also influence a team's performance. For example, an athletic team playing on its home court or field has supportive fans cheering for the team. For a team playing away from home, there are fewer supportive fans. A student team performing in a college environment can find the team's activities competing with many other activities. As a result, finding mutually convenient meeting times can be difficult. A student team whose instructor allows class time for team meetings has a more supportive environment. A team of bank executives, designing a new financial product for their organization, whose CEO indicates the importance of the project for the organization, will be much more involved in the process than will a team in another organization asked to plan a holiday party that the team members know is of little interest to their fellow workers.

> *"A team performs in an environment, generally a larger organization, that usually has an investment in the team's achieving its goal."*

Many factors in a team's environment can facilitate or hinder a team's performance. These are often specific to a particular team. There are four ways in which a team's environment can influence its performance: in the specification of the team's goal and the level of quality expected; in the resources it provides, including personnel to pursue the goal; in the degree of support for the team's goal-directed process; and in its evaluation of and rewards for the products resulting from the team's achieving its goal. These influences need to be considered both as a team is created and as it proceeds toward its goal, since each can significantly impact a team's performance.

Barriers to a team's performance can arise from its environment. For example, a team asked to develop a new information system may find that the team's supervisor, who represents the team's environment, is unclear about whether the goal is to reorganize the existing system or to develop a new one. The team must recognize the confusion and seek a decision from the supervisor. A team given an assignment but given members with inadequate skills to complete the assignment must decide with its supervisor whether to add members who have the relevant skills or to undertake training to develop the skills of members already on the team. A team has the primary responsibility to identify any barriers to high performance and to address them.[14] A team's relationship to its environment is considered in more detail in Chapter 10.

The Challenge Revisited
Creating a Team

1. A team can be effective when its members are clear about its goal and how the team will get there, when it has members with relevant capabilities, and when it establishes principles that foster interdependence.

2. To see a team's goal clearly and to proceed toward that goal, team members must recognize and respect each other's capabilities, must trust each other, must be involved, and must be comfortable working interdependently.

3. As a team proceeds toward its goal, obstacles, such as inadequate member involvement, poor communication, and interpersonal differences, can hinder progress.

4. To address these obstacles, a team must develop and use its decision-making and problem-solving capabilities while remaining clearly focused on its goal.

EXERCISE 2.1 • *Observing Communication Interactions*

1. Appoint one member to observe the communication patterns on your team. For three consecutive 5-minute periods, the observer should record the direction and frequency of communication interactions among team members, according to the procedure that follows:

   a. On three pieces of $8\frac{1}{2}$- × 11-inch paper, the observer draws a diagram, similar to the one illustrated.

      • The number of circles on the page represents the number of team members, less the observer, according to where each is seated. Label each circle with an appropriate designation so that you can tell which person is which.

      • Label each sheet by observation period, either 1, 2, or 3. Remember each observation period is 5 minutes. After each period, record new observations on a sheet.

   b. Use this observation method:

      • The first time a member speaks to another member (speaker to receiver) draw an arrow ➤, showing who speaks to whom. The arrow points from the speaker to the receiver.

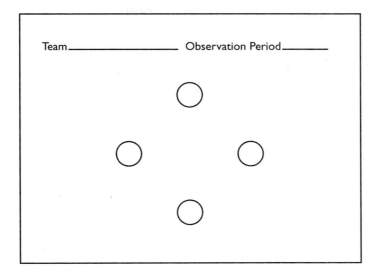

- If the receiver replies, draw a second arrow showing that reply.
- After the first communication between two members (when the arrow is already drawn), keep a tally next to the arrow indicating further communications in that direction as shown here:

- If a speaker speaks to multiple members or all members of the team, all receivers are given a tally.

2. Now jump to Exercise 2.2 and begin observing. When the observation period is finished, total the number of interactions each member has with each receiver. What differences are seen in the amount of communication among members? Discuss the implications of the prevailing patterns for your team's functioning.

EXERCISE 2.2 • *Identifying and Observing Interdependence*

1. As a team, discuss the meaning of interdependence. Take notes of your discussion as you consider the following questions (later you will use your notes to develop reports and procedures):

   a. What does interdependent behavior "look like" (i.e., what specific behaviors would an observer identify as interdependent)?

   b. Are there "rules" that would help the team to develop interdependence and to perform at high levels? What might these rules be?

   c. Develop a method for observing interdependent behavior in your team's activities. Describe this method.

   d. Consider how this method can be used to gather feedback about the degree of interdependence that is present.

2. Prepare a report describing your team's deliberations. Specifically, document behaviors that represent interdependence among your team's members and give your recommendations about how these behaviors can be observed.

QUESTIONS FOR REVIEW AND DISCUSSION

1. Why is a team's goal (where it is headed) the most important issue for a team? Why are the capabilities of a team's membership also important?

2. What is the difference between *technical skills* and *social skills*? Why are many people more skilled with one than the other? What are the implications of such skill differences for team functioning?

3. What is meant by the term *interdependence*? What is the significance of interdependence for teamwork?

4. What is the difference between structural interdependence and behavioral interdependence?

5. How is structural interdependence created? In creating interdependence, what roles do equipment, the assignment of collective responsibility, and the establishment of rules play?

6. How can the assignment of performance outcomes and of reward assignment be instrumental in establishing interdependence?

7. Why is member involvement crucial for team performance? What are the reasons for reduced member involvement?

8. For a team, what are the primary sources of member satisfaction or dissatisfaction? Under what circumstances can each source result in satisfaction or dissatisfaction?

9. What are the primary influences that can help or hinder member performance?

10. Why is member diversity important for a team's functioning? Under what conditions can such diversity become a barrier to a team's functioning?

NOTES

1. See J. Collins & J. Porras (1994), *Built to Last: Successful Habits of Visionary Companies*, New York: Harper Business, for a discussion of goals and vision.

2. The issue of *equifinality*, that is, of a team's having multiple paths to its goal, is discussed in H. Arrow, J. McGrath, & J. Berdahl (2000), *Small Groups as Complex Systems*, Thousand Oaks, CA: Sage, p. 80.

3. The distinction between technical and social skills has a long history. See L. Ketchum & E. Trist (1992), *All Teams Are Not Created Equal*, Thousand Oaks, CA: Sage, pp. 28–29. Also, J. McGrath (1984), *Groups: Interactions & Performance*, Englewood Cliffs, NJ: Prentice Hall, has

described a series of social skills. More recently, D. Goleman (1997), *Emotional Intelligence*, New York: Bantam Books, has described social skills. A portion of the framework for this chapter was summarized from B. Morgan & D. Lassiter (1992), Team composition and staffing, in R. W. Swezey & E. Salas (Eds.), *Teams: Their Training and Performance*, Norwood, NJ: Ablex.

4. See R. Wageman (1995), Interdependence and group effectiveness, *Administrative Science Quarterly*, 40, 145–180.

5. Argyris, among others, has addressed the issue of hidden agendas. See C. Argyris (1982), *Reasoning, Learning and Action*, San Francisco: Jossey-Bass, pp. 82–106.

6. The topic of low member involvement or *social loafing* is discussed in a variety of sources. See, for instance, B. Latane, K. Williams, & S. Harkins (1979), Many hands make light the work: The causes and consequences of social loafing, *Journal of Personality and Social Psychology*, 37, 822–832.

7. The framework for this discussion of interdependence comes from R. Wageman (2001), The meaning of interdependence, in M. E. Turner (Ed.), *Groups at Work*, Mahwah, NJ: Erlbaum, pp. 197–217.

8. Norms are described in a variety of sources. See Arrow et al., op. cit., pp. 115–118. See also K. Bettenhausen & J. Murnighan (1985), The emergence of norms in competitive decision-making groups, *Administrative Science Quarterly*, 30, 350–372 and in Chapter 8 of this book.

9. Wageman's framework for establishing interdependence also provides a framework for operationally defining each of the features of interdependence outlined; Wogeman, (2001), op. cit. To the author's knowledge such an operational definition has yet to be developed.

10. Diversity for a team means first and foremost diversity of skills, knowledge, experience, and perspectives, among other characteristics. The assumption is that this diversity provides resources to a team. See J. McGrath, J. Berdahl, & H. Arrow (1995), Traits, expectations, culture and clout: The dynamics of diversity in work groups, in S. E. Jackson & M. N. Ruderman (Eds.), *Diversity in Work Teams: Research Paradigm for a Changing Workplace*, Washington, DC: American Psychological Association, pp. 14–45. Diversity also refers to differences in characteristics such as gender and national or ethnic background. Although the latter focus is an important topic, the emphasis of the present discussion is on diversity in the former sense.

11. T. Brown & C. Miller (2000), Communication networks in task performing groups, *Small Group Research*, 31, 131–157.

12. For the effect of reduced involvement on communication, see S. Schachter (1959), *The Psychology of Affiliation*, Stanford, CA: Stanford University Press.

13. The consequences of team size for team performance are considered in a variety of sources. See I. Steiner (1972), *Group Process and Productivity*, New York: Academic Press. Also, see Morgan & Lassiter, op. cit.

14. There are various perspectives from which a team's relationship to its organizational environment can be considered. See, for example, M. D. Yeatts & C. Hyten (1998), *High-Performing Self-Managed Work Teams,* Part IV, Thousand Oaks, CA: Sage.

The Challenge
Goals, Vision, and Values

A team's goal is at the core of its functioning. Its vision gives significance to its goal and to the activities by which the goal is achieved. A vivid vision activates a team's energies. It defines a team's identity and its character. A team's values are reflected in the way it pursues its goal and in the value added by its product. If members believe that the product and their vision for it adds value, they will be committed and involved. If members' interactions are supportive, cooperative, and interdependent, members will be energized. The challenge to a team is to arrive at a mutual agreement about their team's goal and about their vision for the goal's achievement. A team's charter specifies members' agreement about the goal, the vision, and the values and principles on which pursuit of a team's goal is based.

chapter 3

Goals, Vision, and Values

A team's **goal** specifies what the team is to accomplish. A team is defined by its goal, which is either assigned from outside or brought to a team by its members. A team's goal gives direction and meaning to members' efforts to achieve it. If a team's members agree on its goal, that is, on what the team is to accomplish, mutuality among team members is fostered. When its goal is clear and members unite to pursue it, a goal can be a powerful motivating force. When its goal is unclear or members disagree about it, a team's goal loses its power, since the team does not know what it is to accomplish.

Some goals are clear; others are not. For example, an athletic team typically has a clear goal: scoring more points than the opposing team. For such teams, identifying and proceeding along a path to their goal is the challenge. Other teams' goals can be unclear. For example, a team of automobile design experts, given the goal of designing a new model SUV, must decide how

> *"When its goal is clear and members unite to pursue it, a goal can be a powerful motivating force."*

"new" the design is to be. This in effect means deciding what its goal is. Is its goal to make modest changes in an existing model or to develop a radically new design? How this question is answered will define what the team is to accomplish and the meaning of the undertaking for the team. It will also have serious cost implications for the team's company.

To understand what a goal is and how it relates to a team's functioning, several issues are considered. First, what is meant by the term *goal*? Second, how do members reach agreement about their team's goal? Third, what gives a goal its significance? Fourth, how does a team pursue its goal?

THE MEANING OF *GOAL*

"A goal is an abstract future state that requires performance over time of one or more tasks to be attained."

A *goal* is an abstract future state that requires performance over time of one or more tasks to be attained. It is abstract because it is not yet accomplished. It is also abstract because it is a conception in team members' consciousness. Although abstract, a goal must be clear and objective for a team to pursue it. "Clear and objective"[1] means that the actions necessary to achieve the goal are identifiable and that the extent to which a particular sequence of actions will move a team toward its goal can be specified. It may also mean defining and testing alternative courses of action for achieving a goal.[2] Finally, "clear and objective" means that there are indicators of the degree to which a goal has been achieved that are specific, observable, countable, and preferably multiple.[3]

A team cannot function without at least one goal that is understood and agreed to by at least some members, and ultimately every member must agree if a team is to function efficiently. "Agree" here means that members have the same conception of what the team's goal is.

A goal has several features that give it significance for a team's functioning. A clear goal *reflects expectations*. It helps members understand what is required of the team and of them as individual members. A goal is a *guide for action*. A goal requires a team to decide how to achieve it. Usually, there are multiple paths to a goal. Differences among team members about the best path to follow can be resolved by deciding which path enables a team to achieve its goal most efficiently. A goal also provides a *point of reference* for organizing members' activities and it provides a *basis for judging the effectiveness* of performance in moving the team toward completion of the goal. Information about how well the team is proceeding, called feedback, is developed for this purpose. Finally, a goal becomes an *incentive for team members*. Team members must commit to achieving the goal and engage in activities to do so.[4]

"Team members must commit to achieving the goal and engage in activities to do so."

When members commit themselves to achieving a goal, a tension is aroused in them. This tension continues until the goal is reached, resolving the tension and giving team members satisfaction.[5] This intrinsic incentive of satisfaction combines with extrinsic incentives, such as recognition or monetary rewards, to motivate members. For example, the automobile design team, mentioned earlier, decides in consultation with top company executives to develop a next-generation SUV. This goal means something "really new." Their point of reference is existing models. The team must decide how dramatic changes are to be and which features of the vehicle will be changed. Finally, after making these decisions the team must design the changes and develop strategies for manufacturing them. For team members committed to achieving this goal, the prospect of such an accomplishment can be very motivating.

REACHING AGREEMENT ON A TEAM'S GOAL

A team's goal, even an attractive goal, can be difficult to pursue for several reasons. Because a goal is an abstraction, members can readily perceive it differently and disagree on how to proceed. For example, a team asked to develop and implement an electronic data system for keeping track of customer service inquiries might have members who differ on the meaning of "develop and implement a system." Some members interpret this to mean developing an innovative system specifically for their organization while two members interpret it to mean identifying a system already operating successfully elsewhere and implementing it. The conflict between these two views, if not addressed, could be costly in wasted time and effort.

A major difficulty with this team's stated goal—"to develop and implement an electronic data system for keeping track of customer service inquiries"—is its vagueness. It specifies more a path than a clear goal. The goal can be more clearly specified by the answer to this question: What is lacking in the current method of keeping track of customer inquiries? The answer could be that customer inquiries are being lost, that customer representatives need more ready access to data when customers call, or that there is a need to analyze the issues about which customers are inquiring. This team's goal is to develop a system that will accomplish whichever one or combination of these issues is the organization's concern.

Underlying the differing views of the team members is a less obvious, but important, issue. As indicated earlier, some members of the team developing an electronic data system want to develop an innovative system specifically for their organization while two members want to identify a relevant system operating in another organization and adapt it for their organization. These differing views reflect an underlying difference in personal goals. Those who want to custom build a system for the organization are skilled computer scientists who are drawn to an interesting design problem. The two members who wish to adapt an existing system for their organization have few computer science skills and fear either having to learn new skills or becoming minor contributors to the project. In other words, at stake in this difference of approach is a difference of individual goals.

Distinguishing Individual Goals and Team Goals

Any individual who becomes a team member has his or her own goals (that is, reasons), for participating.[6] How do individual goals relate to team goals? One might assume that a team goal exists when all members have the same goal. This is unsatisfactory. For example, three students, each running for the same position of class president, have the same goal, but their similar goals hardly make them a team. Theirs are individual goals that can only be achieved individually.

> *"An individual's goal specifies a preferred, future state for that individual and guides that individual's action toward its attainment."*

The difficulty arises from the nature of a goal. A goal is a preferred, future state that guides action toward attaining that state. An **individual's goal** specifies a preferred, future state for that individual and guides that individual's action toward its attainment.[7] In the customer service computer system example, the individuals opting for implementing an existing system seek their own goal, a future state in which a new computer system is implemented without their having to develop additional computer science skills. The individuals who wish to develop an entirely new system want to pursue their individual goals of creative development.

A **team goal** specifies a preferred, future state for a team as a *unit* and guides members' *collective* action to achieve it. An intervening situation between individuals' goals for themselves and a team's goal is another form of goal, an individual's goal for his or her team. In the preceding example, the members with few computer science skills want their team to proceed along a path that fulfills their individual goals, that is, not being required to learn new computer science skills. This individual goal is reflected in their wanting their team to develop a new customer service system by adapting an existing system, because this particular team goal will result in fulfillment of their individual goals.

Individuals' Goals for Their Team

As just discussed, an individual's goal for his team reflects that individual's desire to have his team satisfy his individual goals. The latter goals represent an important stage in an individual committing to a team goal. When an individual joins a team, he generally has in mind what he would like to achieve as a team member. This is that person's individual goal for his team. It serves as a bridge between the individual's goal for himself and the team's goal. Several

> *"The more concerned individuals are about fulfilling their goals for themselves, the less involved they will be in achieving their team's goal."*

considerations influence the choice of this goal. An individual's motives influence his choice of a goal for the team much as they influence the individual's choice of a goal for himself.

An important difference between an individual's goals for herself and her goal for her team is that the team, not the individual alone, must agree to and perform activities to achieve the individual's *goal for the team*.[8] Individuals are dependent on their team for attaining their individual goals for their team. Consequently, an individual estimates the probability that her goal for her team will be attained. Several conditions influence this estimate, including whether the team will stick together to the end and whether the members possess the necessary skills and other resources needed to achieve the team goal. Doubt about any of these can result in individual members becoming more concerned about their goal for themselves than about their team's goal. The more concerned individuals are about fulfilling their goals for themselves, the less involved they will be in achieving their team's goal.

Another influence on an individual's involvement in a team's goal is the team goal's dominance. Established teams often have clearer, more dominant goals than newly formed teams. For example, a team that has for many years planned a company's holiday party will readily focus on the tasks required to achieve its goal, spending little time clarifying the goal itself except possibly for a new member. New members are likely to have little latitude to shift the team's orientation to a different definition of the goal. By contrast, newly formed teams may spend considerable time and effort on clarifying team members' understanding of the team's goal and on deciding how to achieve it. A team in a company that has never had a holiday party will spend time defining and agreeing on the goal, then spend more time planning the steps required to achieve its goal. In this situation, members do have more latitude to orient the team toward achievement of their individual satisfaction.

To arrive at their preference for a team goal, different individuals may weight the various influences differently. An important factor in this process is an individual's comfort with a shared accomplishment. If an individual has a strong need for sole ownership of accomplishments, he is more likely to focus on his own goal of, for example, receiving recognition. Distrust about receiving the desired share of the credit may dominate his view of the activities. If, however, an individual is reasonably comfortable with shared accomplishment, then she will orient more to her goal for the team, trusting that she will share in the credit received by the team.[9]

Converting Individuals' Goals for a Team into Team Goals

Once individuals are members of a team, they generally convert their individual goals for the team into a single goal capable of steering team activities.[10] Two broad criteria are used to accomplish this. One is the **fairness criterion.** This seeks a goal that represents the individual interests of all members. This criterion requires that each member's preferences be clear to and be equally weighted by other members. Most teams fail, to some degree, to meet this criterion due primarily to members having differing degrees of influence in a team's decision process. These differences result from members' differing levels of participation, of skills and knowledge, and of interpersonal competence. For example, members who are hesitant to participate in team discussions are less likely to have their preferences given serious consideration by other team members than are more active participants.

A different criterion, effectiveness, specifies that a team's perspective on its goal should be to optimize its ability to accomplish its main objectives. The **effectiveness criterion** is met through a team problem-solving process to formulate a goal that can be realized most efficiently. Teams fail to meet the effectiveness criterion because of inadequacies in their problem-solving process. These inadequacies can result in choosing a less than efficient path to the goal or failing to choose a path to which all members will commit.

The fairness criterion and the effectiveness criterion can be difficult to reconcile and might even be incompatible. Consider again the example of the software design team. If an analysis of what a new customer service data system is to accomplish results in the goal being to design an innovative system, the team

"The fairness criterion and the effectiveness criterion can be difficult to reconcile and might even be incompatible."

must find a path to the goal that is efficient and affords satisfaction for all members. Specifically, the team must find an efficient path that allows the two less skilled members to be equal contributors without undertaking the extra tasks of learning more computer skills. This can be difficult to achieve.[11]

People attempting to formulate a team goal reveal differences in their cognitive and motivational characteristics. Cognitive processes are reflected in the search for agreement about facts relevant to a decision. In the software design team illustration, the less skilled members focus on the additional training needed, whereas the more skilled members focus on the exciting challenges offered by an innovative system. The quality of any group decision depends on an accurate assessment of the facts and competent problem solving based on those facts. Furthermore, if members' motives are to some degree in conflict, identifying a mutually agreed-on team goal can be difficult. Members are likely to engage in bargaining, maneuver for power over the decision, or form coalitions among members to seek to sway a decision. These processes use resources and can divert a team from efficient pursuit of its goal.

The following hypothetical case provides an example of such a problem. Barbara, Sam, and Joe have recently obtained graduate business degrees. Each has interviewed for several jobs, although none of those offered has met their expectations. Each worked for several years prior to graduate school. Joe was an assistant financial officer in a bank. Barbara worked for a company that designs Web pages. Sam was in the marketing department of a large retail chain. During graduate school they had talked about starting their own company and they continued to talk as they did their job searches. In their discussions each had spoken about what was of interest about owning a business. Barbara is interested in trying out some innovative design ideas and she wants to be her own "boss." Joe has not had direct experience with venture capitalists, but he wants some experience raising money to start a business and he wants to lead a company. Sam would like to develop and implement a really successful marketing

"Members are likely to engage in bargaining, maneuver for power over the decision, or form coalitions among members to seek to sway a decision."

plan and he also wants the prestige of being a top executive. After another week, during which they discuss their goal of establishing their own company, they decide to proceed. Figure 3.1 depicts their goals.

They face, however, a difficulty. Among the three friends' six individual goals, some are more compatible than others. Barbara's desire to develop Web sites, Joes's to raise venture capital, and Sam's to develop a marketing strategy appear compatible, but careful planning will be required to coordinate those individual goals into their mutual goal to establish and run a viable company. The remaining three goals, Barbara's to be her own boss, Joe's to lead a company, and Sam's to have a prestigious executive position appear incompatible because each tends to view the fulfillment of his or her own goal as being the new company's chief executive. If this potential conflict is not addressed, the result could be divisive and destructive of effectiveness.

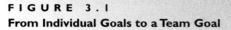

FIGURE 3.1
From Individual Goals to a Team Goal

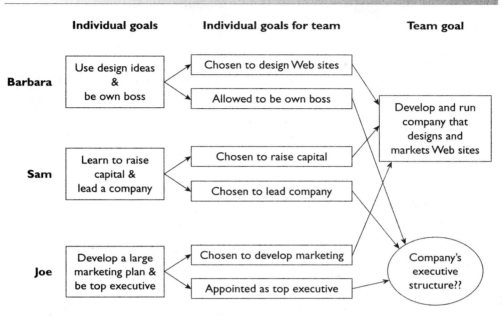

To enhance team effectiveness, these team members need to increase their consensus about the team's goal and minimize incompatibility between members' goals and the team's goal.[12] To address these potentially conflicting goals, openness, discussion, and negotiation are needed to arrive at an arrangement that optimizes team effectiveness and offers some satisfaction for each individual's goals. Non-complementary individual goals that are not discussed can readily become *hidden agendas*. These are individual goals that are pursued covertly by team members solely for their individual satisfaction.

When a team is first formed, it is important to discuss its goal thoroughly. Discussion is important, even when a superior specifies the goal. Discussion helps to remove misunderstandings and encourage ownership. Team members can identify attractive aspects of their team's goal, even some that were not previously seen. They can also consider which of their personal goals can be satisfied.[13] For example, the three cofounders of a hypothetical business need to discuss first their team's goal to establish and run their own business and then consider how some of their individual goals can be met in the process. They also need to discuss what status means for each of them and how each can achieve what he or she desires. Possibly, Barbara can be her own boss as far as technical design issues are concerned. Joe can be responsible for the financial operations. Sam can be responsible for sales. Beyond this they will then need to negotiate a plan for an executive structure in which each can find a reasonable degree of satisfaction, although compromise is likely to be needed.

"When a team is first formed, it is important to discuss its goal thoroughly."

> *"When a hidden agenda has the potential to reduce team effectiveness, the time required to address it is time well spent."*

One objective for a team is to develop its capacity to recognize and address constructively non-complementary goals, including hidden agendas. This should be done in a manner that improves a team's problem-solving ability concerning personal and interpersonal issues. It is not productive to criticize a member when a hidden agenda is recognized. These are to be expected and must be worked on in much the same manner as other team tasks, that is, as challenges to be resolved and problems to be solved. The time spent addressing hidden agendas depends on their influence on team effectiveness. When a hidden agenda has the potential to reduce team effectiveness, the time required to address it is time well spent.[14]

A Team's Vision: The Significance of Its Goal

Saying that a goal is an "abstract future state" is like saying a team *will* prepare a report, or *will* produce an electronic controller, or *will* perform as a string quartet, or *will* reach point B. Such goals can sound rather dull and uninteresting. Described this way these accomplishments have little or no meaning. The report, the controller, the quartet, or reaching point B can be completed just to get finished. What if they had meaning, real significance? What would that be like? The report would be prepared to help the company significantly improve its market share. The electronic controller would be part of a major safety improvement in a vehicle. The string quartet would be awarded a prestigious prize. Point B is the site of a major disaster to which a large quantity of relief supplies is delivered. Described in these terms these goals are engaging and important.

> *"A team's vision provides meaning and significance to a team's goal and its achievement."*

A team's **vision** provides meaning and significance to a team's goal and its achievement. High performance and continuous effort are required to make the vision real. As noted previously, a team's vision embodies what it means for that team to accomplish its goal. This is not just where the team is going, but how it thinks of itself on the way and once it gets there. Its vision provides a team its dynamic. For example, a team with the goal of planning a new information technology system for its division may seek to produce not just a plan (which represents achievement of the goal), but to develop a plan that significantly improves the quality of communication in the division (which is its vision). A team's vision defines the significance of its activity.

Core Ideology

A well-articulated vision consists of two major features.[15] One is a **core ideology.** The other is an **envisioned future.** Core ideology is what drives or motivates a team. For example, a team that envisions developing a plan that improves its company's market share has a core ideology of doing something that *makes a difference.* Just as an individual's "character" reflects *who* the person is, a team's core ideology defines "who" it is. This ideology consists of three interrelated issues: core purpose, core values, and operating principles.

Core purpose gets at the deeper reasons for a team's existence beyond just reaching its goal. In the previous example the team's purpose is to "make a difference." Goals are achieved but purpose is ongoing. Purpose does not change, but it can inspire change. To live up to its purpose, changes in clarity of goal or of member commitment can occur but the core purpose of making a difference remains the same. Effective teams are always "becoming" as they pursue their core purpose.

> *"Core ideology is what drives or motivates a team."*

Core values are closely related to core purpose. They are a small set of guiding principles that indicate how a team goes about realizing its core purpose. They have intrinsic value and importance for those on the team. Ralph Larson, CEO of Johnson and Johnson, said: "The core values embodied in our Credo might be a competitive advantage, but that is not why we have them. We have them because they define for us what we stand for, and we would hold them even if they became a competitive disadvantage in certain situations."[16]

A team's core purpose and core values are embodied in its **operating principles.** These govern how team members perform their tasks, relate to each other, and relate to others outside the team.[17] A team's operating principles must be developed, practiced, and often refined. They apply both to the technical side of its activities and to the social interaction side. Serving both the technical and the social sides is a challenge; it means striving for a level of functioning that is both technically excellent and socially competent.[18] A team's capability to do both represents a major step toward its achieving the considerable advantage that it potentially holds.

An example of an operating principle is provided by an experience an observer had attending a technical problem-solving session at Boeing Commercial Aircraft. During a group evaluation session a participant commented to the observer, jokingly so it seemed, that the observer's presence could distort the problem-solving process. The observer was aware of the so-called "Hawthorne effect" and took little note of what was said. Later the observer learned, when the person who made the remark apologized, that his comment was judged by one of the session's organizers to sound inhospitable and contrary to the company's standards for behavior toward visitors. This illustrates how principles can be applied in a technically-oriented setting.[19]

Envisioned Future

The second major feature of a team's vision is an envisioned future. This is what a team expects to experience when its vision is achieved, when the abstract future state becomes real. There is a risk that the vision may not be accomplished; for example, the report may be accepted but put "on the shelf." It is, however, a condition that those who envision it believe can be achieved. Envisioned future is vivid and engaging. It is not simply preparing a report, that is, achieving the team's goal, but producing an outcome that *makes a difference.* Henry Ford envisioned a future that he described as: "I will build a motor car for the great multitude. . . . It will be so low in price that no man making a good salary will be unable to afford one—and enjoy with his family the pleasures of the great open spaces. . . . When I am through, everybody will be able to afford one, and everybody will have one."[20] This picture embodies a very bold vision for what was in the early 1900s a small auto company. There is also Bill Gates' vision of "personal computing" which, when proposed in an era of room-sized mainframe computers, seemed inconceivable.

Effects of a Team's Goal

Once a team's goal and the associated vision are defined, they can be expected to influence team members' behavior and their interactions with and evaluations of each other. Their influence derives from members aligning their individual goals with the team goal. "Good" team members are expected to work to attain the team goal, even when their preferred goal is not chosen. They do this in the expectation that their team is committed to each member's realizing some aspect of their individual goals, such as experiencing the satisfaction from performing well, receiving recognition for their performance, or obtaining monetary reward.

In reality, a team's goal influences members but the magnitude of the influence can vary. If a team's goal is unacceptable to a significant proportion of the team, the result can be more frequent individual goal-oriented behavior and less team goal-oriented behavior. A team's goal that is accepted by its members has power to influence their behavior, to elicit members' involvement, and to motivate high performance.

"A team's goal that is accepted by its members has power to influence their behavior, to elicit members' involvement, and to motivate high performance."

A clear team goal induces interdependence. It is the focus for a team's collective responsibility. When members accept a team's goal, they experience satisfaction or frustration, depending on what happens to the team. This mutual dependence on the fate of the team reflects interdependence. If one member performs an activity that helps the team reach its goal, the probability of other members gaining satisfaction increases. Interdependence here means cooperation rather than competition.[21] Cooperation means that there is a desire to support each other's activity. There is a readiness to teach others ways to improve performance. There is a readiness to substitute, where useful, one member's activities for another's. Members like one another. There is a readiness to be influenced by other members. The development of cooperative interdependence is important if a team is to improve its effectiveness and achieve its goal and associated vision.

ACHIEVING A TEAM'S GOAL AND VISION

A team's goal and its vision for its goal are intimately intertwined. If a team's vision for its goal is "just to get it done," the accomplishment and the path to it will be flat, not engaging. If the vision is "to get it done in a way or at a level of quality seldom achieved," the path to the accomplishment and its realization can be difficult, but also exciting and engaging. The accomplishment will be one that the team's customer will value because the accomplishment "adds value" often beyond what the customer expects. The accomplishment will be one in which the team takes pride.

For different types of teams, realizing a vision involves different accomplishments. For a surgical team, realizing its vision can mean not simply removing disease, but restoring health and lengthening life expectancy. For a manufacturing team, realizing its vision can mean not simply producing a specified quantity of a company's product, but doing so at a level of quality previously not achieved. For an urban planning team, it is not simply developing a plan for reconstructing a historic area of a community, but planning in a way that makes the area historically authentic and attractive to visitors. For a personnel selection team, it means not simply finding a person to fill a vacancy, but finding a person whose technical skills and interpersonal competence challenge coworkers to previously unachieved levels of accomplishment. For a sports team, it is not simply winning the game, but winning with an exciting, superior performance.

To achieve its goal, a team must select an appropriate path and proceed along it until its goal is reached. To realize its vision, a team must both reach its goal and do so in a manner that makes the vision a reality. Performance that is carefully planned and executed can result in a team's achieving its goal. Only increasingly effective performance can enable a team to realize its vision. Enhanced effectiveness enables a team to reach its goal in a shorter period of time, with greater efficiency, at a higher level of quality, or in a way that is more innovative. A team's reaching its goal and achieving its vision result in a feeling of pride and accomplishment and should also result in the team's customer being satisfied with the outcome and viewing the team as having "added value," that is, as having gone beyond the minimal requirements of the undertaking.

> *"To realize its vision, a team must both reach its goal and do so in a manner that makes the vision a reality."*

A Team's Charter

Out of a team's deliberations about its goal, its discussion of its member's goals, its formulation of its vision, and its definition of a set of values and operating principles should come a consensus about where the team is going and how the team will behave in the process of getting there. To bring the results of these deliberations into sharper focus, many teams take the further step of developing a team contract or **charter.** This is a document that spells out the agreements reached. In the process of preparing the document, differences or misunderstandings may be identified and these can be resolved. As a team proceeds toward its goal and realizing its vision, and as it seeks to act on its principles, further clarification may be needed. A charter can be amended as a team gains experience on which to base a more precise statement.

A team's charter can consist of several parts:

- *Team goal*: a precise statement of what the team seeks to accomplish. What abstract state does the team seek to make real?

- *Team vision*: a precise statement of what the team seeks for its accomplishment to mean. What is to be the significance of achieving its goal?

- *Team operating principles:* a precise statement of the values and principles that will govern the team's actions. What values and principles will govern behavior among team members, in performing its tasks, and between the team and its environment?

- *Team logo:* a team often designs a logo or symbol that, for the team, embodies its goal, vision, and operating principles.

The Challenge Revisited
Goals, Visions, and Values

1. Goals can be difficult to define because they are imprecise or because members focus more on their own goals than on the team goal.

2. A team's vision specifies the meaning and significance of a team's achieving its goal.

3. Once a team's goal and vision are clear, reaching the goal and achieving the vision require a high level of member commitment and effort.

4. When a team's goal and its vision are aligned with members' individual goals, members can be more committed.

5. A challenge for a team is to have a singular goal and an engaging vision, and to choose a path to the goal that utilizes members' knowledge and skills and provides them satisfaction in the process.

EXERCISE 3.1 • *Defining the Team's Goal*

The purpose of this exercise is to prepare a goal statement on which all members can agree. Don't be tempted to take this exercise lightly. Goals can be difficult to define precisely.

1. Have individual team members write a one-sentence statement of what they perceive the team's goal to be.

2. Each member next takes a turn describing to other members what he or she believes the team's goal is.

3. Engage in further discussion until the team arrives at a mutually agreeable definition.

EXERCISE 3.2 • *Developing a Team Charter*

A team's charter is an agreement among its members about where the team is going and how it will conduct its activities.

1. Develop a team charter that covers the following four points.

   a. *Team goal:* Develop a precise statement of what the team seeks to accomplish (see Exercise 3.1). What abstract state does the team seek to make real?

   b. *Team vision*: Develop a precise statement of what the team seeks for its accomplishment to mean. What is to be the significance of its accomplishment?

   c. *Team operating principles*: Develop a precise statement of the values and principles that will govern the team's actions. What values and principles will govern behavior among team members, in performing its tasks, and between the team and its environment?

   d. *Team logo*: Develop a team logo that depicts for the team the essence of this charter.

2. Prepare a presentation and present your team's charter to the class as a whole.

3. Solicit feedback and adjust your charter if others' remarks convince you to do so.

QUESTIONS FOR REVIEW AND DISCUSSION

1. What is meant by the statement "a team is defined by its goal"?

2. What is the difference between a team goal and an individual goal?

3. Why is it necessary for team members to reach agreement about their team's goal? Why can reaching agreement be difficult?

4. What is an individual's goal for his/her team? How do such goals serve as a bridge between individual goals and a team goal?

5. By what criteria can individual goals be converted to a team goal? What are the difficulties inherent in each criterion?

6. What are non-complementary goals? How can they be addressed by team members?

7. What constitutes a well-articulated vision? How does a team's vision give a team's activity significance? What comprises a vision's core ideology? Why are operating principles important for how a team achieves its vision?

8. Why and how can a team's goal and vision influence members' behavior? Why can this influence vary? How does a team's goal relate to members' interdependence?

9. What is required for a team to both reach its goal and achieve its vision?

10. What is a team's charter? Why is it important for team performance?

NOTES

1. J. G. March & H. A. Simon (1958), *Organizations*, New York: Wiley. See also D. Johnson & F. Johnson (1987), *Joining Together: Group Theory and Group Skills*, 3rd ed., Englewood Cliffs, NJ: Prentice-Hall, pp. 164–166.

2. See H. Arrow, J. McGrath, & J. Berdahl (2000), *Small Groups as Complex Systems*, Thousand Oaks, CA: Sage.

3. Goals are a point of reference in determining progress. See D. Yeatts & C. Hyten (1998), *High Performing Self-Managed Work Teams,* Thousand Oaks, CA: Sage, pp. 139–141.

4. See Johnson & Johnson (1987), op. cit., pp. 164–166. Also A. Zander (1980), The origins and consequences of group goals, in L. Festinger (Ed.), *Retrospections on Social Psychology,* New York: Oxford, pp. 205–235.

5. See D. Cartwright & A. Zander (1960), Individual motives and group goals: Introduction, in D. Cartwright & A. Zander (Eds.), *Group Dynamics: Research and Theory,* Evanston, IL: Row Peterson. Also Zander (1980), op. cit., pp. 205–235; and Johnson & Johnson, op. cit., pp. 130–170.

6. Cartwright & Zander, op. cit., p. 347.

7. Cartwright & Zander, op. cit., p. 347.

8. Cartwright & Zander, op. cit., p. 356.

9. Individual differences in the willingness to share recognition and reward have received little examination, although personal characteristics that reflect on the inclination to be cooperative have been examined. See D. Johnson & R. Johnson (1989), *Cooperation and Competition: Theory and Research,* Edina, MN: Interaction Book Company, pp.77–86.

10. Cartwright & Zander, op. cit., p. 359.

11. While fairness is seldom examined, see L. Thompson & C. Fox (2001), Negotiation in and between groups in organizations, in M. Turner (Ed.), *Groups at Work,* Mahwah, NJ: Erlbaum, p. 239, which examines effectiveness in detail. For recent studies, see M. Campion, E. Papper, & G. Medsker (1996), Relations between work team characteristics and effectiveness: A replication and extension, *Personnel Psychology,* 49, 429–452; and J. Choi (2002), External activities and team effectiveness: Review and theoretical development, *Small Group Research,* 33, 181–208.

12. Zander, op. cit.

13. Johnson & Johnson (1987), op. cit., pp. 138–140.

14. See C. Argyris (1982), *Reasoning, Learning, and Action: Individual & Organizational,* San Francisco: Jossey-Bass, pp. 82–106.

15. This section briefly summarizes a discussion of vision by J. C. Collins & J. I. Porras (1994), *Built to Last: Successful Habits of Visionary Companies,* New York: Harper Business.

16. Collins & Porras, op. cit., p. 222; also Yeatts & Hyten, op. cit., pp. 228–229.

17. Collins & Porras, op. cit., pp. 221–232.

18. Development of technical and social competencies; see R. Swezey & E. Salas (1992), Guidelines for use in team training development, in R. Swezey & E. Salas (Eds.), *Teams: Their Training and Performance,* Norwood, NJ: Ablex, pp. 219–245.

19. Author observations at session held by Boeing Commercial Aircraft, Kent, WA, July 30–August 1, 1996.

20. Collins & Porras, op. cit., p. 97.

21. Johnson & Johnson (1987), op. cit., pp. 152–154. Also, M. Deutsch (1949), A theory of cooperation and competition, *Human Relations, 2,* 129–152.

The Challenge
Task Skills and Behavior Styles

Individuals who become members of a team bring to the team's activities their knowledge, skills, and styles of participating in team activities. Members' technical skills can include quantitative, analytic, and design capabilities as well as capabilities in the use of different technologies. These enable a team to perform the range of tasks needed to achieve its goal. Members also possess social skills, such as decision making, problem solving, and planning and negotiating, that enable them to work together productively. An important challenge for a team is to define the tasks and roles needed to reach its goal, to decide which each member is most qualified to perform, and to gain members' commitment to perform their tasks and roles effectively.

chapter 4

Task Skills and Behavior Styles

Individuals who join a team either volunteer because they have an interest in what they believe the team will accomplish or because they are assigned to participate. In either case, to reach its goal a team must perform one or a series of tasks and the team's performance depends on the skills of its members. The tasks teams perform are varied although inevitably they involve two broad types of skills, described previously as technical and social. Different tasks require different technical skills and different mixes of technical and social skills. An important advantage for a team is the range of skills its members offer.

An example of the many skills needed by a team was observed during a three-day technical "problem-solving" session.[1] The research division of a major manufacturing company, seeking ways to cut the cost of its product and to improve the product's quality, focused on the way it machined parts for its products. Increasing the speed of machining without reducing the quality of the parts was the goal. Although many experts did not believe

> "Different tasks require different technical skills and different mixes of technical and social skills."

this goal could be achieved, there were those who felt that it could. To explore the possibilities, the company convened a team of researchers. In overview, the meeting involved two days of the researchers exchanging relevant information. The third day was spent exploring ways to solve the problem.

Initially, a broad range of information was presented and examined. During this phase, a group decision-making process was used to identify the most relevant information. This process accelerated when one expert described equipment he had developed that machined parts as desired. This revelation focused the group on experimenting with his equipment. At another point in the proceedings, another expert described research that changed the way the group thought about the impact of the machine tool on the metal. This provided more focus for the group. On the third day, in a brainstorming session, a variety of strategies for conducting experiments to test the ideas were listed. This was followed by a decision-making process to select a limited set of experiments. The third day ended with a planning session to assign research subgroups to design and conduct a series of experiments.

These sessions involved highly skilled technical specialists who used both their technical and their social skills to achieve the team's goal—finding a solution to a technical problem. Their technical skills included evaluating information about how metal responds to machining, reviewing how the machines function, and defining experiments to test the different proposed solutions to the problem. Their more social skills included generating ideas (brainstorming), team decision making, team planning, and negotiating when differences arose about how to proceed. Fundamental to all of these activities were members' communication skills. The specialized technical information and skills are specific to this team's problem. The more social skills are relevant to most, if not all, team activities. The following section considers the types of tasks and the skills required of members if teams are to achieve their goals.

> *"Fundamental to all of these activities were members' communication skills."*

TEAM TASKS AND THE SKILLS NEEDED TO PERFORM THEM

Technical Skills

Team members are generally—and sometimes exclusively—chosen for their technical skills. **Technical skills** are those required to perform the specialized, technical tasks needed by a team to reach its goal. For example, members of a manufacturing team that produces electronic controllers are chosen for their ability to operate sophisticated production equipment. Members of cardiac surgical teams are selected for their specialized skills related to performing surgery. Members of musical ensembles are chosen for their ability to play the instruments required for a particular piece of music. Members of automobile design teams are chosen for their skills in designing a new model. Team members are selected on the basis of who has the technical skills needed to reach the goal. Teams are formed to achieve a variety of goals. To do so, however, requires a variety of skills in addition to technical skills.

Social Competencies

Teams must perform, in addition to technical tasks, a variety of tasks that are more social in nature. Which of these tasks a team will encounter as it proceeds toward its goal can be difficult to predict, since these tasks arise from the nature and quality of the interactions that take place between members. The following subsections describe tasks that can be encountered by teams and the **social skills** required to perform them. Included are planning, creating, decision making, problem solving, negotiating, and performing. When performed by a team, they are decidedly social in nature.[2]

Generating a Product or Outcome

When a team's task is to generate an outcome, two broad strategies are available. One is to *plan* a strategy by which to achieve the outcome. The other is to *create* the outcome itself.

Planning Tasks.   **Planning** is a crucial part of team performance. For some teams their only goal is to develop a plan. Other teams both develop and carry out a plan. For example, an architectural team develops a plan for a new building, but does not do the actual construction. In a factory a manufacturing process design team develops a plan for manufacturing a product, but the actual manufacturing takes place on the factory floor. By contrast, a mountain-climbing team develops a plan for its climb and proceeds with the climb according to the plan. Similarly, a team of smoke jumpers develops a plan for fighting a forest fire and after jumping into the fire zone carries out the plan.

> *"Planning is a crucial part of team performance."*

Planning involves several steps. The first step is for all team members to be clear about and agree on the goal the plan is intended to achieve. If the goal is unclear, it must be clarified. Other steps are to identify possible alternative paths to the desired outcome, to choose one of those paths, and to detail the steps that, if taken, will result in the desired outcome. Specifying the alternative paths to a goal or specifying the steps to be taken on a single path may, depending on the amount of relevant knowledge and experience members possess, require a team to develop relevant background information. These planning steps are considered in more detail in Chapter 5.

Creating Tasks.   These tasks involve generating an outcome from a less structured beginning. A team is creative when, for example, it lists a set of possible explanations for a problem. An example of a **creating task** is **brainstorming**. This approach is exemplified in the machining research session described earlier. At several points in the deliberations, researchers used brainstorming to develop a list of alternatives. In such situations, members bring different perspectives to the task that enable a team to view the problem in different ways. This increases the probability that among the responses listed will be a correct or best possible formulation.

Some approaches to creating tasks are better than others. Consider, for example, some rules for effective brainstorming. The goal is to generate as many ideas as possible. Participants are not to criticize their own or others' ideas. Finally, participants are to build on the ideas of others. As one member reports an idea, other members may come up with additional ideas. Members are polled for ideas until no additional ideas can be elicited. The result is often a lengthy list of ideas.

The rules for brainstorming are designed to do two things. One is to ensure that the creativity of each individual is not stifled by any social influence processes at work in the team, for example, fear of social embarrassment, conformity pressures, or status systems that inhibit participation by low-status members. Every idea is acceptable. The other is to take advantage of whatever creativity-enhancing forces are operating. These include social support for and reinforcement of individuals' contributions, as well as cross-stimulation of each other's efforts. Praising each other's contributions can help members to feel comfortable contributing their ideas to the team's deliberations.[3]

"Praising each other's contributions can help members to feel comfortable contributing their ideas to the team's deliberations."

Choosing between Options to Arrive at an Outcome

When a team must choose an outcome from a set of previously specified outcomes, two broad strategies are available. Which is used depends on the situation. One strategy is simply to select among pre-specified options. This is **decision making.** When the options are less clear, the task becomes **problem solving.** This means formulating either, or sometimes both, the problem and multiple solutions, and then choosing one to work with.

Decision-Making Tasks.   Teams are often confronted with decision-making tasks. These involve choosing between two or more reasonably clear alternatives. For example, the list of possible solutions generated by brainstorming, such as that described earlier, can be reduced to a single set of best solutions by progressively discarding poorer solutions until only the best solutions remain. A single best solution is then selected.[4]

A team provides several advantages when using this approach. First, with members' broader range of relevant skills and knowledge, teams can make better decisions. Second, a team can acquire and process a larger amount of information by subdividing the responsibility. Third, decisions reached by teams are likely to be regarded as legitimate and worthy of being followed because the decision reflects multiple interests and views, rather than a single viewpoint. There are also disadvantages. First, a team may fail to use the full range of skills or knowledge available to it because one or more members are not motivated to contribute or feel that their contribution will not be acceptable. Second, some team members may influence the decision process more than others. Third, team members may rush to reach agreement and limit consideration of alternatives. Fourth, the diversity of members' views and values can be so broad that they are difficult to reconcile, resulting in an inability to reach closure. Finally, as opposed to individuals, teams tend to make more extreme decisions (either more risky or more conservative).[5]

"Reaching a consensus has the advantage of unanimity, however, reaching it can be time consuming, especially when a team is large."

Guidelines (or rules) for decision making, developed by a team, can help to guide the process to a successful conclusion. For example, a team needs to decide whether decisions are to be arrived at by consensus, that is, by having all members agree, or by majority rule. Reaching a consensus has the advantage of unanimity, however, reaching it can be time consuming, especially when a team is large. By contrast, reaching a decision by majority rule can be more efficient, but it requires acceptance of the majority's view by the minority, which can present difficulties.

Problem-Solving Tasks.   The goal of a problem-solving task is to arrive at a single correct answer rather than choose a single solution from among a list of possible solutions. Problems can be of several types. There are those for which there is a demonstrably obvious correct answer. For example, the answer to the questions, "Is it raining?" and "What time is it?" For such problems, when a correct answer is identified, the correctness of the answer is sufficiently obvious that team members readily agree to its correctness. This type might be labeled *truth wins*. There are also problems, such as algebraic proofs, that have difficult-to-arrive-at, but demonstrable and culturally accepted, correct answers. For these problems, the answer that most members support is taken as the correct answer. This type might be labeled *truth-supported wins*.

Still other problems have correct answers that can only be arrived at by experts. For example, the answer to the question "If wrecked on the moon, what is needed to survive?" could be provided by experts from NASA. When the correct answer lies beyond the team's capabilities and the knowledge of experts must be relied on, teams operate as if the consensus of experts provides the weight needed to select an answer. This might be labeled *truth with much support wins*. It is important that team members be able to identify the different types of problem/solution combinations and to understand how each type of solution is reached. This can enable a team to arrive at a solution in an efficient way.[6]

"Problem solving involves developing and carrying out a strategy that solves, that is, removes, the problem as a barrier."

For a team, a problem can arise in one of two ways. One is when the problem poses a barrier to the team's achieving its goal. The other is when a team's goal is to solve a problem. Problem solving involves developing and carrying out a strategy that solves, that is, removes, the problem as a barrier. Problem solving tends to proceed through three phases. The first is to develop a clear answer to the question "What is the problem?" The second phase is to evaluate the problem, that is, answer the question "What is the significance or what are the implications of the problem?" Finally, there is the issue of addressing the problem. The question here is "How is the problem to be solved or removed?" Depending on the knowledge, experience, and skills of team members, each phase may require that a team develop background information before proceeding.[7]

Negotiating to Achieve an Outcome

Another type of team task involves **negotiating** differences to reach agreement. This includes resolving differences in how an issue is viewed, that is, **cognitive**

conflict, and resolving differences of opinion and negotiating differences that arise from conflicting interests or motives, that is, **mixed motives**.

Cognitive Conflict Tasks.   When team members see an issue differently, a cognitive conflict arises. For example, two team members differ on the way the team chooses its leader. One member considers technical skill to be the most important qualification. The other considers popularity with other members to be most important. This was not an issue in the past because their current leader, who is stepping down, is both technically the most capable and the most highly regarded by other team members. Now that he is about to leave the team, no one member has both qualities, and the different perspectives must be resolved.

Cognitive conflicts are frequent and can often be difficult to resolve, precisely because team members tend to misunderstand each other. To resolve a misunderstanding, discussion is required to clarify the different perspectives, followed by a negotiating process that begins with clearly understanding the different positions, then proceeding to compromise and, it is hoped, to agreement. Failure to negotiate carefully can result in intransigence or in superficial conformity. An individual who experiences real change is able to view the problem from a new perspective and to appreciate its advantages. When there is conformity, the person merely acquiesces to views held by other team members. This can result in inconsistent support for a particular view and possibly even resentment.[8]

> *"Cognitive conflicts are frequent and can often be difficult to resolve"*

Mixed-Motive Tasks.   Team members can also have conflicting motives or interests. These can result in very disruptive disagreements. The tasks discussed previously presume that all members want the same outcome for the team. Mixed-motive tasks, however, involve situations where the best outcome for one team member is not the best outcome for another. Members' interests are pitted against each other although they are interdependent as to outcome. This means that the outcome for one member is dependent on the behavior of other members, such that, if one member "wins," the other "loses."

> *"Team members can also have conflicting motives or interests."*

Such conflicts can be approached as negotiation tasks, as bargaining tasks, as dilemma tasks, or as coalition tasks. These are discussed in order of increasing degree of conflict. This gradation arises from both an increase in the degree to which one member's actions affect another's outcome and a decrease in the flexibility of how payoffs are distributed.

Negotiation seeks to resolve conflict by considering various trade-offs between multiple dimensions. For example, one team member wants the leader reelected monthly, wants longer team meetings, and wants more cross-functional training. Another member wants the leader elected for a two-year term, fewer team meetings, and no cross-functional training. Resolution of this conflict can be accomplished by having the two parties rate the importance of the issues and then negotiate which and to what degree different expectations in each person's set will be met. For example, one member ranks leader term, number of meetings, and cross-functional training in that order. The other ranks them in the reverse order. Negotiation could give each their first ranked choice. A middle ground or compromise on team meetings could then be selected.[9]

Bargaining involves addressing, on a single dimension, disputes between two or more persons. For example, some members want no designated leader. Other members want a leader. In the bargaining process it is important for each side to understand what about a team leader is of concern to the other side. Knowing what one group finds troubling about having a leader may make it possible to devise a solution that minimizes the concern. For example, the group that does not want a leader may fear that a leader will not represent their interests. If a way is found to assure them that the leader represents all members' interests, resistance to having a leader may be reduced or removed.[10]

Dilemma tasks involve two or more persons making choices independently of one another. Their decisions, however, jointly determine the outcomes for each of them. This can happen when a team subdivides responsibilities. In such situations subgroups are interdependent in terms of outcome but not in terms of the process by which the outcome is reached. For example, a team planning its company's holiday celebration sets a limit on spending. Two team members decide to take up money to give to custodial staff as a gift. Two other team members decide to take up money to have a holiday party. If each subgroup wants to spend as much as possible, how does the team hold to the team's spending limit? A way to control spending must be agreed to by team members. The team could agree on an upper limit for each or establish communication between the groups to maintain the spending limit.[11]

Winning **coalition payoff allocation tasks** occur when a subset of members forms a coalition or subgroup that totally controls payoffs to members. This subgroup can deny any positive payoffs to members who are not a part of the coalition while at the same time allocating payoffs among members of the coalition in ways that reflect their relative power, strength, or resources. An example is a team that decides to operate by majority rule and finds the same group voting in the majority each time and also allocating to themselves the most desirable work schedules and overtime. How is this dilemma to be addressed? Unless the controlling coalition is willing to relinquish control, change the allocation of payoffs, or some combination, the negative effect on team performance is likely to be considerable, especially because the performance of excluded members is likely to diminish. Only a renewed focus on the team's goal and the realization of the goal-oriented effort that is being lost will realign the arrangement.[12]

A central problem with mixed-motive tasks is how to get each party to give up some of its ideal solution. There are several considerations. One is whether one or many issues are involved in the dispute. Bargaining is useful when there is one dimension. When several dimensions are involved, negotiating is needed to resolve the differences. The more dimensions to the conflict, the more complex the dispute. A greater number of dimensions can potentially give greater flexibility for negotiating a resolution to the conflict since the different parties to the conflict can more readily gain a part of their desired outcome. Another feature is whether issues are dealt with one at a time or collectively. Satisfactory resolution of either type generally requires compromise.

Performing to Achieve Outcomes

When a team's task is to perform to achieve an outcome, the outcome can be of two types. One involves performing to surpass another team, or **contests**. The other involves **performance** to meet or surpass a standard.

Contests. The goal of contests is to resolve conflicts of power, to win. There is a distinction between how well a group performs and how the contest comes out. A team might perform poorly but still win. Several conclusions can be drawn about task performance in contest situations. One is that success at a competitive task can increase within-group cohesiveness (attraction) but the reverse is not necessarily so. Another is that intergroup competition can increase within-group cohesion but may not affect level of group performance. Also, groups do not always distinguish between good performance and winning in their evaluation of their own and other's performance, although competition with an opponent and cooperation with teammates can lead to individual motivation gains. However, when contests involve coordinating complex, multiple tasks, competition can lead to serious coordination losses unless offset by extensive practice.[13]

> *"A team might perform poorly but still win."*

Performance. Teams can also perform tasks with the goal of achieving a specified standard. Performance is influenced by a variety of factors. The physical features of a work environment, such as noise level, can influence performance. The amount of member experience or training is influential. Social processes are also influential. For example, teams influence their members toward conformity with the team's norms or standards. Team members can also develop positive group feelings called **group cohesion**. Group cohesion, in turn, enables a team to keep its members' performance in accord with the standard established by the team. The more cohesive the team, the more social pressure the team can exert on member performance. If a team receives special recognition for its performance, it may also set higher and higher standards. For cohesive teams this can result in enhanced team performance.[14]

Identifying and Developing Task-Relevant Skills

Some individuals are better at performing some tasks than others. Persons with prior planning experience bring that skill to a team. They are more inclined to plan before acting. They can identify different paths to a goal and see the steps needed to proceed along that path. Some individuals have experience negotiating and are able to analyze a conflict and propose a resolution. It is important for team members to learn who among their group is good at and gains satisfaction from using each of the skills described. Although individuals who join a team bring with them valuable skills and perspectives, it is important for all members to develop new skills and practice existing skills. Doing so increases a team's resources and increases the probability that the team will have the resources needed to reach its goal.

> *"Although individuals who join a team bring with them valuable skills and perspectives, it is important for all members to develop new skills and practice existing skills."*

BEHAVIOR STYLES

Skills are not the only resource team members bring to their team. Two people, each with the relevant knowledge and skills needed to perform a task, may approach that task quite differently. One person plans extensively before beginning. The other begins immediately, making needed adjustments as he or she proceeds. These different ways of performing a task are matters of "style" rather than knowledge or skill. Individuals who become members of a team bring to the team, along with their knowledge and skills, their particular way of performing tasks, their behavior style.[15]

The term **behavior styles** refers to consistencies in an individual's manner of doing work and interacting with other people. A person who is the "life of the party," talking to everyone and telling jokes in one situation, is likely to be that way in most social situations. By contrast, a person who is shy and rather withdrawn in one social situation is likely to be that way in other social situations. Such consistencies do not reflect anything about other individual characteristics (e.g., intelligence or skills) but only how the person goes about performing a task or interacting with others. Their style may not be evident in every situation. For example, a person may be somewhat different in a family situation and in a business situation, but it is likely that in most business and social situations their behavior style will be consistent.

"Styles differ from individual to individual."

Behavior styles arise from an individual's motives in the sense that behaving in a certain manner provides satisfaction or avoids dissatisfaction. Styles differ from individual to individual. For example, some individuals are strongly motivated to test and demonstrate their ability to achieve specified outcomes. They are attracted to and are comfortable in achievement-oriented situations. By contrast, others are strongly motivated to interact with people and seek social situations. They may organize as well as participate in social activities. Some persons may combine both the achievement-oriented and the socially-oriented styles. Some may have little of either orientation. Those who have neither will have some other style—of which there are many.

Behavior styles are important for team members to understand for several reasons. First, styles develop, generally in childhood and young adulthood, and become a part of *who* a person is. They reflect what is for them a source of satisfaction. When a person becomes a member of a team, he needs to find some satisfaction from the team's activities for his particular behavior style if he is to become and stay involved. Second, different behavior styles find satisfaction in different types of activities and responsibilities. For example, a person who has a **task-oriented style** of behaving will be concerned about how team tasks get done. This person will find satisfaction in helping and feeling that she has helped to accomplish a team's tasks. A person who has a social **relationship-oriented style** will be concerned with keeping relationships among group members pleasant and satisfying. This person will find satisfaction by working to maintain harmony among group members. Put more broadly, members' behavior styles influence the different responsibilities, often referred to as "roles," that they assume and find satisfying. Third, each style can be useful to a team if different styles can be made compatible, complementary and positive for a team's performance. If they are not complementary, their effect on performance can be negative.[16]

For this reason it is important for each team member to be aware of his or her style and to compare it with those of other team members. If there is a style match, little conflict is likely. If there are differences, one team member may find it difficult to understand why another member performs tasks in the way he or she does. Members should identify their own styles, discuss similarities and differences with other members, and from this identify the tasks each can best perform. Doing so will enable members to work together more productively and to experience greater satisfaction.

There can be difficulties, however. One is that, although there is general agreement that team member behavior styles are influential, it is unclear what combination of behavior styles is optimum. Some companies have identified combinations of behavior styles that they feel work best for them. It is likely, however, that even within the same company, different situations can require different combinations of styles. For example, a team under the pressure of a very tight deadline may find the task-oriented style very helpful. Another team, required to perform tedious tasks over an extended period of time, may find the relationship-oriented style very helpful.

Another difficulty is that not all styles can be made compatible. For example, a person whose style is very directive, that is, who tells other team members what to do, may be in conflict with another member whose style is to seek comments on an issue from every team member before making a decision. While it is clear that some individuals can change their style of behaving, especially in the context of a team activity, to achieve such changes can be difficult to do without upsetting a team member's ability to perform effectively.

Changes take time and usually occur in social environments in which members are comfortable and trusting of each other. Change can occur when an individual is motivated to change and when team members both expect and support evidence of change. For example, at a team development seminar a corporate human resources manager reported to the total group how members of his team expressed their resentment of his overly directive style. He reported how he was very upset by this and decided to change. His team encouraged and supported his efforts to change and by the end of the week's program both he and his fellow team members felt that he had changed.[17] During the change phase, behavior may alternate between the previous and the new behaviors. Group support for the desired changes is very important.

"Changes take time and usually occur in social environments in which members are comfortable and trusting of each other."

When a team member has a behavior style that is not compatible with the styles of other members and resists change, the individual may need to make other arrangements. Recognizing that some creative individuals do not work comfortably with others, some companies seek ways to utilize an individual's capabilities under circumstances that are more conducive to the individual's behavior style. For example, a company may find a way for such persons to use their creativity in more solitary work.

Characterizing Behavior Styles

Behavior styles can be characterized in many different ways. One widely used method is the Myers-Briggs Type Inventory.[18] This characterizes individuals along four dimensions. The first dimension is *extrovert* versus *introvert*. An introvert is a reflective, internally focused person. An extrovert is more sociable, externally focused, and gregarious. The second dimension, *sensor* versus *intuitor*, concerns information gathering. Sensors tend to be practical, realistic, factual, and specific. Intuitors are more conceptual, theoretical, general, and random. The third dimension, *feeler* versus *thinker*, pertains to decision making. Feelers are humane, harmonious, subjective, and involved in decision making. Thinkers are firm, clear, and detached. The fourth dimension, *perceiver* versus *judger*, is concerned with how individuals deal with their environment and create their lifestyles. Perceivers tend to be more adaptable, flexible, spontaneous, and open. Judgers emphasize control, planning, structure, and scheduling in their lives.

The focal style issues identified by this characterization—sociability, information gathering, decision making, and dealing with their environment—are undoubtedly important. This assessment method results in a large variety of behavior styles, however. Furthermore, individuals are not necessarily at the extremes of any dimension. Rather, they may be closer to the middle. This results in ambiguous characterizations.

A simpler procedure characterizes individuals along two dimensions.[19] One is *assertiveness* (asking versus telling) and the other is *responsiveness* (feeling versus facts). This results in four types. *Drivers* want challenges, authority, and freedom from controls. They are the task-oriented individuals who are concerned with keeping the team's activities on track toward its goal, although they are less inclined to size up a situation and plan. *Analyticals* are fact finders who want high standards, details, and perfection. They are concerned with obtaining data relevant to team functioning, but can get bogged down in gathering data. Both drivers and analytics are *performance-oriented* in contrast to *expressives* who are *people-oriented*. The latter are verbal, enthusiastic, and want social recognition, freedom from details, and to be with people. Expressives seek coordination. They attend to the needs of team members to enjoy both task activities and working with each other. *Amiables* are patient, loyal, sympathetic, and desire guarantees, security, and appreciation. Amiables attend to team members' feeling a part of a group that is highly regarded by its members and by those outside the team. They focus on recognition for the team and for its members.

"Both drivers and analytics are performance-oriented in contrast to expressives who are people-oriented."

Another characterization of behavior style concerns how individuals in social situations, such as a team, orient to interdependence and to goal attainment. For example, some individuals perceive any group task as an opportunity for cooperation. By cooperating, the group accomplishes its goal. Others perceive a group situation as an opportunity for competition. By competing, one or a few members demonstrate their superior skill and gain the goal for themselves. Still others prefer to work alone and reject interdependence altogether. These latter types want to do their part of the task with a minimum of interaction with others.[20]

Cooperative and competitive styles approach interdependence in different ways. One finds cooperation to be more satisfying. The other finds competition more satisfying. Each tends to shape social situations to provide the satisfaction they desire. Those with cooperative styles tend to see goal achievement as a mutual accomplishment in which members support and encourage each other to achieve their goal. Those with competitive styles tend to see goal achievement as a singular accomplishment in which members demonstrate their superior task-related skills. These individuals may also resist giving assistance to other members. These styles can be incompatible.

> *"Cooperative and competitive styles approach interdependence in different ways."*

Emotional Intelligence

Another perspective on performance "styles" is termed **emotional intelligence.**[21] It is comprised of five features. *Knowing one's emotions* is self-awareness and the ability to recognize a feeling as it happens. *Managing emotions* is handling emotions so they are appropriate. *Motivating oneself* is the ability to call on one's emotions in the interests of pursuing a goal. This also involves delaying gratification and controlling impulsiveness in the interest of accomplishment. *Recognizing emotions in others* is the ability to put oneself in another's shoes, to be empathetic. *Handling relationships* is largely about the ability to respond appropriately and constructively to emotions in other persons. Taken together, these abilities represent knowledge of oneself and, through that, an understanding of others.

> *"Recognizing emotions in others is the ability to put oneself in another's shoes, to be empathetic."*

Emotional intelligence (EI) is distinct from IQ and is only modestly related to it. IQ concerns the ability to use words and numbers, to see conceptual relationships, and to remember such material. IQ can be loosely seen as the primary basis for technical skills. Emotional intelligence is the basis for more social, interpersonal skills. Although various measures are used for IQ, there are no measures that adequately assess the scope of issues considered part of EI. The fact that the two constructs are relatively independent means, however, that four types of individuals, at least hypothetically, can be broadly identified. There are those who are high IQ and high EI. There are the two types who are high on one dimension and low on the other, and finally, there are those who are low on both.[22]

> *"Emotional intelligence is the basis for more social, interpersonal skills."*

Two important implications should be drawn from this characterization. One is that a team member may be any one of the four combinations. This means that their skills can be strong in one or both the technical and the emotional/social spheres or their skills can be low on one or both. The second implication is that for those who are low (or lower than they wish to be) on a dimension, the requisite competencies can be learned. This is witnessed to by many research findings including those pertaining to emotional intelligence.

There are, however, two important conditions for such learning. One is that individuals have the motivation and discipline to persist at the learning process. The other is that the team's social environment in which the learning occurs supports, encourages, and gives recognition to each member's learning accomplishments. The development of such an environment by the team leader is discussed in Chapter 6.

The Challenge Revisited
Task Skills and Behavior Styles

1. Team members join or are assigned to a team because they have or can develop skills the team needs to achieve its goal. They also bring with them particular styles of behaving.

2. Team members must identify each other's skills and styles, understand how each can contribute to the team's performance, and organize team activities in a way that optimizes each member's contributions.

3. Members' different skills and behavior styles can enhance a team's performance if each undertakes tasks and roles for which they are best suited. When members are involved in tasks or roles for which they are unsuited, performance suffers.

4. An important challenge for a team's members it to appreciate each other's skills and styles and to identify ways to utilize and encourage their use in ways that most benefit the team's performance.

EXERCISE 4.1 • *Developing an Inventory of Member Skills*

1. Have each team member make a list of the skills he or she brings to the team after considering the team's goal and the tasks to be performed to achieve it.

2. As a group, discuss your different skill sets. If this discussion reminds you of skills not on your original list, add them.

3. Develop an inventory of member skills and discuss task and role assignments in light of this inventory.

4. Prepare a report of your inventory and task and role assignments. Explain the decisions made.

EXERCISE 4.2 • *Assessing Social Behavior Styles*

1. Turn to the "Determining Your Social Style" questionnaire in Appendix 1 on page 228. After you complete the questionnaire, you'll be given directions for scoring your responses.

2. Based on your score and the assessment of your social style that goes with it, write a brief description of your style in your own words.

3. When all members of your team have completed the questionnaire and have answered step 2 (above), members should briefly describe their styles to the team.

4. As you listen to each person describe his or her style, record your reactions. List each member's name on a sheet of paper. Next to it write the one-word description of their prevailing style (either *driver*, *expressive*, *amiable*, or *analytical*). Put a plus sign by members' names whose self-assessments coincide with your opinions of that person's style. Use a minus sign to note a difference of opinion.

5. Discuss how this information about each other's social styles can be used to help your team develop effective performance. Consider the following:

   a. Which styles are represented among team members? Which kinds of activities is each style most likely to do well with and to find satisfying?

   b. Are there team members who score relatively high on more than one style? What do these combinations of styles mean for team activities?

   c. What are the technical and social activities that the team needs to perform? Do the activities that members find satisfying coincide with the activities that the team needs to perform?

   d. Are there styles that can be incompatible? How will incompatibilities be addressed?

   e. Discuss the fit of your team's styles to the work it must perform. Should adjustments in assignments and tasks be made?

6. Prepare a description of your conclusions and decisions.

QUESTIONS FOR REVIEW AND DISCUSSION

1. What is meant by the term *technical skills*? Give examples. What is meant by the term *social skills* (or social competencies)? Give examples. Does having a particular set of technical skills indicate something about a person's social skills?

2. Why are good communication skills so important for good social skills?

3. What are *planning tasks*? Why is planning important for a team's successful performance?

4. What are *creating tasks*? What is their role in a team's performance? Why is brainstorming a useful strategy for a team to create an outcome?

5. What is the difference between decision-making and problem solving? Under what circumstances is each skill useful?

6. How is negotiation conducted? What is the difference in negotiation when there is a cognitive conflict and when there is a mixed motive or conflict of interest? Why are such conflicts difficult to resolve?

7. What is the difference between a contest and a performance? What is the effect of each on team performance? On team member interactions?

8. What is a behavior style? What is meant by the phrase "making team members' behavior styles complementary"? How can behavior styles be made complementary? Why is this important? Why are some behavior styles incompatible?

9. What are some different behavior styles that assessment procedures have identified? Consider three or four and describe the different ways each performs tasks and interacts with others.

10. What is meant by the term *emotional intelligence*? How does it differ from IQ? What are the implications of differences in members' emotional intelligence for team functioning?

Notes

1. Sessions observed by the author at Boeing Commercial Aircraft, Kent, WA, 1996.

2. The framework of tasks and associated skills is summarized from J. McGrath (1984), *Groups: Interaction and Performance*, Englewood Cliffs, NJ: Prentice-Hall.

3. On the efficiency of brainstorming see P. Paulus, T. Larey, & M. Dzindolet (2001), Creativity in groups and teams, in M. E. Turner (Ed.), *Groups at Work*, Mahwah, NJ: Erlbaum, pp. 319–338. See also H. Diehl & W. Stroeba (1991), Productivity loss in idea-generating groups, *Journal of Personality and Social Psychology*, 61, 392–403.

4. On decision making see D. Yeatts & C. Hyten (1998), *High Performing Self-Managed Work Teams*, Thousand Oaks, CA: Sage, pp. 289–301.

5. On this polarizing phenomenon, including the risky shift, see D. Myers & H. Lamn (1976), The group polarizing phenomenon, *Psychological Bulletin*, 83, 602–627.

6. McGrath, op. cit., p. 68.

7. An examination of problem-solving competency is given in D. A. Tisdelle & J. S. St. Lawrence (1986), Interpersonal problem solving competency: Review and critique of the literature, *Clinical Psychology Review*, 6, 337–356. See also D. Levi (2001), *Group Dynamics for Teams*, Thousand Oaks, CA: Sage, pp. 191–209.

8. Cognitive conflict tasks are examined in B. Brehmer (1976), Social judgment theory and the analysis of interpersonal conflict, *Psychological Bulletin*, 83, 985–1003.

9. On negotiation see L. Thompson & C. Fox (2001), Negotiation in and between groups in organizations, in Turner (Ed.), op. cit., pp. 221–266. Also, E. Peterson & L. Thompson (1997), Negotiation teamwork: The impact of information distribution and accountability on performance depends on the relationship among team members, *Organizational Behavior and Human Decision Processes*, 72, 364–383.

10. On bargaining see Thompson & Fox, op. cit., pp. 243–244.

11. On dilemma tasks see Thompson & Fox, op. cit., pp. 243–244. See also D. Messick & W. Liebrand (1995), Individual heuristics and the dynamics of cooperation in large groups, *Psychological Review*, 102, 131–145.

12. On coalitions see Thompson & Fox, op. cit., p. 244. Also S. Komorita & C. Parks (1994), *Social Dilemmas*, Madison, WI: Brown & Benchmarks.

13. For a discussion of the effect of intergroup competition, see M. B. Brewer (1979), In-group bias in the minimal inter-group situation: A cognitive-motivational analysis, *Psychological Bulletin*, 86, 307–324. Also M. Turner and T. Horvitz (2001), The dilemma of threat: Group effectiveness and ineffectiveness under adversity, in Turner (Ed.), op. cit., pp. 445–470.

14. On the relationship between cohesiveness and performance, see S. Carless & C. DePaola (2000), The measurement of cohesion in work teams, *Small Group Research*, 31, 71–88; and K. Gammage, A. Carron, & P. Estabroks (2001), Team cohesion and individual productivity, *Small Group Research*, 32, 3–18.

15. For behavior styles and team performance, see D. Levi (2001), *Group Dynamics for Teams*, Thousand Oaks, CA: Sage, pp. 69–70. Also S. Armstrong & V. Priola (2001), Individual differences in cognitive style and their effects on task and social orientation of self-managed teams, *Small Group Research*, 32, 283–312.

16. The fact that a person has a particular style indicates a preference for a particular activity or role but does not mean that the person cannot perform what for that person may be less satisfying activities.

17. Session in which the author participated.

18. The Myers-Briggs Type Inventory is described in P. G. Northouse (2001), *Leadership: Theory and Practice*, 2nd ed., Thousand Oaks, CA: Sage, pp. 207–213. See also D. Keirsey & M. Bates (1984), *Please Understand Me: Character and Temperament Types*, Del Mar, CA: Gnosology Books.

19. This measure of social style was provided to the author by A. K. Prichard, Boeing Commercial Aircraft Associate Technical Fellow. The four types that result from this assessment procedure are described in H. Robbins & M. Finley (1995), *Why Teams Work*, Princeton, NJ: Peterson's Pacesetter Books, op. cit., pp. 54–59.

20. For cooperative, competitive, individualistic styles, see K. Lewin, R. Lippitt, & R. White (1939), Patterns of aggressive behavior in experimentally created social climates, *Journal of Social Psychology*, 10, 271–299.

21. D. Goleman (1997), *Emotional Intelligence*, New York: Bantam Books, pp. 43–44. See also C. Yost & M. Tucker (2000), Are effective teams more emotionally intelligent? Confirming the importance of effective communication in teams, *Delta Pi Epsilon Journal*, 42, 101–109; and P. Jordan & A. Troth (2002), Emotional intelligence and conflict resolution: Implications for human resource development, *Advances in Developing Human Resources*, 4, 62–79.

22. While this conceptualization of behavior style, as well as others, focuses on pure types, there are in fact many individuals who do not fit a clear characterization. They do not fall at the extremes, but closer to the middle of the distribution.

The Teamwork Process

When a team's goal is clear and the resources available to pursue its goal identified, the process of achieving the goal begins. Rather than proceeding immediately to performing tasks, a team must determine the activities required to achieve its goal. Doing this has the dual advantage of using members' varied knowledge and perspectives to select the best path and of having members understand and agree on the path. Effective communication is essential for planning and for the teamwork process generally. During planning most teams choose a leader whose role is to keep the team goal oriented, to facilitate the goal achievement process, and to encourage members' involvement. Proceeding according to its plan, members begin to perform tasks, to coordinate their activities, and to develop cooperative relationships. That members experience satisfaction in the process is essential to their maintaining involvement. How a team relates to its organizational environment and the implications of that relationship for team performance need consideration. A team also specifies and generates evaluative feedback that enables it to maintain a clear direction, to monitor the quality of its performance, and to assess the quality of its product. Mastering and coordinating the different subprocesses that comprise the teamwork process require concentration and effort. The result, however, can be effective teamwork.

The Challenge
Planning, Meeting, and Communicating

Each of the activities of planning, meeting, and communicating, must be understood and practiced for a team's performance to become effective. Planning is a team's preparation for pursuing its goal. Rather than proceeding immediately to the performance of a task, planning allows a team to develop a strategy that orients the team to its goal and enables team members to understand and agree on activities that will make the undertaking successful. Planning usually occurs in the context of a team meeting. A meeting should enable a team to complete a maximum of relevant business in a minimum of time. Underlying all planning, as well as most other team activities, is communication. Effective communication can be learned but doing so can require concerted effort both to send messages clearly and to receive them accurately.

chapter 5

Planning, Meeting, and Communicating

Planning is essential for a team. Planning allows a team to make the path to the "abstract future state," its goal, real. Planning includes identifying the multiple paths to a goal and selecting the best one. Team members then identify mutually agreed-on steps to take along the path. These steps generally require team members to plan for coordinating their individual activities so that each member contributes maximally to the team's goal achievement effort. The plan also provides a point of reference for a team to check that it is on its chosen path. If the team is off the path, appropriate adjustments can be made. Finally, the plan provides a basis for evaluation and learning. As a team looks back on its performance it can ask: Was our planning adequate? Was the chosen strategy the best possible strategy? Was our implementation of the strategy effective? Answers to these questions enable a team to learn and to improve.

Planning requires contributions from each team member. Consider the following hypothetical scenario. Betsy, José, Sarah, Kevin, and Maria are to design a new training program for their division. Each is from a different department in the division. Maria was asked to lead the effort, which is to be completed in six weeks. At the first meeting Maria asks how the team wants to proceed. Kevin says that they should spell out the steps they will take to develop the plan. Betsy adds that, while each member represents a different department, even before designing the steps, they need to inventory what each member knows about their department's training to determine if the relevant knowledge, experience, and perspectives are represented among the members. Sarah adds to that idea by suggesting that, if the training issues are diverse enough, they may need to establish subgroups, possibly with non-team participants, to help formulate a statement of training needs for each department. José then suggests that with the results of the subgroup deliberations, their team can develop a statement on training needs that the new training program should fulfill. Each member can then review the statement with his or her department to ensure that all relevant needs are identified. Their team agrees that they can then develop a proposal for providing the needed training.

> *"Planning requires contributions from each team member."*

Our hypothetical team has as its goal the development of a plan for a new training program. It is just getting started. Members have raised a series of questions about how to proceed. They ask: What needs is the training plan to fulfill? Members then spell out procedures to determine the needs in each department. When the needs have been defined, the planning process can proceed to select a path to the team's goal. It may seem strange but this team is planning how it will develop a plan.

Defining Planning

What is planning? It can be viewed as a tool by which an undesirable state is transformed into a desirable (or more desirable) state. Using the terminology that earlier defined a goal as a preferred future state, planning is a process that informs a team how and where to move from its present state to its preferred, future state. A plan guides the transformation process by which a goal is achieved. Planning requires a team to think through as many of the details of the process of reaching its goal as it can. Because even a well-thought-out plan can lack some details, some planning will continue as a team proceeds toward its goal.

> *"A plan guides the transformation process by which a goal is achieved."*

A team gains several important benefits from having a plan. First, by depicting the steps by which its goal is to be achieved, considerable ambiguity is removed from the process of reaching the goal. Second, because a plan is developed and agreed to in a joint team activity, team members are more likely to envision the same strategy for reaching the goal and to be committed to it. Third, because members have a similar understanding of the strategy, it becomes their point of reference for coordinating their activities in pursuit of the goal. Considered broadly, a team's plan provides members with a common mental map of how the team will reach its goal.[1]

Planning Stages

What does the planning process entail? One author [2] has proposed five stages:

Formulation.   Initially, a team seeks to understand the "gap" between its present state and its preferred state. At the **formulation stage** the problem is explored and the expected achievement described. Team members' different perspectives on characteristics of the gap can provide a more realistic view of relevant issues and interrelationships. For example, the **needs assessment** undertaken by the team developing a divisional training plan (described earlier) involves this stage of their planning activity.

Conceptualization.   The second stage of planning, **conceptualization**, involves creating alternative strategies for closing the gap between present and future states, that is, for reaching the goal. Complex problems often must be broken into smaller, easier-to-understand parts. This may require developing models that depict the major components of the problem. These models suggest different views or "pictures" of possible solutions. They represent different "paths" to a team's goal. From among these possibilities the one that offers the most promise can be selected. For example, the team described earlier may find that when the training needs are defined, there are three paths (or models) for providing training to their division: developing a training resource in each department of the division, developing a training resource for the entire division, and having an external contractor provide the training needed by the division.

Detailing.   In the **detailing stage**, the steps required by the different paths or models are specified. Developing these details can reveal the strengths and the weaknesses of each path or model. Those with serious inadequacies can be dropped. For those that remain, details concerning resource needs and performance requirements can be developed. Considering more than one viable approach can lead to a better final plan than considering only one. For example, the team developing a training strategy considered three possibilities: a training facility in each *department*, a *division* training facility to serve each department, and a contract to an *external* training provider. Some strengths and weaknesses of each strategy are outlined in Table 5.1.

Table 5.1 considers four criteria. *Proximity to need* refers to closeness to and familiarity with the local situation's training needs. *Depth of capability* refers to how concentrated training skills can be for a specified budget. *Can address special needs* refers to the ability to meet specialized needs, such as diversity

---

TABLE 5.1
Three Strategies to Meet Division Training Needs

Criteria	Possible Strategies*		
	Department	Division	External
Proximity to need	High	Moderate	Low
Depth of capability	Low	Moderate	High
Can address special needs	Low	Low	High
Can generate employee involvement	High	Moderate	Low

*High, Moderate, and Low refer to each strategy's ability to meet each criterion.

training. *Can generate employee involvement* refers to the organizational level that is most likely to elicit employee commitment and involvement. *High, Moderate,* and *Low* refer to how adequately each strategy can meet each criterion.

Evaluation. The fourth stage, **evaluation**, involves selecting the best or most efficient alternative. Evaluation can identify costs, benefits, personnel needs, potential sources of satisfaction and dissatisfaction for staff, and other factors that influence the efficiency of each alternative. By evaluating the alternatives, the best alternative can be chosen. Considering the issues in Table 5.1 (and others that could be added), a cost analysis of the different strategies can be made and used to weigh the benefits of each alternative. This analysis is the basis for a final decision (or recommendation).

> *"By evaluating the alternatives, the best alternative can be chosen."*

Implementation. The **implementation stage** involves a detailed examination of how to put the selected model into action. Broadly, successful implementation involves specifying the details of the selected strategy and developing a social environment, both in the team itself and, if necessary, in the team's organizational context, that supports the chosen strategy's successful implementation. Again, to use the team developing a training plan as an example, if a model other than training at the departmental level were recommended, attention to minimizing departmental resistance to having training provided by a source outside the department may be needed.

The planning process spells out as precisely as possible the specifics of how the team will achieve its goal. This enables each team member to develop, as clearly and accurately as possible, a shared mental model of the strategy. A plan reduces ambiguity and helps members to understand where and when coordination among member activities is needed. A plan also provides a basis for evaluating progress and for making adjustments if needed.

The temptation for a team to pursue its goal without planning can be great. What happens when a team does not plan? Consider the following. Ten members of a high school band form a team to raise funds for a band trip. They decide to sell T-shirts to raise money. They meet and decide that they can sell 500 shirts, each member selling 50. They place their order, divided equally among the available adult sizes. After two weeks of sales they realize that 50 percent of the extra-large T-shirts cannot be sold. They also find that each has received requests for infants and children's sizes, which they did not think to order. Overall, the sale loses $100. The team lacked adequate planning, especially the type of needs assessment that the team developing the training plan, described earlier, decided to undertake. Had the band team done such an assessment, their sales effort would have been more successful.

> *"The temptation for a team to pursue its goal without planning can be great."*

MEETINGS AS A CONTEXT FOR TEAM ACTIVITIES

Team planning is most often conducted in a meeting context. A major drawback can be the time required. Knowing how to run an effective meeting can reduce the time required, increase member satisfaction, and facilitate a team's progress toward its goal.

> *"Meetings are interactions between at least two people, often scheduled in advance, to address some mutual concern."*

Meetings are interactions between at least two people, often scheduled in advance, to address some mutual concern. Their simplicity and familiarity makes meetings appear easy to conduct. Meetings can, however, waste time and generate frustration. Businesses that establish work teams are often concerned about the amount of time required by team meetings. Consequently, it is important to learn how a meeting can efficiently accomplish what it is intended to accomplish.[3]

Consider the following example. A five-student team, assigned to develop a proposal for a research project on water pollution, is having its second meeting. The meeting was scheduled for 8 P.M. Four are present by 8:05. At 8:20 the fifth team member arrives and the team begins discussing the results of the previous meeting at which they decided to focus on insecticides in drinking water. One member begins to describe a movie she saw on water pollution (*Erin Brockovich*). A lengthy exchange between two members about the movie follows. At 8:50 a third member asks what the movie has to do with their assignment. One of the members discussing the movie becomes noticeably irritated and stops talking. Another team member notes that they should review the assignment, but after searching they find that no one has a copy. A discussion of what the members *think* was in the assignment follows. At 9:20 two members indicate that they must leave to study for an exam the next day. They agree to meet later that week. As they leave at 9:30 one member comments that the meeting was "a waste of time!"

This team has demonstrated how to spend an hour and a half and accomplish nothing. The meeting illustrates several characteristics of unsuccessful meetings. There is low member commitment (arriving late), no plan for the meeting (no agenda), no preparation (no assignment available), and no one takes responsibility for the meeting (no leader). By contrast, meetings that go well have several important characteristics. There is adequate planning. The team leader and, ideally, a second person consider in advance the reason for having the meeting. They ask: How can this meeting facilitate the team's achieving its goals? Topics can address the goals themselves, strategies to achieve them, obstacles preventing their being achieved, or indicators of progress.

Planning a Meeting

A meeting is most likely to be successful if it is structured. This means establishing clear meeting objectives, which can be difficult for several reasons. Meeting objectives must be relevant to the team's larger goal. A decision must be made concerning meeting objectives and the steps required to achieve them. These steps should be spelled out in a meeting **agenda** that includes items to be discussed and the time allotted to each. Creating a time pressure can result in a more efficient meeting process. The final item on the agenda should be an evaluation of the meeting and its accomplishments. This enables members to review the progress made and to decide on next steps to be completed either before or during the next meeting. Ways

> *"A meeting is most likely to be successful if it is structured."*

to improve future meetings can also be considered. A meeting's agenda should be made available to team members in advance of the meeting.

An important benefit of an advanced agenda is that members can review it, think about it, prepare if necessary, and, if sufficiently concerned, raise questions about it prior to or at the beginning of the meeting. The first item on the agenda should be a review of the agenda to agree that each item is relevant. The team's acceptance reflects a degree of "buy-in" or commitment to the objectives and process reflected in the agenda.

Some may feel that planning a meeting imposes too much structure and risks stifling creativity. There are several reasons this is not so. Well-planned meetings maintain a focus on the meeting's objectives and on the steps required to reach the objectives. Structured meetings also provide some assurance that time will be used effectively. Maximizing progress and minimizing the time spent are crucial. Structure makes this possible.

> *"Well-planned meetings maintain a focus on the meeting's objectives and on the steps required to reach the objectives."*

Other issues, in addition to structure, should be considered. Knowing *who should be present* requires advanced planning. Some meetings require that all members be present, some do not. When items on the agenda pertain to the entire team, everyone should participate. When items pertain to only a subset of members, only those members who are involved are needed. Results of subgroup deliberations can be communicated to the entire team.

Meeting Leader

Understanding the responsibilities of the **meeting leader** is important. This is one of several meanings of *leader* discussed at different points in Chapter 6. The leader assists participants to achieve the meeting's objectives. An effective meeting leader has a clear objective for the meeting, can identify and evaluate paths to that objective, can elicit contributions from all participants, and can negotiate conflicts should they arise. Team members develop confidence in a meeting leader when they experience satisfaction because a meeting efficiently achieves its objectives.

> *"Team members develop confidence in a meeting leader when they experience satisfaction because a meeting efficiently achieves its objectives."*

The entire team should address the selection of a meeting leader. Teams can rotate leaders or settle on a single leader. Rotation enables each member to experience leading and gives other members the opportunity to experience their leadership. Considerable responsibility rests on the meeting leader. If a leader has inadequate skills for handling the responsibilities, the skills can be learned, although not without time, effort, and persistence. The responsibility is not, however, only the leader's. Team members must understand their responsibility to contribute to the meeting activities.

Why Meetings Fail

Meetings can go wrong for any of several reasons. Foremost is a *lack of planning*. Meetings are called, people attend, but nothing tangible is accomplished because what was to be accomplished was never clear. The next reason is *failing to adhere to the agenda*. Participants must hold to accomplishing what is expected. They must ask: How does this discussion move us toward our objective? Productive meetings result in decisions being made. They result in a sense of progress and accomplishment. Decision making may be difficult. It narrows options to two and then selects one. This can be an uncomfortable process, either because of discomfort with the options or because of concern about fallout from the decision. Making decisions is, however, one of a team's responsibilities.

Another problem is *lack of time limits*. Time limits make meetings more efficient. When time limits are not maintained or discussion goes on without progress, participants become frustrated. When this happens, members are likely to find ways to disrupt the process just to maintain their interest. If members are provided information in advance of a meeting, they can think about their contribution. Material provided to attendees in advance should indicate as clearly as possible the options to be considered.

> *"Meetings often involve sharing information."*

Meetings often involve *sharing information*. Team members are responsible for sharing relevant information that derives from their different competencies, experiences, and perspectives. A *low level of member participation* indicates that something is wrong. There are several possible reasons. Some members may feel they have nothing to contribute. Encouragement by the team leader and other members of the team can help to overcome reticence to speak. Some members may lack communication skills. Coaching can help to develop these skills. A leader may run the meeting in a way that tends to minimize participation. This problem should be addressed through leadership training. Also, some members may have their own agendas and hence do not participate. This is a special problem that is discussed later in this chapter.[4]

Another problem is *intense disagreement between members*. Disagreements can require extended discussion. It may even be necessary to do this "off line," that is, outside the context of the meeting. In such a case, unless the meeting can work around the difference and make progress toward its objective, it may be better to adjourn the meeting with the expectation that the difference will be resolved before the scheduled continuance of the meeting. This prospect may in itself reduce the conflict. See the discussion later in this chapter on resolving interpersonal conflicts.[5]

> *"Meetings are essential to effective team functioning."*

Meetings are essential to effective team functioning. Efficient, productive meetings require structured agendas including time limits. If some or all team members feel that the meetings are not productive and do not result in members having a sense of satisfaction, the problem needs to be addressed and solved, much as any other team problem is addressed. Communication is at the heart of this process.

EFFECTIVE COMMUNICATION

Communication is more than an exchange of words. All behaviors in the presence of others convey some message. Behaviors can be gestures (an outstretched hand), body language (turning one's shoulder to someone), or even no behavior (failing to recognize a person). A somewhat limited definition of communication is a message sent by one person (the sender or speaker) to another person (the receiver or listener) with the intent of influencing the other's behavior. This does not mean that there is always a set sequence of events. Communication can be rather fluid. Individuals can receive, send, interpret, and infer—all at the same time.

Effective communication exists between two people when the listener interprets the speaker's message in the same way the speaker intended it. A model of the communication process involves several steps, as described in Table 5.2.[6] Difficulties can arise at any of these steps. A speaker can be unclear about his or her intentions, ideas, or feelings. Even when these are clear, the speaker may be hesitant or unwilling to communicate openly. The channel chosen for communicating the message may be inadequate. For example, a written communication can be more precise than a spoken communication. The listener may misinterpret the message's meaning. As a result, the listener responds to an unintended meaning. The listener may react to a message either openly or may hide his or her reaction. Interruptions and distractions can also make the message more difficult to understand.

Sending Messages Effectively

To send messages effectively, use the first-person singular to clearly own the message. This makes it clear to the listener that these are the speaker's thoughts. Next, the speaker should think about what she wants to say before speaking, then be as complete and precise as possible. Third, it is important to make verbal and nonverbal messages congruent. Asking someone how he is feeling while looking around the room gives a mixed message of interest and disinterest. Fourth, while it is important to be concise, some repetition can help to clarify views. Finally, by asking the listener to indicate what he understands was said, the speaker has the opportunity to correct misperceptions.[7]

"To send messages effectively, use the first-person singular to clearly own the message."

The speaker should also consider how the listener is likely to perceive the message. By appreciating the listener's frame of reference, the speaker

---

TABLE 5.2
Communication Process Model

Speaker
Focuses on intentions, ideas, feelings to be sent.
Encodes intentions, ideas, feelings into message.
Sends message to a receiver through a channel.

Listener
Decodes message by interpreting its meaning.
Responds internally to interpretation of message.
Responds externally to the message.

Noise: Any feature that interferes with the communication process.

---

empathizes with the listener. This increases the likelihood that the listener will interpret the message accurately. Understanding a listener's possible reaction does not mean avoiding expressing what one is feeling or thinking, however. Next, indicate to the listener by name, action, or figure of speech the feelings that are associated with the message. This makes clear what is felt and also makes the feelings more readily addressed. Also, when describing another person's behavior, do so in objective terms. By avoiding evaluation or interpretation when describing another's behavior, the behavior can be examined more objectively and the listener can, if necessary, seek clarification.

> *"When sending a message, the speaker's credibility is an issue."*

When sending a message, the speaker's credibility is an issue. Credibility refers to several things. One is what the listener perceives the speaker's motives to be in sending the message. Does the speaker engender trust? Credibility also involves the listener's perception of the speaker's expertise and reliability. Is what the speaker says true and accurate? There are also issues of the speaker's friendliness, energy level, and involvement in the issue. Is the speaker's manner attractive? Finally, the listener is also influenced by the opinions others have of the speaker. Do others, who are well regarded by the listener, think well of the speaker?

Both the speaker's skill in sending messages and her credibility as a communicator affect the way a message is received. For some, communication in the manner described here can be difficult. However, effective communication is a skill. With effort, it can be improved. These skills, outlined in Table 5.3, apply to all forms of communication.

Receiving Messages Effectively

Listening is a part of communication that is often disregarded. Effective communication is thought of as effective speaking. Listening is, however, as important

---

TABLE 5.3
Sending Messages Effectively

Speaker's Message
Send clearly owned message .
Make messages complete, precise.
Make verbal and nonverbal messages agree.
Use redundance to generate clarity.
Request feedback to verify accuracy.
Consider listener's frame of reference.
Describe feelings associated with message.
Describe other's behavior in objective terms.

Listener's Perception of Speaker's Credibility
Perception of speaker's motives
Perception of speaker's expertise, reliability
Perception of speaker's warmth, friendliness
Perception of others' opinions of speaker

as speaking and especially important when communication is difficult. There are several reasons for this.[8] First, it hurts not be listened to. Most people think of themselves as better listeners than they really are. It is especially hurtful not to be listened to by those persons we count on for understanding. To listen is to pay attention, to be interested in, to care about, to take to heart, to validate, to acknowledge, to be moved, to appreciate what another is saying. Second, individuals have a need for others to validate their experience. By stepping into another's frame of reference—by putting oneself in the other person's shoes—the person who listens well acknowledges and affirms the person speaking, thus sustaining their self-respect. Third, being heard means being taken seriously. Being listened to is how individuals learn whether they are understandable and acceptable or not. Not being listened to makes a person feel ignored and unappreciated.

Effective listening enables the listener to give feedback about the message in ways that clarify and sustain continued discussion. Listening skills are broken down onto two parts. One is communicating the desire to understand the ideas and feelings of the speaker. The other is understanding and interpreting the speaker's ideas and feelings. Communicating the desire to understand correctly and not evaluate a message may be more important for good communication than how one understands and interprets the ideas and feelings.[9]

A major barrier to effective communication is the tendency to judge the message being received. For example, the speaker makes a statement and the listener responds inwardly or openly with "I think you're wrong," "I don't like what you said," "I think you are right," or "That is the greatest (or worst) idea I have ever heard!" Awareness of such evaluation can make the speaker defensive and cautious and reduce openness. When strong emotions are involved, the tendency to evaluate increases. The stronger the feelings, the more likely it is that two team members will evaluate each other's statements from their own point of view only.

> *"A major barrier to effective communication is the tendency to judge the message being received."*

Specific skills enable a person to indicate their understanding of a message. One is for the listener to restate, accurately and without evaluation, the message content and feelings of the speaker. This indicates an understanding of the speaker's frame of reference. The basic rule is: Express your own views only after you have accurately restated the speaker's ideas and feelings to the speaker's satisfaction. The speaker's feelings may be unclear. You should check the accuracy with the speaker without interpreting or expressing approval or disapproval. The listener is in essence saying, "Here is what I understand your feelings to be; am I accurate?"

A third skill is for the listener to interpret the speaker's message and to reach agreement with the speaker on the message's meaning. When the restatement of the message's meaning is inadequate, the meaning must be negotiated until there is agreement. The exchange can be prefaced with "What I think you mean is ...". If the speaker considers the statement accurate, the listener can then reply. If the restatement is considered inaccurate, the speaker should be asked to restate the message until the speaker is satisfied that the message's meaning is understood. These listening skills are summarized in Table 5.4.

TABLE 5.4
Receiving Messages Effectively

Listener's Listening
Speaker needs to feel heard, understood.
Feeling heard validates speaker's experience.
Feeling heard means being taken seriously.

Listener's Understanding
Resist evaluating message as speaker speaks.
Indicate understanding by repeating message accurately, without evaluation.
Empathize with speaker's feelings.
State understanding of feelings and negotiate agreement.

Sources of Team Communication Problems

Communication difficulties can pose serious problems for team performance and interpersonal relations. Resolving such difficulties is another example of the need for team problem solving. These problems can be of several types.

> *"Communication difficulties can pose serious problems for team performance and interpersonal relations."*

Misunderstandings. Two meeting attendees can fail to understand each other because one or the other is unclear in his statement or response. When this happens it is important to ask for a more detailed explanation. When a misunderstanding remains, it may help for the listener to repeat as much as he understands, asking the speaker to correct or explain the unclear parts. The rules for effective communication, described in Tables 5.3 and 5.4, are useful in such situations.

Failure to Listen. Most people fail to listen at some time or other. In a meeting this can happen when one person, who is not speaking, is busy formulating her next statement and fails to "hear" what the speaker is saying. Consequently, the nonlistener's comments miss the flow of the discussion and sound irrelevant.

Attribution of Bias. A more complicated communication problem arises when a listener assumes that a speaker is expressing a biased point of view supportive of his own interests. It is important to remember that everyone speaks from his or her own point of view. If the listener, however, thinks that the speaker is unduly biased, the listener may hear only those parts of the communication that fit the assumed bias. For example, a speaker, discussing the costs and benefits of an environmental regulation, is perceived by a listener to be biased against the regulation. In such a situation, questions to the speaker by the listener can help to clarify the speaker's perspective.[10]

Hidden Agendas. A *hidden agenda* is a more complex form of the bias problem. It involves a team member having an interest or motivation, that is, having a goal for her team, that is not in line with the team's actual goal. Part of the strategy of having a hidden agenda is that meaningful discussion is avoided.

One result can be the member not participating in pursuing her team's goal. This means lost resources. If this happens and performance is negatively affected, it needs to be identified and discussed.[11]

Discounting.   Another challenge to effective communication is what is referred to as **discounting**. This means responding to someone's statement with "Yes, but . . ." Under the disguise of agreement, there is effective disagreement. Extensive use of discounting can be disruptive. In such instances, the "Yes, but. . ." can be addressed as disagreement and the differences of view negotiated to agreement.

"Under the disguise of agreement, there is effective disagreement."

Personality Conflicts.   Conflicts between individuals can go beyond simple disagreement. These often surface when individuals become angry at the lack of progress or there is spillover into team activities from another area of conflict. For example, two team members, having had a heated argument at a company party, find that afterward they disagree more frequently on team matters. Such conflict can be so great that the individuals cannot work together. Conflict can also arise out of frustration with a flawed meeting process or because of differences in members' styles about how to address technical or interpersonal issues. Because these differences can "derail" a meeting, they should be addressed. If necessary, principles designed to minimize conflict can be agreed to by the team.[12]

Resentment of the leader.   Meetings can fail because team members have a negative reaction to the meeting leader. This can occur because the members perceive the leader to have assumed the role without the team's agreement or because the team leader, once chosen by the team, makes decisions without conferring with other team members. Having a team discussion about who is to assume the role of leader or about the leader's role can reduce the likelihood of such resentment. When there is ambiguity about how the leader is to be chosen or about the leader's role, it is important to raise the issue for discussion and agreement.[13]

The Constructive Role of Controversy

The communication problems just described are an inevitable feature of interpersonal interaction, especially efforts by teams to solve problems and make decisions. Such problems can be disruptive and even destructive or they can be constructive and creative. If the controversy arises from competition or from preferring to work on one's own, there is little motivation to maintain constructive communication. These individuals seek essentially to work by themselves. If, however, the parties to the controversy have a cooperative outlook and do want their team to achieve its goal, the chances of resolving the controversy are greatly improved. This is referred to as **constructive controversy.**

To keep controversy constructive several rules are outlined in Table 5.5. It is important to challenge ideas related to opposing views, but to avoid any tendency to reject the person who espouses the view. Keep the focus on coming to the best decision possible. Avoid seeking to "win" the argument. There is often some merit in both points of view. Encourage every member to participate in

> *"Paraphrase or restate what has been said, if it is not clear, to ensure clarity."*

the discussion and to master all of the relevant information. Encourage careful listening to everyone's ideas, even when disagreeing. Resist interrupting. This can imply a "put down." Paraphrase or restate what has been said, if it is not clear, to ensure clarity. Bring out all the ideas and facts supporting both sides, and then put them together in a way that makes sense. Seek to understand both sides of an issue. Finally, members should be willing to change their minds when the evidence supports a different view.[14]

Interpersonal conflict can complicate interpersonal interactions. Each person observes and makes judgments about others present. If individuals know each other from previous interactions, they have prior judgments. Old antagonisms can surface. If individuals are meeting for the first time, they develop first impressions, often quickly. If they respond positively to each other, their interaction is likely to be open and relaxed. If they are "put off" by each other, their interaction will be tense and guarded, even distrustful. In this latter situation the likelihood of controversy increases.

It is important for conflicts to be addressed by team members. Conflicts that are not addressed detract from a team's ability to identify and resolve barriers to high performance. The quality of interactions, whether open or guarded, friendly or distrustful, can facilitate or hinder what a team accomplishes. The quality of interactions also has considerable impact on the satisfaction members experience. While some antagonisms may defy reduction, many can be changed for the better by following the rules for constructive controversy, by maintaining a focus on the team's goal, by members being promotively interactive, and by members experiencing success.

TABLE 5.5
Rules for Constructive Controversy

Be critical of ideas, not individuals.
Focus on making the best decision.
Encourage every member's participation.
Listen attentively to members' ideas.
Paraphrase and restate what is unclear.
Bring out all ideas supportive of both sides of issue.
Seek to understand both sides of issue.
Be willing to change mind when evidence supports another view.

The Challenge Revisited
Planning, Meeting, and Communicating

1. Planning by a team is challenging because tasks and social interactions must be specified and coordinated to specify a path to the team's goal.

2. Meetings are challenging because they must be planned, members must participate, and the meeting's objective must be accomplished.

3. Effective communication is challenging because members must be clear and accurate in sending messages while other members must listen. Poor communication can result in conflict and controversy.

4. A challenge is to strive toward effective communication and to address conflict and controversy using negotiation and problem solving to strengthen rather than weaken team performance.

EXERCISE 5.1 • *Planning a Team Meeting*

1. Develop a plan or model for holding team meetings. In the plan, specify the following:
   - How will meeting objectives be established?
   - How will the meeting agenda be prepared?
   - How will the meeting leader be identified?
   - What will the meeting leader's responsibilities be?
   - What practices or principles should the team follow to make meetings as productive as possible?
   - How will the team determine whether meeting objectives have been achieved?
   - How will the team identify ways in which subsequent meetings can be made more productive?

2. Prepare a report of the results of your team's deliberations.

EXERCISE 5.2 • *Innovation Maze*[15]

The Setup: The team sets up a roughly 13- × 9-foot grid on the floor or pavement, as shown in the following diagram, using one-inch masking tape. Each square in the grid should be approximately 18 inches on each side.

Instructions: This is a team problem-solving exercise about leadership and followership and the mutual support required for teamwork. Your goal is to get all members through "the maze" by following a single path formed by adjacent squares, either side by side or diagonal. The amount of time allotted for a team to proceed through the maze can be from 12 to 15 minutes.

- The path begins at one of the squares in column 1 (**Start**) and proceeds—in a curved, not a straight, line—through the last row, after which a person exits the maze (**Finish**).
- Only the facilitator knows the key that depicts the correct path.
- The diagram below depicts an example of a correct path.
- Time should be allowed at the start of the exercise for planning. A set amount of time, determined by the facilitator, will be permitted before each new member attempts to cross the maze.
- *Remember*: The correct path is one continuous line made up of adjacent or contiguous squares.

Several rules and constraints govern your team's actions while solving the problem.

- Teams will be awarded $1,000,000 if all members get through the maze.
- Teams will be assessed a $100,000 penalty for each rule violation.

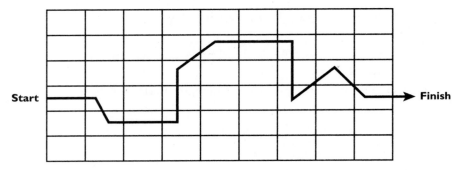

The following rules and penalties apply:

- Only one person at a time is allowed on the maze.
- If a person steps on a wrong square, he or she will be "buzzed" and must withdraw from the maze. There is no penalty for being buzzed. To withdraw successfully, however, a person must follow the exact same path used to get in. If he or she fails to do so, a penalty will be assessed.
- A rotation of "innovators" attempting the maze is required so that once one group member is buzzed off the maze, another tries, until all members have tried. The rotation begins again and continues until time is called.
- No "Hansel and Gretel" is allowed (i.e., no leaving a trail on the maze for others to follow).
- No diagramming the unfolding path on paper or blackboards as it is discovered.
- When in a planning mode, the entire team must be behind the start line and talking is allowed. When implementing, that is, while an "innovator" is on the maze, team members may array themselves in any way they choose around the maze, but no talking is allowed. A penalty will be assessed for talking while executing.

- When an innovator is out on the maze, none of his or her fellow team members may touch the maze with any part of his or her body. A penalty will be assessed for touching the maze while an innovator is on the maze.

An exercise "round" is complete when the time limit is reached. The exercise should be repeated for a second round, after a different "correct" path through the maze has been selected by the facilitator. (Rounds can continue until all members are through the maze, if the facilitator wishes.)

1. Questions for discussion—round 1:

   a. What was the experience like, being on the maze?

   b. What was the penalty for stepping on the wrong square? Why was there hesitation before stepping on a square?

   c. What actions of other team members helped progress? What actions hindered progress?

   d. Did your team have an explicit strategy for helping an innovator through the maze?

   e. What role does planning play in this exercise? How can planning be improved?

   f. What might be done differently in the next round to improve performance?

2. Questions for discussion—round 2:

   a. What did your team do differently in the second round? Did you change tactics? How effective were the changes?

   b. Were any innovations in strategy attributable to individuals or to the team as a whole?

   c. Were members more or less involved in the second round than they were in the first round? What made the difference?

   d. Did your team break any of the "rules"? Were there more or fewer broken rules than in the first round? Why?

   e. Did your team have a leader during the first round? During the second round? How was a leader identified? What does this exercise tell you about leadership?

   f. What are the lessons of this exercise? What have you learned that can be applied in other settings?

QUESTIONS FOR REVIEW AND DISCUSSION

1. Why is planning essential for effective team performance? What is planning? What are the five stages of the planning process?

2. Why are teams tempted not to plan adequately? What can happen when planning is inadequate?

3. The most significant drawback about team meetings is the time they require. What can be done to minimize the time required to have an effective meeting?

4. What is meant by *meeting structure*? How is a meeting structure developed? Why is an advance agenda important for member participation?

5. Why is having a meeting leader important? What are the meeting leader's responsibilities?

6. Why is the participation of all members who attend a meeting important? What are the reasons for members not participating? How can each of these reasons be addressed?

7. What does effective communication involve? What are the steps of the communication process? What are problems that can beset the communication process?

8. What is required to send and receive messages effectively? How can the skills associated with effective communication be developed?

9. Name four problems that can interfere with communication among team members. How can each of these problems be resolved?

10. What is meant by the term *constructive controversy*? Why is it important for a team to address conflict and controversy? What are the rules for keeping controversy constructive?

NOTES

1. Mental maps or mental models are discussed in a variety of sources. See J. Mathieu, T. S. Heffner, G. Goodwin, E. Salas, & J. Cannon-Bowers (2000), The influence of shared mental models on team process and performance, *Journal of Applied Psychology*, 85, 275–283.

2. R. C. Nutt (1984), *Planning Methods for Health and Related Organizations*, New York: Wiley, p. 60ff.

3. See H. Schwortzman (1989), *Meetings: Gatherings in Organizations and Communities*, New York: Plenum.

4. On sharing information, see D. Gigone & R. Hastie (1993), The common knowledge effect: Information sharing and group judgment, *Journal of Personality and Social Psychology*, 65, 959–974. Also C. Connolly (1996), Communication: Getting to the heart of the matter, *Management Development Review*, 9, 37–40.

5. The skills discussed in Chapter 4, especially negotiating, bargaining, and decision making, can be useful in resolving interpersonal conflicts.

6. D. W. Johnson (1986), *Reaching Out*, 3rd ed., Englewood Cliffs, NJ: Prentice Hall, p. 108.

7. This section summarizes a discussion of sending messages effectively in D. W. Johnson (1986), op. cit., pp. 112–114. Also D. W. Johnson & F. P. Johnson (1987), *Joining Together: Group Theory and Group Skills*, Englewood Cliffs, NJ: Prentice Hall, pp. 177–179.

8. M. P. Nichols (1995), *The Lost Art of Listening*, New York: Guilford Press.

9. The discussion of rules for receiving messages effectively is summarized from Johnson & Johnson, op. cit., pp. 179–181.

10. For a description of different forms of interpersonal misperception see D. Levi (2001), *Group Dynamics for Teams*, Thousand Oaks, CA: Sage, p 234.

11. Argyris has written extensively about this problem showing how it can undermine the performance of a consulting partnership. See C. Argyris (1982), *Reasoning, Learning and Action*, San Francisco: Jossey-Bass, pp. 82–106. Also see R. A. Eisenstat (1990), Fairfield Coordinating Group, in R. Hackman (Ed.), *Teams that Work (And Those that Don't)*, San Francisco, CA: Jossey-Bass, pp. 19–35, for a description of a meeting that seemed to go well but manifested underlying antagonisms.

12. On managing conflict, see Levi, op. cit., pp. 115–131.

13. Selection of a leader is discussed by D. Yeatts & C. Hyten (1998), *High Performance Self-Managed Teams*, Thousand Oaks, CA: Sage, pp. 302–308. A somewhat contrasting view is provided in D. Ray & H. Bronson (1995) *Teaming Up*, pp. 144–145, New York: McGraw-Hill.

14. Johnson & Johnson, op. cit., p. 180.

15. This exercise is taken from S. S. Kaagan (1999), *Leadership Games: Experiential Learning for Organizational Development*, Thousand Oaks, CA: Sage, pp. 56–59. Reprinted with permission of Sage Publications, Inc.

The Challenge
Leading a Team

Most teams need a leader (or leaders). Who among a team's members is likely to be the most effective leader depends on the team's experience and maturity, on the difficulties posed by the environment in which the team operates, and on the ability of the leader to adopt a leadership style that can facilitate the team's performance in that situation. In selecting a leader, a team must make a realistic appraisal of the team's leadership needs and select one or more members who can meet those needs. Having chosen a leader, a team must be supportive, recognizing that leading can involve learning and practicing a previously unfamiliar style of leadership in the process of assisting a team to achieve its goal.

chapter 6

Leading a Team

A team just getting started will confront this question: Who will lead? Sometimes a team begins its planning process or even begins performing goal-oriented tasks without considering who will be its leader. The need for a leader to assist the team to keep track of assignments, to facilitate coordination of activities, and to keep the team focused on its goal will, however, become apparent. Consider the following situation.

Sarah, George, Elizabeth, Tyrone, and Amanda are music students working toward master's degrees at a prestigious music conservatory. They have formed a string quintet to fulfill the requirements for their master's projects with the hope that they might continue together after graduation as a professional ensemble. Each is an exceptionally skilled instrumental performer, although most are more comfortable performing solo than as members of a quintet. Working together has been a learning experience for all. As they have grown more experienced and comfortable with each other, the need for a leader has become increasingly clear. They need one of their members to lead discussions on how to perform a piece of music, to set the tempo as they perform, to decide how much practice is needed, and to decide which section needs the most work.

They are now in the process of making this decision. Sarah would like to be the leader, although she has had no experience as a leader and is not quite sure what she should do. George was the student director of his college orchestra, and while he did quite well in the position, he is not sure that he wants to assume the leadership role because he knows the demands it makes. He knows that he becomes impatient with differences between members. Elizabeth was concertmaster, essentially assistant director, in her college orchestra. While in that role she gave considerable thought to what makes a musical group excellent. She also enjoys helping orchestra members improve their coordination. Tyrone also would like to perform the role, especially since he has some ideas about how George and Amanda can improve their performance. He has also been the one to suggest practice dates and to send e-mail reminders. Amanda would like to be the leader. She has had no leadership experience with a musical group although she was president of her sorority her senior year in college.

Each of the members is thinking about how he or she could provide the leadership that would best help the quintet to achieve its goal of being a high-performing musical ensemble. Furthermore, some members would like to be the ensemble's leader and others would not. How does this team decide? [1]

There are several broad considerations. For instance, who actually begins to take responsibility for leadership? Often, one or two members step into the role early in the team's activities. Other considerations include these: Who among the team's members thinks about where the team as a unit is going and how it will get there? Who understands and can encourage interdependent team functioning? What is the response of other team members to the person who is being considered for the position? Who could, as leader, share the role where feasible? Given these considerations, what is it that qualifies and enables a team member to lead his or her team? To answer these questions, we will consider several views of leadership, then return to the quintet's decision.

Perspectives on Leadership

Leadership is a much discussed, much researched, and sometimes greatly misunderstood concept. Authors search for metaphors that capture the essence of leadership. Styles of leadership have been characterized as Machiavellian, authoritarian, charismatic, transformational, and even as that of geese and buffalo.[2] Each characterization falls short by itself because it fails to identify the essence of true leadership.

A basic assumption is that a team functions more effectively with a leader than without. The effect is not always positive, however. Thus, an important issue is how a leader affects team behavior in general and team performance in particular.[3] There are also exceptions—teams that do not have leaders.[4] That a team can perform with a minimum of leadership is due largely to its performance being highly scripted, for example, by a musical score, or to the fact that its members are highly skilled and experienced acting in the situation they are in.

"Leadership is a much discussed, much researched, and sometimes greatly misunderstood concept."

Most teams do have leaders. When goals are imprecise, the process for achieving them ambiguous, and the skills members need to carry out the process still developing, leadership is especially important to keep the activity on track and to keep members involved. The question is this: What characterizes an effective team leader? To answer this question, several perspectives on the nature of leadership are considered.[5]

Leadership Traits

Which traits, either with which one is born or which develop early in life, enable an individual to be an effective leader? For example, Erikson[6] has theorized that leaders as different as Hitler and Gandhi became the individuals they were as a result of early childhood experiences. Are effective leaders more charismatic?

> *"Such leaders have vision and the ability to communicate their vision to followers."*

These are leaders who inspire devotion and offer hope of accomplishment. Such leaders have vision and the ability to communicate their vision to followers. They are self-confident and have practical ability that enables them to inspire others to work to achieve their goals. Attempts to define and measure charisma have, however, generally failed. This underscores a major problem with the leadership trait approach. It focuses on personality characteristics that some individuals may have but fails to specify how they come to be. To lead teams requires behaviors that can be developed and improved with experience.

Leadership Styles

Leadership styles, in contrast to leadership traits, emphasize behaviors that can be learned, although the difference between some traits and styles can be unclear. While an individual may be more comfortable with one leadership style and use it more frequently, he or she may be able to use other styles when a situation requires it. The following are examples of leadership styles.[7]

Leading by Controlling.   The **controlling** (or **directive**) **leader** determines all policies, specific work tasks, and work companions. He or she specifies steps in an activity one at a time so that subsequent steps are largely uncertain. A

> *"The controlling leader remains aloof from team participation except when demonstrating some task or activity."*

leader with this style personally praises or criticizes members' work; however, the reason for the praise or criticism is often unclear. The controlling leader remains aloof from team participation except when demonstrating some task or activity. Under this style members, are dependent on the leader. In response to this style, team members express more discontent and even hostility, although their general reaction is to be submissive. Members also tend to work less when the leader is absent.

Leading by Participating.   The **participatory** (or **democratic**) **leader** encourages and facilitates team activities. Members are encouraged to discuss general steps to the goal. When technical advice is needed, the leader may suggest two or more alternatives from among which members can choose. Members are free to work with whomever they chose. The division of tasks is left up to the team. Praise and criticism by the leader are objective or based on facts and reasons for either are given. This style encourages questions and guides actions with suggestions. Work led by this style can be efficient. Although the quantity of work done under the controlling leader style can be somewhat greater, under the participatory leader style, worker motivation is stronger. For instance, when a participatory leader is absent, work is more likely to continue. With the participatory leader style there is more group-mindedness, more friendliness, greater originality, and more mutual praise.

"The participatory (or democratic) leader encourages and facilitates team activities."

Leading by Staying Apart. The **"laid-back"** (or **nondirective) leader** participates minimally in team activities and gives the team complete freedom to make team or individual decisions. Such a leader provides information only when asked. No attempt is made to appraise or regulate the course of events. Teams with laid-back leaders tend to ask more questions. Few orders are given and little effort is made to stimulate self-guidance. There are few disrupting commands and little criticism, praise, or approval. Less work tends to be done under this style, and that which is done may suffer in quality.

"Teams with laid-back leaders tend to ask more questions."

Leading by Coaching. Another perspective on leadership is the leader as coach. A goal of the coaching leader is to help team members develop the ability to self-monitor, that is, to evaluate their own behavior in the interests of improving. Several core principles are followed in coaching:[8] to provide a context that promotes individual development; to use positive reinforcement, encouragement, and sound technical instruction to create interpersonal attraction between coach and team member; to establish norms that emphasize team members' mutual obligation to help and support one another; to involve team members in decisions about team rules and to reinforce compliance with them rather than punishing noncompliance; and to obtain feedback and engage in self-monitoring to increase awareness of one's own actions relative to established guidelines.

The major shortcoming of the leadership style approach is that different styles are effective under different conditions. A controlling style is more effective when an urgent decision is needed. A participatory style is more effective when member commitment needs to be built. A laid-back style is more effective when the group is committed, has the needed resources, and needs a minimum of direction to work effectively. Coaching is effective when the tasks required to reach a team's goal are reasonably clear and success depends on the quality of task performance.

Leadership in Different Situations

The best predictor of a leader's future success is prior success as a leader. A previously successful leader may, however, fail in a situation that imposes demands that are incompatible with his or her leadership skills.[9] An examination of how the situation influences

"The best predictor of a leader's future success is prior success as a leader."

leader behavior and of how leaders vary their behavior from situation to situation has resulted in several different emphases.

One emphasis proposes that teams have two objectives. One is to complete their tasks and the other is to maintain effective collaborative relationships among their members. For a team to complete its tasks successfully, members must carry out task-related activities, for example, obtain, organize, and use information to make decisions. For a team to be successful, its leader must also help to structure interactions, give directions, and energize the team's task-related efforts. It is counterproductive, however, to complete a task in a manner that alienates team members. Tasks should be completed in a way that increases members' ability to work together effectively in the future. To achieve this, the leader needs to encourage members to participate, facilitate effective communication among members, evaluate the emotional climate of the team, and relieve tension in the team when it gets too high. The leader should also facilitate discussion about how the quality of a team's work can be improved.

From this perspective, any team member may become a leader by behaving in ways that help the team to complete its task and to maintain effective collaborative relationships. Leadership behaviors are specific to a particular team in a particular situation. Under specific circumstances, any given leadership behavior may or may not support a team's functioning. According to this view, leadership involves a learned set of skills. Having diagnosed the needs of a specific situation, anyone who is motivated and perseveres can develop and apply skills relevant to that situation, although support from team members will be needed to do so.[10]

"Teams with little experience working together may need more direction than more experienced teams."

The strengths of the different styles described in the preceding paragraphs suggest how styles can be adapted to a situation. For example, with a deadline looming, a team leader may need to be more directive to complete the work on time. In a situation where much complex work is to be completed, the leader may need to be more involved in specific activities. In a situation where the leader must spend considerable time with the team's supervisor or customer, a more laid-back style that gives more responsibility to a team may be more functional. Also, a team's experience level is a situational consideration. Teams with little experience working together may need more direction than more experienced teams. Furthermore, a team that is having difficulties performing its tasks will require more task-related leadership, whereas a team that is having difficulties maintaining cooperation among members will require more leader attention to interpersonal issues.

Another view of the emergence of leadership focuses on matching leaders to situations in which they will be most effective.[11] According to this view, if five strangers are placed together and assigned a task that requires cooperation, social interactions will occur and become patterned or structured. Some members will interact more frequently, others less frequently. Figure 2.1 (Chapter 2) depicts such a communication and interaction structure. From this patterning, a possible leadership structure emerges: that is, one or two persons assume the leadership roles. They can be identified as the members involved in the most interactions with other members (e.g., member A in Figure 2.1). In some situations there may be two leaders. One assumes the task leadership role and the other assumes the group maintenance role. Such a division of responsibilities can, in appropriate situations, prove effective.

This view makes several assumptions. When a group has a task to complete, its members tend to engage in task-related behaviors on an unequal basis. Some want to "get the task done." Others seek to maintain cooperative relationships among members. Members who are highly task oriented may feel hostility toward members who are oriented to interpersonal satisfaction and appear less committed to the task. Those committed to maintaining interpersonal satisfaction may feel that those who are task oriented don't care about people. Consequently, there is a need to legitimize and support both roles. By differentiating and synchronizing the roles of **task leader** and **maintenance leader,** they can effectively reinforce and support each other.

A related perspective focuses on different situations requiring different leadership styles. In some situations, task-oriented leaders are more effective. In other situations, maintenance-oriented leaders are more effective. A task-oriented leader can be more effective under two conditions. One occurs when the leader is on very good terms with team members, the task is clearly structured, and the leader has a position of high authority and power. Under these conditions, the team is ready and willing to be directed. In the second set of conditions, the leader is on poor terms with team members, the task is ambiguous, and he or she has a position of low authority and power. Under these conditions, an effective leader takes responsibility for making decisions and directing team members in task-related activities. Experiencing success will enhance the leader's status with the team. However, when the leader is on moderately good terms with team members, has moderate authority, and the task is moderately clear, the maintenance-oriented leader, who emphasizes member participation in team decision making and problem solving, will, according to this perspective, be the most effective.[12]

"Experiencing success will enhance the leader's status with the team."

How can one determine what the "situation" is? How is one to know whether task clarity, leader–member relations, and leader power are high or low? This is not easy to answer, although most teams tend to be moderate on all three dimensions. Most important is for the leader to seek to understand the situation by examining these issues: the quality of the relationship between leader and members, the clarity of the task structure, and the degree of the leader's power and authority. Another question is whether these three dimensions are the only ones to be considered. Again, this is not an easy question to answer. These are, however, important questions for a leader. He must regularly scan the team's situational conditions and adjust his behavior to fit the conditions in the interests of enhancing team performance.

Another focus is a team's level of maturity.[13] This refers to a team's level of development as a team and is concerned with a team's capacity to set for itself high but attainable goals and with members' willingness and ability to take responsibility for achieving the goals. Maturity pertains only to a specific goal because a team may have high maturity relative to one goal, but low maturity relative to a different one.

"Communication is primarily from the leader to team members."

When a team has low maturity relative to achieving a specific goal, the leader should engage in *high task and low relationship behaviors* (directing or telling). This means that the leader defines the roles of team members and tells them how, when, and where to do various tasks. Communication is primarily from the leader to team members. At a moderate level of maturity, when task roles are moderately well developed and interdependence is moderately established, the leader should engage in *high task, high relationship behaviors* (coaching or selling). This involves providing clear direction as to task role responsibilities and giving socioemotional support to get group members to psychologically buy into decisions that have to be made. Communication is two way. Also, at the moderate level of maturity, when team members have the ability and knowledge to complete the task but interdependence is only moderately established, the leader should engage in *low task, high relationship behaviors* (supporting or participating). This involves team members sharing in decision making through two-way communication and considerable facilitating behavior from the leader. When team maturity is high, *low task, low relationship behavior* (delegating) by the leader allows team members considerable autonomy to complete the task, since they are both willing and able to take responsibility for directing their own task behavior.[14] Table 6.1 summarizes the leader role for three levels of team maturity.

"Situations differ in terms of the leader's relationship to other team members, the clarity of the task to be performed, and the degree of power the leader has."

To summarize, there are two broad leadership roles. One is that of task leader, the other, that of team maintenance leader. In the early phases of a team's activity, the members who are inclined to do so begin to perform these roles. How the roles are performed depends on the style of the leader, on the maturity of the team, and on features of the situation. Situations differ in terms of the leader's relationship to other team members, the clarity of the task to be performed, and the degree of power the leader has. Less mature or experienced teams require more directive leadership, whereas more mature, experienced teams are able to assume more responsibility for their activities and therefore require less

TABLE 6.1
Matching Leader Style to Team Maturity Level

Team Maturity	Team Maturity		Leader Role	
	Task	*Maintenance*	*Task*	*Maintenance*
Low	Low	Low	High	Low
Moderate 1	Moderate	Moderate	High	High
Moderate 2	High	Low	Low	High
High	High	High	Low	Low

* The two more likely moderate conditions are where both situational conditions are moderate or task capability is high and team maintenance is low.

directive leadership. Effective leadership requires consideration of each of these issues and the application of a style that is most appropriate.

CHOOSING A LEADER

At the outset of this chapter the quandary of the musical ensemble was "Who will lead"? Considering Table 6.1 one would say that this quintet is at a moderate level of maturity. Member skills are well developed, but they are just developing as a performing unit. They would benefit most from a leader who can focus on team maintenance. Taking what the members of the quintet express about the role of leader, a further analysis can be developed.

Table 6.2 outlines some issues to be considered; indicates where each member is relative to the issues, based on available information; and suggests where better information is needed. If one assigns weights (e.g., 3 = high, 2 = moderate, 1 = low) to each member's status on the five issues, a rough estimate of each person's qualifications to lead the quintet can be determined.[15] Doing so suggests that Elizabeth may be the leading candidate.

The information in Table 6.2 should not be the end but the beginning of the discussion. This team needs to discuss several issues. First, at its level of maturity this team needs a leader who can help the team to develop coordinated, cooperative interactions. Three members of the team did not mention the issue. What do they think about the topic? Second, George has the most leadership experience although he does not enjoy an important part of the role. Because his leadership experience is a team resource, how can it be used to benefit the team and provide George satisfaction? Are the dual roles of task and group maintenance relevant here? Third, only one member mentioned a "vision" for the team. What do others think? Can a singular vision for the team be developed? What is the leader's role in developing a vision? Fourth, four members would like to be leader. How can their wishes (their individual goals) be met? Assuming that finding a way to meet these aspirations will be important for keeping members involved, who as leader will be willing to address this issue?

TABLE 6.2
Evaluating Members' Qualifications for Leadership of the String Quintet

	Members				
Member Capabilities	*Sarah*	*George*	*Elizabeth*	*Tyrone*	*Amanda*
Instrumental skill	High	High	High	High	High
Group maintenance concerns	?	Low	Moderate-High	?	?
Leadership experience	Low	High	Moderate-High	Low	Low-Moderate
Motivation to lead	High	Low	High	High	High
Vision for future	?	?	High	Moderate-Low	?
Helping others to lead	?	?	?	?	?
Initiates leadership	?	?	?	?	?

"trust develops because team members experience their team and its activities as a mutually supportive social environment"

Discussing the type of leadership experience each member would like and then discussing how the candidates for leader might satisfy these aspirations is a team problem-solving challenge.

The discussion that the string quintet needs to have will require considerable openness and tact by team members both in offering their thoughts about other team members and in revealing their own desires and wishes (their individual goals). For this to occur, members must trust each other enough to be willing to reveal their personal feelings and observations. Such trust develops because team members experience their team and its activities as a mutually supportive social environment. In choosing a leader, a team is deciding not simply who will lead, but who will create and support the quality of social environment in which the envisioned performance will take place.

THE LEADER'S ROLE IN CREATING A SOCIAL ENVIRONMENT

Leadership proceeds as a process of reciprocal influence. The leader exerts influence over team members and members influence the leader. The leader offers team members a way to achieve a desired outcome. Members in turn offer their support to the "position" (or role) of leader. From this position, the leader begins a process of encouraging team members to set and achieve goals and to work together to achieve those goals. This often means that leaders need to persuade and inspire members to follow their view of what needs to be done.[16]

By this reciprocal process, a leader creates the **social environment** in which a team functions. Creating a social environment is sometimes referred to as **social architecture** with the leader as social architect. Social architecture is defined as the ". . . silent variable that translates the 'blooming, buzzing confusion' of organizational life into meaning. It determines who says what to whom, about what, and what kind of actions ensue. Social architecture is an intangible, but it governs the way people act, the values and norms that are subtly transmitted to group and individuals, and the construct of binding and bonding" that occurs.[17]

The term *social architecture* is preferable to the more frequently used *culture* because it implies a tractability that the term *culture* lacks. Reference to *culture* is most often in the context of how difficult it is to change. Using the term *architecture* does not alter the difficulties. The term *architecture* does, however, clearly imply that the environment is designed and built, and further implies that it can be redesigned and rebuilt.

An illustration of how social architecture can be built is provided by several studies.[18] These examine the effect adult leaders' styles have on participants' performance and interpersonal relations in experimentally created "clubs." Leaders learned to use each of three leadership styles by following one of three scripts: "autocratic," "lassiez-faire," or democratic. In the terminology used here previously, these terms represent "controlling," "laid back," and "participatory." The way each type of leader behaved toward club members created a distinctive social environment or social architecture that resulted in notably different responses by group members.

As described earlier, *controlling leaders* created social environments in which, while directing activities, the leader remained aloof from team activity. Members were dissatisfied and even hostile, while at the same time, submissive to the directions of the leader. Under this style, the quantity and quality of work produced were reasonably high, although members' efforts slacked off when the leader was absent. Member satisfaction was low. *Participating leaders* created social environments in which the leader was involved, encouraging group discussions and group decisions. Members were group-minded, friendly, and more praising of each other's activities. Under this style, the quantity and quality of work were moderate to high, and members continued to work when the leader was absent. Member satisfaction was high. *Laid-back leaders* created social environments in which the leader was minimally involved and members had many questions but received little direction. Under this style, quantity and quality of work were low, as was satisfaction.

> *"Members were group-minded, friendly, and more praising of each other's activities."*

This typology can be applied to members of the string quintet and suggests the social environment that each might create. For example, Elizabeth was aware that Tyrone had some ideas about how George and Amanda could improve their performance, but he tended to *tell* them what to do rather than ask questions (Would such-and-such work better?) or to focus on improving the ensemble's performance (How could we improve this passage?). Tyrone's directive style irritated George especially. Elizabeth felt that Tyrone had some good ideas but his style in presenting the ideas was a problem. Elizabeth was trying to keep the discussion open and constructive and she was talking to Tyrone trying to help him develop a more discursive, participatory style. In sum, Elizabeth was energetically seeking to create a positive, constructive social environment for the ensemble's activities in contrast to Tyrone's more directive style.

THE LEADER'S ROLE IN CREATING A VISION

Leaders not only build a social environment in the present, they also help their team create a vision of the future. David Halberstam, in *The Powers That Be*, describes William Paley, who at age 27 took an almost bankrupt CBS with no radio stations of its own to a $27.7 million business with 114 stations in only 10 years. Halberstam states: "What he had from the start was a sense of vision, a sense of what might be. It was as if he could sit in New York in his tiny office with his almost bankrupt company and see . . . millions of the American people out in the hinterlands, so many of them out there, almost alone, many of them in homes as yet unconnected to electricity, people alone with almost no form of entertainment other than radio. It was his sense, his confidence that he could reach them, that he had something for them, that made him different".[19]

How does a leader create a vision, a desirable future state for the team? A vision is a realistic, credible, attractive future state that is better in some important ways than what now exists.[20] Where does this image of the future come from? An effective

> *"How does a leader create a vision, a desirable future state for the team?"*

leader does not necessarily create her vision although she thinks carefully about it. It often originates from talking with friends and colleagues or from reading, among other sources. A leader rarely creates the vision without material from others.[21] A leader may choose an image from several possibilities available at the moment, then articulate it, give it form and legitimacy, and focus attention on it.

"This decision involves selecting a vision."

For example, consider the musical ensemble again. George had thought about the quintet's desire to be recognized as a high-performing chamber music group and he felt that as a goal, *being high performing* was too abstract, too unreal. He believed that the quintet could be *the* premier chamber ensemble if only they were to choose a specific type of music. He saw several possibilities but he thought that they would best achieve their vision if they focused on Mozart string quintets. This same challenge faces any team. A team of bank executives putting together a plan for a new savings product must consider whether they want the product to be the most lucrative, the most innovative, or the most copied.[22] This decision involves selecting a vision.

Once a vision is articulated, an effective leader begins to develop the details of how to realize the vision. To do this a leader must first be a good and careful *listener*. Many leaders establish both formal and informal channels of communication to access ideas. Successful leaders are also good at asking questions. They also pay attention when others respond to their questions. By paying attention, they gather clues about how to proceed. From these clues and their own thoughts about strategy, they begin to develop different scenarios or processes by which the vision can be achieved.

Three sources guide development of a scenario. Considering the *past*, leaders reflect on their own experiences. They talk to others in similar situations. They look for what their team has been trying to do, how successful it has been,

"the leader selects, organizes, structures, and interprets information about the future"

and why. They develop a model of what has worked and what has not. Considering the *present*, leaders look at what is happening right now. They consider the human and material resources needed for the team to shape its future. They seek to understand restraints and opportunities that will influence the outcome. They may even conduct small experiments. The interpretation of this information is an important feature of leadership. Considering the *future*, the leader selects, organizes, structures, and interprets information about the future. He or she develops scenarios for alternative outcomes and then considers the implications of each for the team's achieving its vision. Discussion of the alternative scenarios and which will be pursued by the team is another decision-making challenge.[23]

A vision provides the team a bridge from the present to the future. On the one hand, a team seeks to maximize its rewards from its external environment; on the other hand, team members seek to maximize their rewards from their participation in the team. When the team has a clear sense of its purpose, direction, and desired future state, and when this image is of such clarity that it can be shared, individuals can more readily find and perform their own roles on the team.

An effective leader keeps the vision before the team. This vision, this clear sense of direction, empowers individuals and confers status on them because they see themselves as part of a worthwhile enterprise. They gain a sense of importance. When individuals feel that what they do makes a difference, they are more likely to bring vigor and enthusiasm to their tasks, and the results of their work will be mutually reinforcing. Under these conditions, the human energies of the team are aligned toward a common end, and a major precondition for success has been satisfied.[24]

> *"An effective leader keeps the vision before the team."*

A shared vision of the future also suggests measures of effectiveness for the team. It helps individuals distinguish between what's good and what's bad for the team, and also what is worthwhile to achieve. Most important, a shared vision makes it possible to distribute decision making widely. People can make difficult decisions without having to appeal to higher levels of authority each time because they know what end results are desired. Individual behavior can be shaped, directed, and coordinated by a shared and empowering vision of the future.[25]

The Challenge Revisited
Leading a Team

1. A team's choice of a leader has serious implications for the team.
2. A leader keeps the team's goal real and its vision clear and fresh.
3. A leader has a significant role in establishing and maintaining a positive, supportive, social environment.
4. A leader assesses the resources the team needs to achieve its goal and to realize its vision.
5. A leader identifies barriers to a team's achieving its goal and energizes the team to address them.
6. A team and its leader must be mutually supportive, recognizing the contributions and accomplishments of every member.

EXERCISE 6.1 • *Who Should Lead?*

Using the information available in the chapter about the musical ensemble (quintet) of Sarah, George, Elizabeth, Tyrone, and Amanda, complete the following tasks:

1. Develop three alternative scenarios depicting the team's future under each of three leadership arrangements. Explain how and why each will work.
2. Select the one scenario that is best for the team. Explain why.

EXERCISE 6.2 • *A Leadership Plan for Your Team*

1. Discuss each member's interest in and qualifications for leading the team.

2. Decide how each member's skills can be used to further the team's goal achievement effort.

3. Prepare a short report on your team's deliberations and decisions about its leadership.

QUESTIONS FOR REVIEW AND DISCUSSION

1. What is the team leader's responsibility? Is this responsibility the same for every team?

2. How does a team go about selecting a leader?

3. What is meant by *leadership traits*? By *leadership styles*? Compare and contrast the two with reference to their implications for team performance.

4. What is the relationship between leadership style and team situation? How does the situation influence leader behavior?

5. What is the difference between task leadership and group maintenance leadership? Why is each important for team functioning?

6. What characteristics of a situation should be considered by a team when it selects its leader?

7. Why is it important for a team to discuss the qualities it needs in a leader? How should such a discussion be conducted?

8. What is a team leader's role in creating a social environment? How is a social environment created?

9. How can a leader help a team to create its vision? Why is a team's vision important for achieving its goal?

10. How does a team develop a shared vision?

NOTES

1. Some team leaders are appointed. The focus in this chapter, however, is on a team's selecting its leader(s).

2. J. Belasco & R. Steyer (1993), *The Flight of the Buffalo*, New York: Warner Books. These authors discuss "leadership is learning" (pp. 80–84) and contrast "geese," which adapt to conditions, to "buffalo," which are less adaptable.

3. See R. Hogan, G. Curphy, & J. Hogan (1994), What we know about leadership, *American Psychologist*, 49, 493–504. See also M. M. Chemers (2000), Leadership research and theory: A functional integration, *Group Dynamics*, 4, 27–43.

4. There are musical ensembles without a leader, for example, the Orpheus Chamber Orchestra (described on *NPR Morning Edition*, June 1, 2000).

There are also work groups without leaders, for example, see C. J. G. Gersick (1990), The bankers, in J. R. Hackman (Ed.), *Groups that Work (and Those that Don't)*, San Francisco: Sage, pp. 112–125.

5. See P. Northouse (1997), *Leadership: Theory and Practice*, Thousand Oaks, CA: Sage, for a summary of a variety of leadership theories.

6. E. Erikson (1950), *Childhood and Society*, New York: Norton.

7. K. Lewin, R. Lippitt, & R. K. White (1939), Patterns of aggressive behavior in experimentally created "social climates," *Journal of Social Psychology*, X, 271–299. These authors demonstrated that the different styles can be created using scripts. There have been many variations of this approach since then. See, for example, R. Foels, J. Driskell, B. Mullen, & E. Salas (2000), The effects of democratic leadership on group member satisfaction, *Small Group Research*, 31, 676–701.

8. R. E. Smith and F. L. Smoll (1997), Coaching the coaches: Youth sports as a scientific and applied behavioral setting, *Current Directions in Psychological Science*, 6(1), February, 16–21.

9. Distributing leadership responsibilities among members is proposed as a way to address the demands of the situation. See D. Johnson & F. Johnson (1987), *Joining Together*, 3rd ed., Englewood Cliffs, NJ: Prentice-Hall, pp. 55–57.

10. Johnson & Johnson, op. cit., pp. 55–56.

11. Interaction process analysis identified these different objectives. See R. F. Bales (1950), *Interaction Process Analysis*, Reading, MA: Addison-Wesley. For a more recent version see the description of SYMLOG in P. Hare (1992), *Groups, Teams, and Social Interactions: Theories and Applications*, New York: Praeger.

12. See Johnson & Johnson, op. cit., pp. 58–60; also F. Fiedler (1967), *A Theory of Leadership Effectiveness*, New York: McGraw-Hill. See also Northouse, op. cit., pp. 74–87.

13. See Johnson & Johnson, op. cit., pp. 61–62; also P. Hershey and K. Blanchard (1988), *Management of Organizational Behavior: Utilizing Human Resources*, Englewood Cliffs, NJ: Prentice-Hall. See K. H. Blanchard (1985), *SLII: A Situational Approach to Managing People*, Escondido, CA: Blanchard Training and Development. See also Northouse, op. cit., pp. 53–73.

14. This characterization is described in Northouse, op. cit., Chap. 4, especially pp. 54–58.

15. Such a weighting procedure is rough but can give a useful overview of member qualifications for leadership.

16. The reciprocity between leaders and followers has been examined extensively. See G. Homans (1961), S*ocial Behavior: Its Elementary Forms*, New York: Harcourt, Brace, p. 286. See also A. Zander (1979), The psychology of group process, in M. R. Rosenzweig & L. W. Porter (Eds.), *Annual Review of Psychology*, Vol. 30, Palo Alto, CA: Annual Reviews, pp. 417–451.

17. W. Bennis & B. Nanus (1985), *Leaders: The Strategies for Taking Charge,* New York: Harper and Row, pp. 110–111. These social structural features are discussed in more detail in Chapter 8 of this volume.

18. Lewin, et al., op. cit., pp. 271–299.

19. Cited in Bennis & Nanus, op. cit., pp. 87–88.

20. Bennis & Nanus, op. cit., p. 89.

21. Bennis & Nanus, op. cit., pp. 95–96.

22. See Gersick, op. cit., pp. 112–125.

23. Bennis & Nanus, op. cit., pp. 97–101.

24. Bennis & Nanus, op. cit., p. 89.

25. Bennis & Nanus, op. cit., pp. 91–92. The "shared" quality of team members' performance has more recently been examined under the heading of "shared mental models." See J. A. Cannon-Bowers, E. Salas, & S. Converse (1993), Shared mental models in expert team decision making, in N. J. Castellan (Ed.), *Individual & Group Decision Making: Current Issues,* Hillsdale, NJ: Erlbaum.

The Challenge
Performing Team Tasks

Team members perform tasks to reach their team's goal. Part of a team's planning process is to decide which tasks are to be performed, how they are to be performed, and the standard of performance by which they are to be judged. After identifying relevant tasks a team must decide whether or not to subdivide tasks. The sequence of tasks or subtasks must be decided as well as how to perform tasks efficiently. A team must also assign members with appropriate skills to perform each task or subtask. Having made these decisions, a newly formed team must also decide how to implement its decisions and might even want to practice performing tasks before proceeding toward its goal.

chapter 7

Performing Team Tasks

Performing tasks is at the core of what a team does to pursue its goal. How a task is structured (or designed) and a team's understanding of that structure can determine how effectively a team performs and how satisfying team members find participating in that performance. Sometimes the structure of a team's task is the team's responsibility. Sometimes, it is specified for a team. In either case, to achieve an efficient level of performance a team must understand how its tasks are structured and how that structure affects its performance.[1]

Some teams' tasks are structured by "rules" that specify how the task is to be carried out. For example, a basketball team's task is to get the ball through the "hoop." This task is structured by rules that specify the boundaries of the court, the height and size of the hoop, and the number of players on the court, among other rules. The "plays" a team learns and practices are specific paths to scoring points. These plays must be carried out in conformity with the game's rules. A team must understand these rules before it can perform its task efficiently.

Some tasks do not have prespecified rules. Teams performing the tasks are responsible for specifying the rules. For example, a mountain climbing team is

> *"A team must understand these rules before it can perform its task efficiently."*

free to choose any path to the top of the mountain. In making its choice, however, it must take into consideration terrain, weather, members' capabilities, and safety precautions, among other issues. The practices (or rules) a team follows are agreed to by the team. If a misjudgment is made, the success of the endeavor—and even the welfare of its members—can be placed in jeopardy. The following is a simple example of a team that is free to structure its task as it chooses.

The parent–teacher association (PTA) of Mountainview School has agreed to raise money to equip a new weight and exercise facility for the school gymnasium. To do so, they have decided to make and sell submarine sandwiches (subs). The children and the parents have sold orders for 840 subs, to be delivered between 9 A.M. and noon on a Saturday. Several parents are in charge. They need to answer this question: What is the most efficient way to make and deliver the subs?

The general procedure is to slice the roll, place the filling, either ham, cheese, or turkey, on the roll, put lettuce and tomato on the filling, close, wrap, place packets of mustard and mayonnaise in the wrapping, and then attach a label to indicate the type of filling. As part of planning for the task, the parents tried two methods of preparation. One was for one person to complete the entire process (i.e., slice, fill, wrap, and label). The other was to create an assembly line in which one person slices the roll, the next places the filling on the roll, the next places lettuce and tomato on the filling, and the last person wraps and labels the package. Additional people to keep the process supplied and to deliver the subs are required by either strategy. The parents found that one person doing the entire job could make 20 subs an hour. Using the assembly line with four persons, the group could make 120 in an hour, an average of 30 subs per hour per person.

The assembly line was chosen as most efficient and two refinements were introduced. One was to have two persons wrapping and labeling. This addressed the slowest step, a bottleneck, that could be removed by adding a second person to perform the step. This increased production to 155 subs per hour, or 31 per person per hour. The second adjustment was to form three assembly lines, one for each filling. This removed the decision about which filling to use and reduced mistakes in labeling. The labels were to be printed beforehand. Based on these calculations, three teams could make the 840 subs in less than two hours. Beginning work at 8 A.M. and allowing some time for breaks, the 840 subs could be prepared by 10:30 A.M. Delivery of those prepared early could begin at 8:30 A.M. with all of the deliveries completed by 11:30 A.M.

The parents have addressed the decision of how to organize their task performance to achieve their goal most efficiently. Their planning activity included experimenting to find the most efficient way to organize the task. This enabled them to understand why they did the task a particular way. In effect, they established a set of "rules" for performing their task. These rules structure the task, that is, they specify the steps and constraints along a path to their goal, as depicted in Figure 7.1. The discussion that follows considers different types of tasks and the general rules that structure the way each type is performed.

F I G U R E   7 . 1
Steps to Goal (Submarine Problem)

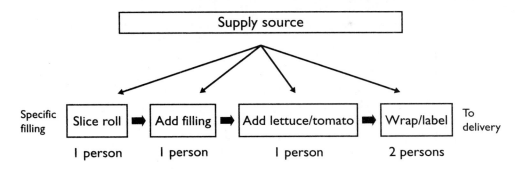

TASK STRUCTURE

Broadly, a team must make two decisions when choosing a path to its goal. One is to determine what tasks must be performed to reach the goal. In the case of the parents making subs, the tasks chosen were fairly standard for making subs: slice roll, place filling, put on lettuce and tomato, and package. They could have added other steps, such as adding relish, but they chose not to. The other decision involved determining how these tasks were to be organized. The parents focused most of their planning on this decision because it enabled them to achieve the greatest efficiency.

Sometimes a team's tasks are designated and have prespecified rules that constrain a team and its members. For example, team sports have rules that constrain team behavior. A team playing a sport must decide how best to perform given these rules. For some activities, specific tasks are not designated and team members must make both decisions we discussed: what the subtasks will be and how they will be organized. For example, a team developing a new product design must decide the subtasks to be performed and the process by which they will be completed. These decisions represent a team's choosing a path to its goal. The importance of a team's selecting a path to follow and deciding how it will proceed along that path most efficiently cannot be overstated.

Classifying Task Types

One system for classifying task types distinguishes two broad categories of tasks.[2] **Unitary tasks** are tasks for which a division of labor is not feasible. These are tasks for which the team must arrive at a single team outcome or product. For example, in a team math challenge, the goal is to give a correct answer. For a business team, the goal is to make a correct decision. For a mountain climbing team, the goal is to move a load of supplies from

"Sometimes a team's tasks are designated and have prespecified rules that constrain a team and its members."

"The importance of a team's selecting a path to follow and deciding how it will proceed along that path most efficiently cannot be overstated."

"Divisible tasks are tasks for which a division of labor is feasible."

the valley to a mountain base camp. **Divisible tasks** are tasks for which a division of labor is feasible. Divisible tasks can be broken into subtasks. For example, manufacturing processes are most often divisible. Different team members do different steps (subtasks) in the process. For such tasks, especially where technical skills are needed, a team with members having varied skills may succeed even though none of its members can do the entire job alone.

Consider the parents preparing for the sub sale. They had a choice between reaching their goal either by making the task unitary (one parent made an entire sub) or divisible (having several parents do separate steps to make one sub). They chose the latter and established rules they followed as they proceeded along that path. The parents decided to subdivide the task into four steps, then to further subdivide into three processes depending on the filling to be used. Furthermore, they assumed that any parent had the skills and knowledge to perform any step.

Variations in Unitary Tasks.   Unitary tasks can be designed in several ways. One variation is when *a team's product is the members' combined output*. In this variation, each team member performs the same task and members' contributions are added to make a team product. A team's performance of **additive tasks** depends on the ability of its average member. For example, if the parents who were making subs had decided that each member of their group would make complete subs and all worked until the 840 subs were ready, the task would have been unitary and additive. Parents' calculations indicated that by that procedure each parent could make an average of 30 subs per hour. Figure 7.2 depicts this task design.

"Each team member performs the same function and all members must succeed in their performances for the team to be successful."

A second type of unitary task is one in which *members work together to produce a group product*. These are sometimes referred to as **conjunctive** (or **connected**) **tasks.** Each team member performs the same function and all members must succeed in their performances for the team to be successful. With this type of task, a team's performance depends on the performance of the poorest performing member. For example, in the sub-making example, the rule could be that each parent must prepare the entire sub in a prescribed way. If each parent had a quota of subs to fulfill and the subs could not be delivered until all 840 were ready, the task would be conjunctive. The slowest member constrains the whole team. In such situations, it is critical that the least competent member perform as close to potential as possible. Whatever the team can do to assist the poorest performing member to achieve the best possible performance will benefit the team as a whole. Figure 7.3 depicts this task design.

A third type of unitary task is that of *a single member producing an outcome*. These unitary tasks, referred to as **disjunctive** (or **not connected**), impose a rule that if one member completes the task, the task is accomplished for the team. For example, on a quiz show where a team of individuals represents a college, any one member can answer a question, and this answer is the answer for the team. The performance of disjunctive tasks depends

FIGURE 7.2
Unitary, Additive Task Performance

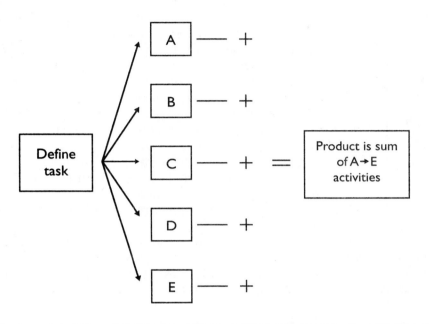

Each Does Same Task

FIGURE 7.3
Unitary, Conjunctive Task Performance

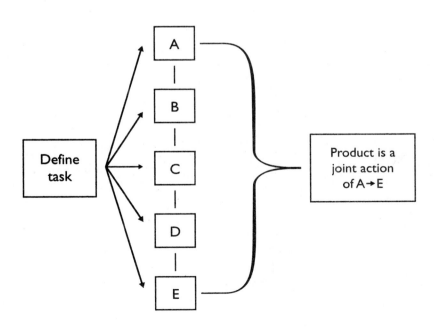

Each Does Same Task

on the team's best member although more than one team member may arrive at the same correct outcome. Furthermore, a team presented a problem to solve must have at least one member who can arrive at the correct solution. A team must find a way to identify this member.

> *"A person is more likely to speak up when she expects to be listened to and/or is confident in her solution."*

An additional rule can be that the team must decide which member's response is correct or best and will be the team's response. When the solution is not obvious, there are two hurdles. One is the willingness of the member with the correct solution to voice it. A person's doing so depends to a degree on their perception of other members' receptivity and on their perception of their own capabilities. A person is more likely to speak up when she expects to be listened to and/or is confident in her solution. Once the solution is offered, a second hurdle is the team's willingness to accept the solution as its own. The more members who reach the correct solution, the greater the likelihood that the team will accept that solution. Having a discussion leader, who can ensure that everyone has a chance to speak, increases the likelihood that the correct answer will receive a hearing. Figure 7.4 depicts this task design.

A fourth type of unitary task, referred to as **discretionary**, is that of the *team deciding how members' contributions will be combined*. Judgmental tasks are more likely to be discretionary than motor tasks. For example, a planning task force responsible for developing a new marketing strategy for a company's

FIGURE 7.4
Unitary, Disjunctive Task Performance

Each Does Same Task

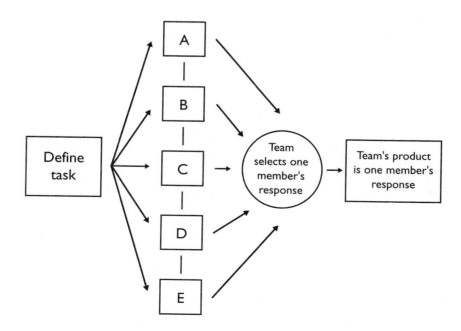

product must decide what combination of each member's proposed solution will be part of the task force solution. There are several strategies for making such judgments or decisions. One strategy is to have one member do all of the work and other members acquiesce. A second strategy is for several members to produce alternative possibilities and have the team select one of them. A third strategy is for all members to produce alternative possibilities. The team then formulates a combination to be the team's choice. One difficulty with this latter approach is that some members are likely to make better or more accurate choices. Determining who the more able members are can be difficult. Figure 7.5 depicts this task design.

Additional Rules.   Unitary tasks can have rules that further define success beyond simply completing a task. **Maximizing** rules make success a function of how much or how rapidly something is accomplished. For example, for teams racing to the top of a mountain, the team with the fastest member to the top or the one that carries the greatest load to the top wins. Another example is a quiz show where a team that comes up with the correct answer first wins.

Another rule might be concerned with how precisely a team's outcome meets some specification. These are **optimizing tasks.**

"Judgmental tasks are more likely to be discretionary than motor tasks."

"Maximizing rules make success a function of how much or how rapidly something is accomplished."

FIGURE 7.5
Unitary, Discretionary Task Performance

Each Does Same Task

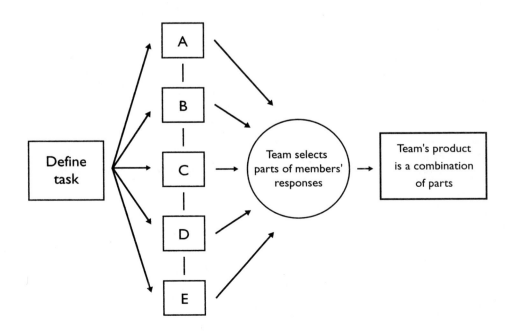

For example, for online grocery deliveries, the team that makes the most deliveries closest to the specified time for delivery is the most successful. Another example is cost estimation. The team that estimates costs of construction closest to the actual cost of construction is judged to be best. Maximizing and optimizing rules can apply to all four types of unitary tasks. Table 7.1 outlines the rules for each type.

Divisible Tasks.   Tasks that can be broken into subtasks are labeled *divisible*. For example, tasks that comprise manufacturing processes such as assembling electronic components into a single electronic unit are often divisible. Many other tasks, such as compiling a report, can be divisible. On these tasks, a group may succeed because as a group its members have the skills to do so, yet no one of its members could do the entire task alone. With divisible tasks there are two important issues. One is how the tasks are subdivided. The other is how team members are "assigned" to subtasks. Steps in performing a divisible task are depicted in Figure 7.6.

> *"A team's product can be very good if each member works on that subtask that he or she can do better than other members."*

Divisible tasks are not necessarily performed well. How tasks are actually divided and who performs each subtask are complex issues that bear directly on a team's level of performance. A subtask division may not be optimum for the task. A team's supervisor or the team members themselves may not know who is best qualified to perform a subtask. The rules under which the team operates may require members to take turns performing all subtasks, resulting in less qualified members performing some subtasks. For these reasons, planning for a divisible task is important. When team members are not well-known to each other, planning should include a process for learning about members' relevant skills and knowledge. A team's product can be very good if each member works on that subtask that he or she can do better than other members.

When tasks are divisible, subtask specification and assignment or matching of team members to subtasks can be decided either by the team or by some source outside the team. This latter type of matching is referred to as **prespecified,** and there are four possible combinations. One combination, prespecified matching to subtasks that are team specified, is only hypothetical. The remaining three combinations can actually occur and are discussed next.

TABLE 7.1

Rules for Maximizing or Optimizing Unitary Tast Performance

Unitary Task Type	Maximizing	Optimizing
Additive	Most product produced	Product closest to standard
Conjunctive	Fastest response by entire team	Entire team closest to standard
Disjunctive	Member making fastest response	Member response closest to standard
Discretionary	Selection of best or fastest response	Selection of response closest to standard

F I G U R E   7 . 6
Divisible Task Performance

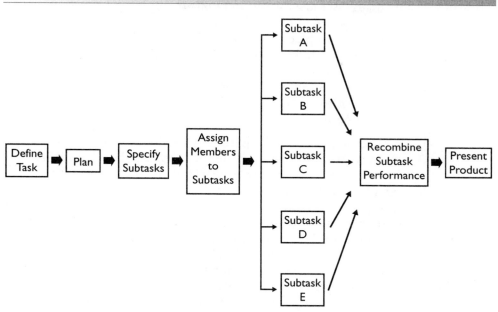

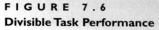

Team Matching with Prespecified Subtasks.   Sometimes the rules pertaining to task performance clearly specify the subtasks into which a total endeavor must be divided, but team members must decide for themselves who will perform each subtask. In a case where each member performs each subtask and then the team makes a decision as to which performance will be the team's product, effectiveness is maximized. For example, if two members of a golf team can each take a shot and then choose the best shot as their team's shot, their score is likely to be much better than it would be if they had to decide in advance of each shot whose shot would count for their team. If, however, one player is known to be best at long drives while the other is best on the green, this information can help considerably in deciding who should take which shot.

In general, the appropriate process for a team to use to match its members to prespecified subtasks is fairly evident. If a member possesses the capability to successfully perform a subtask, he should do so and present the result (for example, a correct solution) to the team. The team should, in turn, accept the solution and proceed to the next problem. The process should then be repeated for each subtask.[3] The challenge is for a team to follow this "rational" path. When, however, several subtasks must be performed simultaneously and the rules dictate that everyone should do their "fair share," and the team is to proceed as rapidly as possible (a maximizing rule), this rational path may be difficult to follow.

Team Matching with Team-Specified Subtasks.   Sometimes the rules allow for the division of tasks into countless parts. The team is required to define a set of subtasks, organize them in a manner that is manageable by the team, and then perform them. For example, a task force assigned to study a topic generally has

> *"The team must define the relevant issues and organize its activities into subtasks that address them."*

a range of issues to consider. The team must define the relevant issues and organize its activities into subtasks that address them. Once subtasks have been defined, members must assign themselves or be assigned to the subtasks in a manner that makes it possible to complete them. If the subdivision process fails to provide a set of tasks that can be performed efficiently by the resources (member skills) available, the outcome will suffer. Furthermore, even with an optimum subdivision, if the resources to carry out the subtasks are either not available, are misassigned, or fail to perform, the outcome will also suffer.

Prespecified Matching with Prespecified Subtasks. Sometimes task rules specify how the total task must be subdivided and who must perform each subtask. This is common in industry, for example, when a group of specialists are placed on a team to perform a task. A group's performance may be strongly influenced by the particular division of labor that is used. One study[4] compared individuals who performed all aspects of the task with individuals who performed only a specialized portion. The former was slightly more efficient when tasks were easy; however, the latter was better when tasks were more difficult.[5]

> *"A group's performance may be strongly influenced by the particular division of labor that is used."*

Matching team members to subtasks may be very effective when a pattern of specialized subtasks fits the specialized resources of team members and quite ineffective when it does not. This mismatch may occur because a person is unqualified to do the work, lacks relevant information, or dislikes doing it. For example, even with high motivation, if an individual lacks relevant skills, performance will not be effective.

Division into subtasks usually results in the poorest performer determining the overall team performance level and product. "Poor" can mean either or both quantity and quality. Subtasks are **conjunctively interdependent,** to combine terms described earlier, when all subtasks must be completed to produce a single group product. Conjunctivity also exists if some members cannot perform their specialized tasks until others have performed theirs or if several subtasks must be performed simultaneously, in synchronization with others.

> *"Interdependence associated with conjunctivity in divisible tasks can buffer a team's dependence on its weaker members."*

Interdependence associated with conjunctivity in divisible tasks can buffer a team's dependence on its weaker members. As described in Chapter 2, interdependence involves not only connectedness but also collective responsibility. This means that a team can and should support and assist its weakest members as a means to enhance the team's performance. For example, if one task force member, assigned a portion of a report to write, cannot find relevant material, then another member who knows of relevant sources should share this information with the member having difficulty. This is shared responsibility and results in a better team report.

Temporal Programming. When several subtasks must be performed simultaneously, a single person cannot ordinarily be matched with more than one subtask. A team must have as many members as there are subtasks. When subtasks can be performed sequentially, that is, one after the other, a single person may sometimes be successfully matched with all of them or as many as her capabilities permit her to perform. Consequently, sequentially ordered subtasks permit greater flexibility in matching members to subtasks than do subtasks that must be performed simultaneously. For example, a track team competing in a meet has two exceptional middle distance runners. They can run in the 220-yard individual event, the 440-yard individual event, and on the mile relay because the events are **temporally programmed,** that is, not run simultaneously.

Team Size and Task Performance

A team's ability to perform relevant tasks is impacted by the number of its members.[6] Will an increase in team size improve its performance? Does a decrease in team size cause performance to deteriorate? The answers to these questions depend on the nature of the task, the initial size of the team, and the resources, that is, the knowledge and skill, of the team members involved. Adding people when the task is simple (unitary and additive), for example, shoveling snow from a large and long driveway, can reduce the time needed to complete the task. If the task is more complex, for example, developing a task force report, increasing the team size can create serious coordination or motivation problems and result in deterioration of performance. For example, adding people to a committee of 10, whose task is to make a complex decision, is likely to prolong the process because of the need to coordinate the larger number of members and to keep them all involved.

> *"A team's ability to perform relevant tasks is impacted by the number of its members."*

When unitary tasks are *additive*, one person's accomplishment is added to that of others to arrive at a team product, for example, total amount of snow shoveled. Potential output is expected to increase as a linear function of team size. Assuming equality of capability, if the size of the team is doubled, its potential ability to perform a task is doubled. There are limits to this generalization, however. Additivity generally occurs only when the team's size and the outcome to be achieved fall within a restricted range, for example, the amount of snow to be shoveled is limited. With additive tasks there appears to be an upper limit (or ceiling) on the amount or quality of work larger teams can do. Tasks that are additive for teams of certain sizes will lose their additivity if team size is drastically increased. This means that the average member will produce less. For example, doubling the number of parents producing subs is unlikely to reduce by half the time required to do the task. There may also be a threshold. For example, to pull a one-ton boulder quickly, team size is increased until the team can pull the weight. After that, additional members are useful only insofar as they can be substituted for others who are slow runners or for anyone who tires.

> *"Tasks that are additive for teams of certain sizes will lose their additivity if team size is drastically increased."*

When unitary tasks are *disjunctive,* that is, when any single member of a team can supply the team product, success depends on the most competent member. Larger teams have a greater likelihood that at least one member will be able to do the task.[7] When a unitary task is *conjunctive* and easy, the potential for successful performance of very small teams is relatively high, but decreases rapidly as size increases. As the size increases, even with an easy task, some members will be less able than others. The less able members will slow the whole team. When the task is difficult, potential performance is low, even for two-person teams, and this potential decreases as additional members are added. This is because each additional member may be less competent than those already on the team, limiting the whole team's performance.

When a unitary task is *discretionary,* a team is free to select or combine members' performance in any way. When this unusual condition exists, a team has the potential to reach the most preferred conclusion, because there are always ways by which the judgments of individual members can be combined to produce that conclusion. Consequently, when tasks are discretionary, team size is unrelated to potential performance.

"when tasks are discretionary, team size is unrelated to potential performance"

Divisible tasks can be divided into two or more subtasks. At an early stage, the larger the team available to work on a divisible task, the larger the number of subtasks into which the total can be broken but the greater the number of persons to be matched with each subtask. There is, however, a point beyond which further subdivision becomes meaningless. At this point, additional members add nothing. This varies with the specific task.

A further complication arises when recombining the results of subtask performance. At some point, the outcomes generated by the various subtask performances must be combined to yield a team product. At this point, the more subtasks there are, the more complex the recombination process. The processes involved in this final stage are not those involved at earlier stages. If at earlier stages larger teams can achieve greater efficiency by increasing the number of subtasks, the outcomes to be combined in a final team product will be more numerous, making assembly of a finished product more difficult. This may cancel the advantage that larger teams enjoy because they are more likely to contain members who are especially competent to perform their subtasks.

Although larger teams as compared to smaller teams have superior resources and thus a higher level of potential performance, size also tends to complicate the procedures by which resources are used so as to obtain maximum efficiency. The larger a team is, the greater the variation of ability among its members and the more members to be matched with specific subtasks and to be assimilated within a delicately balanced pattern of ongoing activity.

Organizational problems (who will do what when) are less readily solved when teams are large. If only one person is available to perform a task, organizational problems are likely to be comparatively simple. An individual decides what should be done, how to do it, and when. Actual performance may fall below potential because the individual does not perform the steps to the best of his or her ability or because steps are not performed in the right order. There are no process losses due to inappropriate matching or to poor interpersonal coordination. When two persons work collectively on a task, however, all of the decisions required of a single person are pertinent, and others are added. If the task is unitary, a productive way to combine individual outcomes must be discovered and adopted. In some cases coordination must be established. If the task is divisible, the most appropriate members must be assigned to each subtask and the most appropriate procedure found for assembling subtask outcomes into a team product.

> *"Organizational problems are less readily solved when teams are large."*

The Challenge Revisited
Performing Team Tasks

1. Before proceeding toward its goal, a team must plan for its task performance.

2. Planning for task performance involves group decision making to identify relevant tasks, to design the tasks appropriately, and to assign appropriately skilled members to perform each task.

3. Planning also involves determining or setting the standards by which the performance will be judged and developing a performance strategy that can meet or surpass the standards.

4. As a team begins to implement the performance strategy, practice of less familiar features of the performance strategy may be needed and necessary adjustments made.

5. Increasing the number of team members can enhance the team's resources, but can also increase coordination difficulties.

EXERCISE 7.1 • *Event Planning*

A committee of five students and two faculty has been created to plan the college homecoming celebration. For a Saturday in October they are to plan the following:

- A morning activity to showcase some new academic activities of the college
- An afternoon activity centered around the college's football team
- An evening dinner and social activity

1. As a team, outline several different paths this committee could follow to ensure that homecoming is a success. Your outline must include
   - The task design of each path
   - The issues the committee should consider as it follows each path
2. Prepare a short report of your deliberations.

EXERCISE 7.2 • *New Product Development*

Your team has been asked to develop packaging for a fragile object (an egg). The objective is to prevent the egg from breaking during shipment. An egg that can be dropped from eight feet onto a hard surface without breaking satisfies the minimum packaging specification. Your team is to do the following:

1. Develop a package using only soda straws and masking tape.
2. Develop a cost analysis. Straws are $100 each; tape is $20 per inch; team salary expense is $5 per minute, per person. Overhead is 75% of the total cost of producing the package.
3. Develop a sales presentation for your team's packaging product. Include a brand name and logo for the product.
4. Be prepared to present your product to the class.
5. Develop a written analysis of the task design that your team used in this exercise on product development. Describe two other designs that might have been used, describing the strengths and weaknesses of each.

QUESTIONS FOR REVIEW AND DISCUSSION

1. What is the relationship between a team's task performance and its goal achievement?
2. What is meant by *task structure*? Give examples of different task structures. Why is it important for a team to understand the structure of the tasks it performs?
3. What is the difference between a unitary task and a divisible task? What are the "rules" that govern each task type?
4. Define the following types of unitary tasks: additive, conjunctive, disjunctive, and discretionary. Give one or more examples of situations that involve each type.
5. What are the differences between optimizing rules for success and maximizing rules for success?
6. What are the two most important issues for a team to consider in planning for divisible tasks?
7. Describe problems that can occur when planning for and performing divisible tasks.
8. What is meant by *conjunctive interdependence*? What are its implications for a team?
9. What is the significance of temporal programming for a team's task performance?
10. How can team size benefit or hinder team performance? How does team size influence performance of the different types of task structure?

NOTES

1. The present analysis is drawn largely from I. D. Steiner (1972), *Group Processes and Productivity*, New York: Academic Press. For more recent discussions of task design in general, see D. Levi (2001), *Group Dynamics for Teams*, Thousand Oaks, CA: Sage, pp. 25–29; and L. L. Thompson (2000), *Making the Team: A Guide for Managers*, Upper Saddle River, NJ: Prentice Hall, pp. 61–67.

2. Steiner, op. cit.

3. On the topic of matching members to subtasks, see D. C. Barnlund (1959), A comparative study of individual, majority, and group judgment, *Journal of Abnormal and Social Psychology*, 58, 55–60; also Rychlak (1965), The similarity, compatibility, or incompatibility of needs in interpersonal selection, *Journal of Personality and Social Psychology*, 2, 334–340.

4. On the topic of how tasks are subdivided and their difficulty level, see J. T. Lanzetta & T. B. Roby (1956), Effects of work-group structure and certain task variables on group performance, *Journal of Abnormal and Social Psychology*, 53, 307–314.

5. See also S. G. Cohen (1994), Designing effective self-managing work teams, in H. M. Beyerlein & D. A. Johnson (Eds.), *Advances in Interdisciplinary Studies of Work Teams: Theories of Self-Managed Work Teams*, London: JAI Press, pp. 67–102; also P. Tesluk, J. E. Mathieu, & S. J. Zaccaro (1997), Task and aggregation issues in the analysis and assessment of team performance, in M. T. Brannick, E. Salas, & C. Prince (Eds.), *Team Performance Assessment and Measurement*, Mahwah, NJ: Lawrence Erlbaum, pp. 197–224.

6. Steiner, op. cit., chap. 4; see also D. E. Yeatts & C. Hyten (1998), *High-Performing Self-Managed Work Teams: Comparison of Theory to Practice*, Thousand Oaks, CA: Sage, chap. 24.

7. See Steiner, op. cit., pp. 68–69; and I. D. Steiner & N. A. Rajaratnam (1961), A model for the comparison of individual and group performance scores, *Behavioral Science*, 6, 142–148.

The Challenge
Coordinating and Structuring Team Activities

Achieving a team's potential for high performance is a major challenge. To do so requires team members to have a mutual commitment to reach the team's goal, to trust each other to support the team's activities, and to coordinate and cooperate in performing the team's tasks and interpersonal activities. Coordination requires cooperation and cooperative learning to make activities compatible. Coordination and cooperation support team members' interdependence. Efficiency is achieved by setting high standards for performance and by having members take specific responsibilities for facilitating each other's performance.

chapter 8

Coordinating and Structuring Team Activities

THE PERFORMANCE PROCESS

To be successful, a team's task performance must produce a product. This can occur in different (often many) ways. Some proponents of team-based management contend that a team of five can achieve a level of performance that surpasses the combined performance level of the same five individuals working individually on the same tasks. The assumption is that there is something in the team-based performance process that is lacking when individuals perform singly. In other words, the expectation is that there are performance "process gains" when working as a team that do not occur when the same number of individuals work singly.[1]

Relevant evidence, however, is mixed. Workers can experience more satisfaction working with others.[2] Teams of workers given responsibility for detecting and remedying lapses in quality can improve quality.[3] Working in teams can also reduce the need for direct supervision.[4] However, much of the evidence relating to team performance indicates that teams experience "process losses." When a team does not achieve its potential level of performance, that is, the level one would expect, the difference between actual level of performance and potential level of performance is attributed to process losses. These losses arise from a variety of sources related to team members' activities. Such losses do not affect individuals working alone.[5]

Process losses arise broadly from two sources. First, some factors associated with teams prevent an individual from performing well. These include unclear goals, inadequate knowledge and skills, and reduced motivation. Second, some factors specific to the teamwork process prevent a team from performing well. One author describes these factors as ". . . all the interpersonal and intra-personal actions by which people transform their resources into a product and all of those non-productive actions that are prompted by frustration, competing motivation, or inadequate understanding."[6]

These individual and team-related factors reflect a tendency toward less effective functioning by a team.[7] They disrupt and distort the process of a team's working toward its goal. To reverse this tendency, teams need more effective communication, better coordination, increased cooperation, and also the selection of task performance strategies that support and encourage enhanced interdependence on which effective teamwork is based. Consider the following team.

Inez, Norman, Amy, Brian, and Carlos are to develop a new set of up-to-date personnel guidelines for their company. The existing guidelines are overly detailed and some are no longer in compliance with recent labor laws. Inez is a labor lawyer from the company's legal department. Norman is a training specialist from the company's human resources department. Both are in the company's large central office. Amy, Brian, and Carlos are from three relatively small branch human resources offices. All three are generalists who must address any human resource problem that arises. Although most personnel issues are common to the four sites, a few are specific to individual sites. For example, one branch site has several workers with disabilities.

The five members know each other but have not worked together before. They share a desire to prepare a report that is an exemplary model of current human resources practice. Each knows that the personnel issues they are to consider are complex. They are to examine five subtopics: legal issues, compensation and benefits, training, employee evaluation, and special issues, such as disabilities. They are also to consider the concerns of both the central office and the branch offices. By what task performance process can this team proceed most effectively toward its goal? Because multiple performers are involved, the team must decide how the tasks will be designed and how the performances will be coordinated so as to achieve the team's goal.

Different teams face this challenge differently. Football teams decide whether to run, pass, or kick. A strategy for coordinating team members' contributions is then chosen. An executive management team, seeking to increase its company's market share, must select a set of activities by which to reach its goal and decide how the activities will be coordinated. The human resources team,

"Much of the evidence relating to team performance indicates that teams experience 'process losses.'"

"How can this team reach its goal and achieve its vision?"

described earlier, must also select a set of activities by which to reach its goal. It must then decide on a strategy for coordinating member performance so as to optimize the quality of its product, its report. Overall, this is a maximizing task, since the team desires its report to be "exemplary," that is, the best. How can this team reach its goal and achieve its vision?

The team begins by brainstorming **task strategies.** From among these the team selects four for further consideration. Finally, they must choose one as the team's strategy. The following are four possible strategies:

Strategy 1.   Each member writes a report, covering all five topics, and these are combined in a final report. This strategy is unitary and additive. Each member does the total activity and the results are combined as the team's product. This strategy involves minimal coordination. The overall task is conjunctive since the team's report is not complete until all members finish their report. There is likely to be considerable variability in quality across the individual reports, however.

"Coordination is needed for members to identify points needing improvement and to take the steps to make those improvements."

Strategy 2.   Each member writes his or her own report, covering all five topics as in strategy 1. Additionally, an executive summary is prepared to present the key points of each member's report. Developing the summary requires coordination among members to decide which points from each member's report are to be specified in the summary. The efficiency of this decision process is important for this team's effectiveness. The individual reports are included as appendices in the final document. To enhance the quality of the summary, members as a group can discuss each point in the executive summary, then improve any statement needing clarification. Coordination is needed for members to identify points needing improvement and to take the steps to make those improvements. Including the executive summary reduces the effort required for readers to understand the report's key points. Also, the quality of the summary is improved by the team's coordinated, collective effort.

Strategy 3.   Each member is to develop a subreport on one of the five subtopics. Members are to choose the most qualified member to write about each subtopic. An executive summary will highlight key points from each subtopic report. The subreports are included as appendices in the final report. This strategy considers the initial task divisible; each member works on a different part, and the team decides who is to do each part. A second task, preparing an executive summary, is discretionary. As in strategy 2, the team decides which points from members' reports to highlight. The issue of quality is not addressed except in the team's effort to select the "most qualified" person to write on each subtopic. The team notes that there are only two specialists among its five members. Members collaborate in selecting points for the executive summary. How the executive summary can be improved is not addressed, although ways to improve it, described in strategy 2, could be used.

Strategy 4. Team members are assigned in pairs to prepare a subreport on one of the five subtopics. As far as possible, a representative from the central office is to be paired with a representative from a branch office in order to have both perspectives represented in each subreport. To cover the five topics, each member must work on two subtopics. An executive summary will provide an overview of the main points from each subreport. This strategy is divisible but assigns two team members, rather than one, to develop each subreport. There are several advantages to having two members work on each subreport. The perspectives of both the central and branch offices are available to most subgroups. If responsibilities are shared equally, only one subgroup pair will have two branch representatives. This means that a combination of more technical and more general experience is reflected in the majority of the report. The two-member subgroups can also provide each other support. If the three members not on a particular subgroup review each report and make suggestions, each subgroup can then make additional improvements in its report. An executive summary will be developed as described in strategies 2 and 3.

The benefits of strategy 4 to this team's effectiveness are considerable. The skills and experience of each member are used maximally to improve the team's product. Interdependence, that is, members feeling collective responsibility for all aspects of the project, offers greater assurance of the team's achieving both its goal and its vision. Team members may appear to take on additional responsibilities, however, compared to strategies 1 and 2, in which members primarily work alone. In strategy 4, members share responsibility by supporting and helping each other to improve their performance. This strategy requires the greatest coordination of member activities, because members work together considerably more than in the other three strategies.

> *"The skills and experience of each member are used maximally to improve the team's product."*

COORDINATION

Interpersonal Coordination

Developing Relationships. In laying out possible paths by which a team can reach its goal and then by selecting one that offers the greatest likelihood for success, relationships develop among team members. These relationships in turn shape members' behavior in performing the activities that move the team toward its goal. As members' relationships improve, a network of relationships becomes evident (see Chapter 2, Figure 2.1). It is important that these relationships facilitate, rather than interfere with, efforts to achieve the team's goal. At issue is **interpersonal coordination.**

The first step for our human resources team is to get to know each other. Developing new relationships involves exploring outcomes for the relationship, assessing their adequacy, and estimating their stability. Individuals often enter the process of building a relationship with ambivalence. A new relationship, particularly in the context of a team, can mean abandoning ways of making

> *"Individuals often enter the process of building a relationship with ambivalence."*

decisions, possibly leaving previous working relationships, or just losing a feeling of independence. Increasing interdependence may feel like dependency. This may be especially true for individuals who feel that having to wait while another person makes a decision or completes a task *is* dependency. This feeling can result in conflict.

The potential for conflict exists because of uncertainty as to whether the new relationship is the best available and uncertainty about the possibility of being forced to endure low or even negative outcomes. A situation is most threatening when there is concern that, having become dependent on a relationship, it will be arbitrarily disrupted by the other person or become one sided. To resolve the uncertainty, the team as a whole must address members' concerns about poor outcomes. Members must discuss their team's goal, members' goals for themselves, and their goals for the team. Out of this discussion should come a mutually shared view of the team's goal and a realistic view of how members' goals for themselves can be satisfied in the process of achieving the team's goal.

Social Appraisal.   These discussions involve social appraisal, a process that, if it goes well, enables members to become better acquainted, more comfortable with each other, and as the process proceeds, more trusting of each other.[8] Several factors affect an individual's appraisal of another person. A general rule is that some items of information are given more weight in the judgment than others. The core of one person's view of another is often the earliest information received, the "first impression," although it need not be. For example, descriptions of individuals as warm or cold can affect initial impressions. As the relationship proceeds, however, someone originally considered "cold" may be seen as warmer than was originally thought.

> *"Unfamiliarity tends to delay the formation of relationships, to inhibit inventiveness, to cause team members to limit themselves to low-cost behaviors, and to depend on politeness and more stereotyped forms of behavior."*

Other factors, such as the nature of the task or of the setting, can influence a person's appraisal of another person. For example, a person who places high value on task completion will reveal this in the course of a decision about task performance. A person who places high value on maintaining positive relationships among group members will reveal this in the same discussion. The unfamiliarity of a task or of the circumstances in which a task is performed increases uncertainty about outcomes from a relationship and its future stability. Unfamiliarity tends to delay the formation of relationships, to inhibit inventiveness, to cause team members to limit themselves to low-cost behaviors, and to depend on politeness and more stereotyped forms of behavior.

Another influence on the development of a relationship is an individual's use of self-protective hostility. This is often manifested in reduced interpersonal communication that tends to insulate the hostility. More open communication can change the feeling. When team members take time to discuss their observations and reactions to the task and to the situation, the effect can to be to break through the hostility and allow relationships to develop. As a result, members become more attracted to the situation and more productive.

Social influence.   The development of a relationship between two individuals that both are desirous of preserving introduces another ingredient, **interpersonal influence**.[9] More precisely, when participants in a relationship wish to further the relationship, each becomes to some degree subject to the influence of the other. For team members, such influence extends to both choosing and pursuing the most mutually advantageous path to the team goal. "Advantageous" refers to that path which involves at a minimum the least cost to an individual and preferably provides satisfaction. Individuals must negotiate the choice of a path and their part in pursuing it.

> *"Individuals must negotiate the choice of a path and their part in pursuing it."*

Once decided, pursuit of the choice is also subject to influence. If all parties contribute their fair share of the resources needed to achieve the goal, there is little need for interpersonal influence. However, if one person slacks off in his or her contribution, the other person may begin to exert pressure to encourage the lower contributor to regain the expected level of contribution. For example, a team member who consistently fails to prepare for team meetings will be pressured to do so. If this pressure is not effective or if those who prepare for the meeting exert no pressure at all, those who prepare may try to compensate for the other's lack of preparation by preparing more, although generally not without increased irritation.

Efforts by those who are prepared (the nondeviating team members) to influence those who are not prepared (the deviating member) to pursue the team's path or to make a greater contribution will continue to a point. Such efforts are characterized by increased communication. A limit will be reached, however, and efforts to influence the deviating or unprepared member will cease. This is indicated by reduced communication. This may be followed by a neutral stance by the nondeviating members toward the deviating member. There may even be rejection of the deviating member with an associated tendency to see that person as contributing even less than he or she did in reality.[10]

Task Coordination

When two or more individuals work together on a task, greater social complexity is present than when individuals work alone. If individuals are to work together, their activities must, to some degree, be coordinated. As the number of persons increases, the **task coordination** complexities increase. When two persons, A and B, are working together, their behaviors can be either compatible or incompatible. Compatible responses involve B's behavior contributing to the furtherance of A's behavior or vice versa. Incompatible behavior means that B's behavior does not contribute to or even detracts from A's behavior or vice versa. For example, A and B are planting a garden. A begins by preparing the soil. B then digs holes in which to plant the seeds. Person A drops the seeds in the holes and covers the seeds. B follows by watering the planted area. The activities of A and B are compatible and, in combination, enable them to achieve their goal more readily. Were A to begin to prepare the soil and B to start watering the area before the seeds were planted, the result would be a great deal of mud and a much more difficult planting situation. The actions of B would be incompatible with the actions of A and would interfere with the planting process.

The coordination of task-related activities is built on positive working relationships and effective communication among team members. These provide the basis for coordinating a team's task activities. Figure 8.1 depicts open communication among team members that enables them to coordinate their activities.

Figure 8.2, by contrast, depicts a lack of communication between team members B and C. As a result, the coordination of B's task activities with those of C suffers. In a task design such as that depicted in Figure 8.2, A's contribution to B's activity is lost in B's uncoordinated activity, and C has no activity from B on which to build.

The central issue for task coordination is **response compatibility,** that is, whether the behaviors of two or more team members further members' efforts to achieve their team's goal or whether they hinder that effort. When responses are incompatible, team members must both identify the incompatibility and solve the problem that leads to the incompatibility.

When incompatible behaviors cannot be avoided or eliminated from an interaction, they must be synchronized. This means that they do not occur simultaneously or do not occur in ways that introduce interference. Under some conditions, the environment provides cues that enable individuals to adjust their behavior to minimize or remove the interference. For example, in a movie theater friends do not talk while the movie is in progress. A variation is when one member of a pair gives cues as to behavior and the other member of the pair adjusts to those cues. In an employment interview an interviewee takes his cues as to acceptable behavior from the interviewer and adjusts his behavior to fit.

Synchronization is more difficult to arrange when both members of a pair are governed by strong need states, since the needs themselves are unlikely to be synchronized. For example, a person who takes pride in being strongly task oriented and wishes to begin performing the task immediately may find herself in strong conflict

---

FIGURE 8.1
Coordinated Task Activities

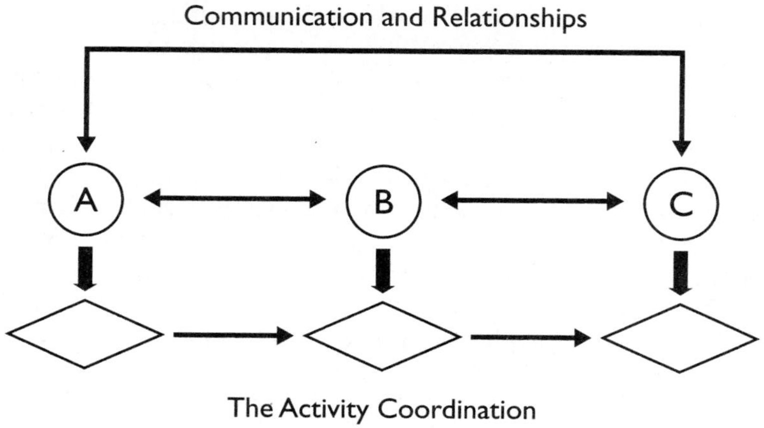

Communication and Relationships

The Activity Coordination

FIGURE 8.2
Uncoordinated Task Activities

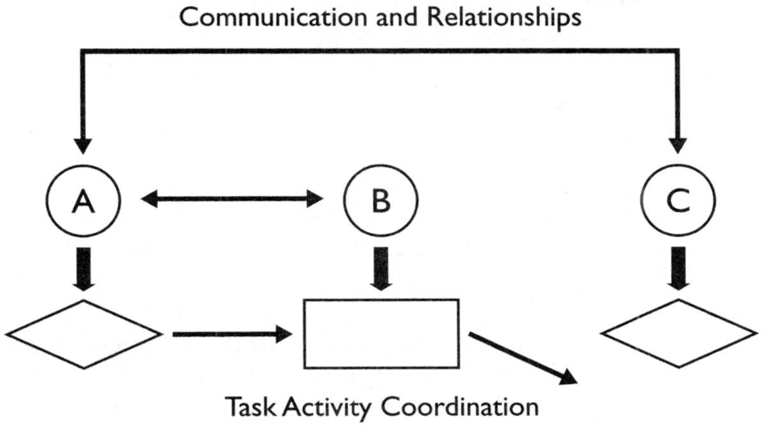

Communication and Relationships

Task Activity Coordination

---

with another person who is strongly inclined to plan each detail of the task before starting. Even when such differences are addressed, both sides may offer strong resistance to changing. Each perspective has much to offer. If a way can be found to synchronize the two orientations, team functioning will benefit.

Incompatibility can be converted to compatibility by carefully planning synchronized sets of behaviors. Synchronization can also be achieved by practicing to reduce or remove incompatibility. This means practicing the behaviors until they are synchronized in a manner that results in effective performance, that is, until they become routine. Behaviors that become routine are less susceptible to interference and should result in enhanced rather than deteriorated performance.

Teamwork is a social undertaking. The effect that the presence of others has on performance is often referred to as **social influence** or sometimes as **social facilitation.** This latter terminology is misleading because the presence of others can either detract from or interfere with performance or enhance or facilitate performance. An explanation for this difference[11] is that the presence of others has a motivating effect. When the responses involved in performance are *well learned,* the presence of others can enhance performance. For example, a well-practiced athletic team may perform better before spectators. When the responses are *in the process of being learned,* the presence of others can disrupt and inhibit performance. For example, a theater group in the early stages of rehearsing a new play is likely to consider an audience an interference.

This distinction is important. While the ongoing performance of a team that has worked together for a long time is likely to be enhanced by the presence of others, a team just getting started or confronted by a major problem for which it has no immediate, goal-oriented response is likely to be distracted and hindered by the presence of others. Teams just beginning to work together or beginning unfamiliar tasks need to understand how the presence of others (including other team members) can be disruptive. Ways to reduce the disruption must be found.

"Incompatibility can be converted to compatibility by carefully planning synchronized sets of behaviors."

"Ways to reduce the disruption must be found."

These can include discussing the discomfort that is felt, even with fellow team members, and/or secluding the team as it solves problems and learns new behaviors. Taking these steps can facilitate a team's identifying incompatible behaviors and finding ways to replace or synchronize them.

COOPERATION

Cooperative Interaction

Cooperation is intended to facilitate team members' activities. It involves members encouraging and helping each other to complete tasks and is often reciprocal. One member helps another with a task at which the former is more skilled. On a different task the roles may be reversed. **Cooperative interaction** can be a powerful influence toward developing mutually supportive relationships that form the basis for effective interpersonal coordination.[12]

"Emotional bonds form that result in concern for each other's welfare and success."

Cooperative interactions can also help team members commit to working with each other to achieve a mutual goal. Emotional bonds form that result in concern for each other's welfare and success. **Interpersonal trust** develops by placing consequences for oneself in the control of others and having one's confidence in others confirmed. Interpersonal trust is destroyed when others behave in ways that ensure harmful consequences for oneself.

Peer feedback is an important feature of cooperative interaction. *Feedback* is information that makes possible comparison of actual performance with some standard of performance. While individuals intrinsically give themselves feedback, the most powerful and effective source is others, especially those involved in a mutual undertaking whom one trusts. Feedback can extend to challenging each other's conclusions in the interests of promoting higher quality decision making. Such controversy occurs when involved team members have different information, opinions, reasoning processes, theories, and conclusions, and they must reach agreement. When managed constructively, such challenges create uncertainty about the correctness of one's views, generate an active search for more information, give rise to reconceptualizing one's knowledge and conclusions and, eventually, lead to greater mastery of relevant issues. For the team the result is more effective decision making and problem solving.

Cooperative Learning

Learning new behaviors requires more effort than performing previously learned behaviors. **Cooperative learning** is a way to reduce that perceived effort. Within most task situations, performance is enhanced when individuals give each other relevant, efficient, and effective task-related assistance. In these situations team members can exchange ideas, conclusions, information, and resources that are relevant to the completion of their tasks.

Cooperative learning situations are more supportive of members' seeking information from each other, and members make better use of the information.

Cooperative situations provide a positive environment that supports more accurate communication of information, more attentiveness to other's statements, more acceptance of and willingness to be influenced by others' ideas and information, and more confidence in one's own ideas and in the valuation of others' ideas.[13] Teaching others also increases mastery of the material and promotes higher level reasoning.

Cooperative learning requires **perspective taking,** the ability to understand how a situation appears to another person. This ability increases mastery and utilization of others' information. Messages are more easily understood by others and the information is retained longer. More creative and high-quality solutions and more accurate problem solving result when perspective taking is done. Misunderstandings are more readily clarified, and attitudes toward the information exchange process, fellow problem solvers, and the problem-solving experience tend to be more positive.

> *"More creative and high-quality solutions and more accurate problem solving result when perspective taking is done."*

STRUCTURING INTERACTIONS

Over time team behaviors and activities become *structured*. This means that patterns and consistencies develop in team behaviors that are repeated. Structure can make a team more efficient or it can make it less efficient. More efficient teams do not need to make decisions about frequently occurring behaviors, and members know how others will behave in such situations. Less efficient teams develop structures that do not engender high performance, or a team, having an efficient structure, departs from it. Three features of team social structure are discussed here.

A team's **communication network** is a structural feature, described previously, that refers to who speaks to whom and with what frequency. These networks come about in several ways. They can develop spontaneously because some team members speak more and some speak less or not at all. Those who speak direct their comments primarily to one or a few group members. After a period of time these patterns take on the quality of a "rule" of communication. "This is just the way our team is," team members will say. Networks can also be imposed. This can occur because, for example, physical features of the space in which the group works require it. When team members are placed in different offices, those in the same office will communicate with each other more frequently than with members in a different office.[14]

Communication networks can influence the emergence of leadership. For example, the team member who is central in a communication network, that is, the person who receives and sends the most messages, usually emerges as the leader. Because the central member has more information, he or she can coordinate team activities more effectively. There are two broad patterns of communication: *centralized* and *decentralized*. Centralized patterns are those where information passes through a central person.

Decentralized patterns are those where information is more flexibly shared. When a task is simple and requires only the gathering of information, a centralized

FIGURE 8.3
Communication Networks

Centralized

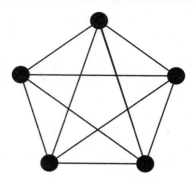

Decentralized

network is faster and has fewer errors. When, however, a task is complex and requires the analysis of information, a decentralized network is more efficient. With a complex task, members in centralized positions may receive more messages than they can handle. An overloaded network limits communication and reduces efficiency. Figure 8.3 depicts each type of network.[15]

> *"Norms develop when individuals who have not previously worked together become a team."*

Norms develop when individuals who have not previously worked together become a team. Members may, sometimes subtly, and sometimes not so subtly, begin to test each other for limits and for expectations. There are questions such as "What will this person contribute?" and "What does this person expect me to contribute?" This testing provides group members with information about how other members address different issues, who has strong views, and who tends to lead discussions, among other things. Such testing is necessary, but can be stressful, because it requires each member to consider, step by step, the implications of his or her behavior as well as the implications of other team members' behavior. If this testing continues, it is also time consuming.

To reduce the testing and related stress, behavioral consistencies, or norms, develop as standards of behavior. For example, a newly formed team must decide when to meet, but it first must decide how the decision will be reached. Will it be by consensus, by majority, or by the team's more outspoken members? Initially, the team may decide to make decisions by, for example, consensus. If this decision-making strategy is repeated, it may become the standard because it is more efficient to agree how, on a continuing basis, the team will make decisions, rather than deciding each time. Whenever a decision needs to be made, this rule or norm is called into play.[16]

Norms can develop by deliberate agreement (as in a team's charter), by trial and error, or by importing them from another setting, such as a previous team experience. It is structural because it shapes the way the team members interact. For example, a team may decide to have its meetings begin promptly at the specified time. Knowing this, members can plan their arrival accordingly. Punctual members will pressure tardy members, subtly and not so subtly, to be on time. Eventually, members begin to perceive a norm with a sense of obligation as "right" for the team.

Adhering to norms has several important consequences for a team. There is more behavioral uniformity and a shared frame of reference about how to behave. Both of these enable a team to be more efficient in coordinating its activities. Furthermore, transgressions of norms, for example, repeated lateness, result in expressions of censure by members who are on time. A team's failure to address such transgressions can lead to lowered performance and member dissatisfaction.

> *"Adhering to norms has several important consequences for a team."*

A norm can also be inefficient. For example, a team's having to reach consensus on all decisions can be time consuming in ways that decision by majority is not. However, having taken on the status of a rule or norm, efforts to change from consensus to majority rule can meet resistance. Allowing itself flexibility about when to decide by consensus and when to decide by majority can make a team's decision making more efficient. A team's ability to examine its norms and to revise them or to initiate new ones enables a team to improve its performance.

Roles develop when members assume different responsibilities within a team. For example, the first responsibility or role created by a team is often that of the team leader. This role may be assigned or simply be assumed by a person with superior task skills, with previous task experience, or with superior socioemotional task skills. Team members assume different roles for several reasons. Different members have different skills that qualify them for different responsibilities. Different members must carry out different responsibilities more or less concurrently. For example, a team charged with designing a new product, developing a cost analysis for the product, and developing a marketing plan will find it more efficient to have different team members specialize on one of the subtasks.[17]

> *"Roles develop when members assume different responsibilities within a team."*

Teams function well when roles are assigned to appropriately skilled members, and they function poorly when they are not. The greater the number of role–member combinations from which a team must choose, the less likely it is that the best possible combination will be chosen, or the greater the effort needed to identify the most effective combination. Team members can also perform more than one role. In industry, learning multiple roles and related skills is referred to as **cross-training.**[18] This has several advantages. A team's skill base is increased. Whenever the need arises, for example, when a team member is ill, other members can fill the vacant role. Performing different roles can also reduce the tedium of repeating the same job, benefiting motivation and morale. Team members can also be used more efficiently. For example, when a person's role is inactive, the ability to perform another role can increase efficiency.

When *interdependence* develops, members see the achievement of the team's goal as a collective responsibility and seek to coordinate their activities and behaviors in ways that facilitate goal achievement. A feature of interdependence is interacting cooperatively in pursuit of the goal and feeling satisfaction from shared accomplishments. These behaviors and perceptions develop and are sustained in an environment in which members trust each other and respect the resources that each brings to the team's activities. Members value coordination as an effective means to achieve their mutual goal, and interactions are structured in ways that facilitate interdependence.

The Challenge Revisited
Coordinating and Structuring Team Activities

1. Coordination is essential for a team to achieve high performance.

2. Effective coordination of team tasks and interpersonal activities requires members committed to achieving their team's goal and confident of each other's efforts to do so.

3. Developing coordination and cooperation as a team involves mutual openness, interpersonal appraisal, and exposure to each other's influence.

4. Coordination also depends on cooperation among members who support and promote each other's activities and interactions and who assist each other to develop new perspectives and to learn new ways of responding.

5. Effective coordination and cooperation also depend on high standards of team behavior and on members who accept specific responsibilities for facilitating their team's goal-directed activities.

EXERCISE 8.1 • *Coordination and Structure*

Strategies 1 through 4, described in this chapter, require that members of a human resources team coordinate their efforts to create a new set of personnel guidelines in different ways.

1. As a team, analyze the different ways in which member coordination is needed in each of these four strategies.

2. As a team, specify the structural properties that can be used with each strategy to aid and improve coordination.

3. Document your decisions and recommendations.

EXERCISE 8.2 • *Involvement and Commitment: A Case Study*

Your team is consulting with Sandra's team about how to solve the problem she presents (see case study on next page). Your team is to develop a written proposal and then report to Sandra's team. Consider all of the following:

1. What is your team's goal in this exercise?

2. What is the *problem* confronting Sandra's team?

   a. What is the problem that has resulted in the situation described in the case study?

b. List as many ways to define the problem(s) as your team can identify. (Use brainstorming to develop the list. *Brainstorming* involves (1) listing, without evaluation or comment, as many ideas as members can identify; (2) organizing a nonrepetitious list; and (3) selecting the best approach from the list.)

c. Discuss the list of possibilities and select one that seems most to the point.

d. Prepare a problem statement.

3. What is the *solution*?

a. What should the solution accomplish?

b. List as many ways as possible to achieve this objective. Brainstorm.

c. From among this list choose the best solution.

d. Prepare a proposed solution statement.

4. How can this solution be *implemented*?

a. What result is the implementation intended to accomplish?

b. List as many ways as possible to implement the solution. Brainstorm.

c. Which strategy does your team recommend as most likely to be effective? Are there possible negative effects? What are they?

d. Prepare an implementation plan, describing the positive and negative aspects of the plan.

5. As a team prepare a written report of your team's deliberations that includes the following:

- List of different possible problems considered and statement of problem selected

- List of different solutions considered and description of solution chosen

- List of implementation strategies considered and description of strategy chosen

- Recommendations about how to prevent the situation described in the case study.

INVOLVEMENT AND COMMITMENT

As told by Sandra, a team member

My group was made up of one female, two guys, and myself; for convenience sake, Mary, Joe, and Bob. We had never met before. Our goal was to write a marketing memo from a case study that we had received a week prior to the assignment being given out. Our first meeting was on a Monday night. Mary did not show up because she had an away game. Joe was late. Upon arriving he immediately informed Bob and me that he was going home for the weekend and he was not going to be around to help us write or type the memo. We spent this meeting discussing how we would tackle the assignment—who would do research and how we should organize it. Bob and Joe just sat there and had blank stares. Keep in mind, the day before we had met for a few minutes after class and agreed to read the seven-page case study and take a few pages of notes so *that we could come together* the next night with different ideas and would spend less time discussing and more time assembling the memo.

Basically, everything that could have gone wrong did. At first, I tried to lighten the mood by cracking jokes and laughing and encouraging them to tell me how they felt about the case—but still they said nothing. I thought it might be because they felt uncomfortable, but after many attempts to engage them in the conversation, I realized they just were not into the assignment. I finally decided to start reading my notes and telling them how I felt while making frequent pauses to ask them if they agreed or disagreed. They nodded their heads in agreement at every point I presented. This not only made me uncomfortable because I didn't see it my place to take over the entire project, but I couldn't understand why the two guys had not disagreed with anything I had said. Both guys had different agendas and goals (one of which was to get this memo done quickly and get out of the library) than I had. They obviously did not want to be there and wanted to push the work off onto someone else. At the end of our first meeting we had accomplished nothing. The only information we had was mine. At this point, I didn't really care if they expected me to write the whole report, I just wish that they would have contributed, so that we would have had more to work with and more perspectives with which to view the situation. We set up a meeting for the next night.

The next day, only Bob and I showed up, which was funny to me because that morning I had left a voice mail on everyone's machines to remind them of the meeting. We decided to meet in the computing center so that we could type the memo. Bob offered to take the three sheets of data that Joe had collected and type them into spreadsheets. Remember, this is a task that should at best take no more than an hour. While he did this I offered to write the introduction. When I had finished the introduction, he had still not finished so I just continued to write the report. Two hours later I had finished writing the majority of the report as he sat beside me—saying nothing and twirling his pencil. His only comment was "Well, Sandra, you *are* the journalism major. Writing is easy for you and you have to be good at it, so I know our group will get a good grade." I just brushed off his comment, because at this point I was so frustrated that if I let it get to me I knew I would blow up at him. Just then, the other girl in our group walked in. She apologized profusely and asked if there were anything she could do. At this point Bob and I had to spend 45 minutes catching her up on what was going on. I was relieved that she was nice and offered to do some work. She wrote the last paragraph of the analysis section while I wrote the conclusion. At the end of the meeting she offered to type the entire memo because she wasn't at the other meeting.

When all was said and done, we all had different agendas, lacked commitment, had *too* much consensus, and had no plan as to how to accomplish our task. The kicker of the whole experience is that Joe lied to the group saying he would be home all weekend because I saw him out on Friday night!!! Maybe it was because some members felt uncomfortable around each other, or maybe it was because some were too lazy or because I may have been too into the assignment and I came on too strong. To me, the experience was more disheartening than it was frustrating.

QUESTIONS FOR REVIEW AND DISCUSSION

1. What is meant by *process losses* or *process gains*? Why is either assumed to occur?

2. How does a team design a strategy for reaching its goal? What are the issues a team should consider in selecting a strategy?

3. What is the role of coordination in the strategy a team chooses? Do all task designs require the same degree of coordination? Discuss examples.

4. What is meant by *interpersonal coordination*? What is the role of interpersonal relationships in interpersonal coordination? What can interpersonal conflict do to interpersonal coordination? How can such conflict be addressed?

5. What is *social appraisal*? How can the results of social appraisal affect coordination? How can social influence have a negative or positive effect on interpersonal coordination?

6. What is *task coordination*? How are task coordination and interpersonal coordination related? Why is response compatibility a central issue for task coordination?

7. When responses are incompatible, *response synchronization* can be an alternative. What is response synchronization? Under what conditions is it possible and how is it achieved?

8. What is meant by *social facilitation*? How does social facilitation "work"?

9. What is meant by *cooperation*? Why is it important for coordination? What is *cooperative learning*? What is its role in coordination?

10. What are *structuring social interactions*? What is a *norm* and what is its significance for social structure? What is a *social role*? How do roles help to structure social interactions? How can both norms and roles make interactions more efficient?

NOTES

1. See L. D. Ketchum & E. Trist (1992), *All Teams Are Not Created Equal*, Thousand Oaks, CA: Sage, chap 2.

2. On satisfaction working with others, see M. T. Iaffaldano & P. M. Muchinsky (1985), Job satisfaction and job performance: A meta-analysis. *Psychological Bulletin*, 97(2), 251–273. See D. Yeatts & C. Hyten (1998), *High-Performing Self-Managed Work Teams*, Thousand Oaks, CA: Sage, pp. 231–232.

3. On improving quality, see J. A. Cannon-Bowers, R. Oser, & D. L. Flanagan (1992), Work teams in industry: A selected review and proposed framework, in R. W. Swezey & E. Salas (Eds.), *Teams: Their Training and Performance*, Norwood, NJ: Ablex Publishing.

4. On teams reducing the need for direct supervision, see Cannon-Bowers et al., op. cit.

5. For a discussion of process losses, see Steiner (1972), *Group Process and Productivity,* New York: Academic Press; and L. A. Penner & J. P. Crayer (1992), The weakest link: The performance of individual team members, in R. W. Swezey & E. Salas (Eds.), *Teams: Their Training and Performance,* Norwood, NJ: Ablex Publishing.

6. Steiner, op. cit., p. 63.

7. On factors influencing team effectiveness, see E. Sundstrom, M. McIntyre, T. Halfhill, & H. Richards (2000), Work groups: From the Hawthorne studies to work teams of the 1990's and beyond, *Group Dynamics,* 4, 44–67.

8. On social appraisal, see M. Argyle (1969), *Social Interaction,* Chicago: Aldine, chap. IV.

9. On social influence, see W. D. Crano (2000), Milestones in the psychological analysis of social influence, *Group Dynamics: Theory, Research and Practice,* 4, 68–80.

10. See S. Schachter (1951), Deviation, rejection, and communication, *Journal of Abnormal and Social Psychology,* 46, 190–207.

11. R. Zajonc (1965, July 16), Social facilitation, *Science,* pp. 269–274.

12. On effective interpersonal coordination, see D. Johnson and R. Johnson (1981), The effects of cooperative, competitive and individualistic goal structures on achievement: A meta-analysis, *Psychological Bulletin,* 89, 47–62.

13. On more confidence in one's own ideas and in their valuation of others' ideas, see D. Johnson & R. Johnson (1974), Instructional goal structures: Cooperative, competitive, and individualistic? *Review of Educational Research,* 49, 51–70, cited in D. Johnson & F. Johnson (1987), *Joining Together,* Englewood Cliffs, NJ: Prentice-Hall.

14. On communication networks, see Johnson and Johnson (1987), op. cit., pp. 213–214.

15. H. Leavitt (1951), Some effects of certain communication patterns on group performance. *Journal of Abnormal and Social Psychology,* 46, 38–50; and M. Shaw (1964), Communication networks, in L. Berkowitz (Ed.), *Advances in Experimental Social Psychology,* Vol 1, New York: Academic Press, pp. 111–147.

16. On norms, see M. H. Colman & A. V. Carron (2001), The nature of norms in individual sports teams, *Small Group Research,* 32, 206–222.

17. On roles, see M. R. Beauchamp & S. R. Bray (2001), Role ambiguity and role conflict within interdependent teams, *Small Group Research,* 32, 133–157.

18. On cross-training, see Yeatts & Hyten, op. cit., p. 176; J. Klein (1994), Maintaining expertise in multi-skilled teams. In M. M. Beyerlein & D. A. Johnson (Eds.), *Advances in Interdisciplinary Studies of Work Teams: Theories of Self-Managed Work Teams,* London: JAI Press, pp. 145–166.

The Challenge
Team Member Satisfaction

The satisfactions a team's members experience directly influence their involvement. Sources of satisfaction are members' attraction to working to realize an important vision, their sense of cohesion with other members when pursuing their team's goal, and the sense that each member is helping to accomplish the tasks required to achieve the goal. Members also derive satisfaction from the rewards and recognition that the team receives. Members who experience few or no satisfactions tend to lose interest, thus denying their resources to the team and in the process reducing the satisfaction experienced by other members. A team's leader is responsible for helping members to experience satisfaction.

chapter 9

Team Member Satisfaction

TEAM COHESION

When the quality of relationships among team members and their attraction to the team and its activities are positive, a mutual sense of team cohesion results. Team members' *liking* each other is sometimes noted as the basis of cohesion. In teamwork, trust and respect may be more important than liking. Their importance derives from members' needing to depend on and expect certain types and levels of behavior from each other. Team cohesion also derives from members' satisfaction with the task(s) involved in working toward and accomplishing the team's goal. Lacking any of these, attraction to the team and its activities is reduced and cohesion suffers.[1]

> *"In teamwork, trust and respect may be more important than liking."*

Cohesive teams have important positive qualities. Members are more committed to and attribute greater value to the team's goal. They are more willing

"Members of cohesive teams tend to communicate more frequently and effectively and to listen to and accept the opinions of other members in making decisions."

to work toward a common goal and accept assigned tasks and roles more readily. They are more motivated to accomplish the team's tasks (if for no other reason than to live up to the expectations of fellow group members), and they persist longer in working toward difficult goals. Members of cohesive teams tend to communicate more frequently and effectively and to listen to and accept the opinions of other members in making decisions. As team norms or standards develop, members conform to them more readily and protect their team's norms by putting pressure on members who violate them.

A cohesive team environment supports the mutuality and interdependence that are essential to effective team functioning. Members are aware that each is liked, accepted, and valued and that others hold similar goals and values to theirs. Members are more satisfied with the work of their team and experience greater security and less tension when the team is cohesive. Cohesive teams also give more latitude to the development and expression of hostility and conflict than do noncohesive groups. This latter underscores the importance of team members being able to identify, understand, and use positive strategies of conflict resolution.

Cohesion is an ideal that is infrequently achieved, however. There are a number of barriers to cohesion. Consider the following team. Sami, Sally, Clara, George, and Ellen are volunteer members of an environmental awareness group. Their group's goal is to conduct workshops to raise awareness about water quality. Each has concerns about the environment, however, each is drawn to this group for additional reasons. Clara and Sally are especially interested in water quality. Ellen is interested in learning more about how nonprofit groups organize and operate. George joined the group to be with Sally. Sami joined to develop his leadership skills. Each of the team members, except Sami, is enjoying the experience. Sami finds that leading requires an unexpected amount of effort. He also sees that Ellen and George tend to take the leadership role and to do the required work. After a period of ambivalence, Sami begins to lose interest in the group's activities.

This team lacks cohesion because Sami's individual goal is unfulfilled. Leading the team requires a degree of effort he did not expect. Others have assumed the role he desired to perform. As a result, Sami is losing interest. Assuming that the team wants Sami to continue and that Sami wants to continue (which may require a team discussion of the issue), there are several possible approaches that might provide Sami more satisfaction. One is to find an alternative leadership role for him. Since the leadership role is sometimes divisible, there may be a leadership subtask, such as workshop leader, that Sami would enjoy. It might involve, say, preparing a discussion of some important environmental issue.

Another possibility is to look at Sami's interests more broadly. What motivates Sami, other than his desire to lead? More broadly, what type of experience does a particular individual find interesting or satisfying such that he or she will exert effort to enjoy the experience? An answer involves Sami's motivational make-up. More broadly, what motivates individuals generally?

MEMBER MOTIVATION

One often-cited perspective on human **motivation** is that of Maslow.[2] In his **hierarchy of needs**, Maslow distinguishes several types of human motives or "needs." He describes as *basic needs* those that are physiological such as the need for food and water. When unsatisfied, these become dominant. When the organism needs food, all other capacities are put into the service of obtaining food. *Safety needs* are a second priority. If the physiological needs are relatively well satisfied, a new set of needs emerges for security, protection, and freedom from fear. If both the physiological and safety needs are fairly well satisfied, there will emerge *needs for love, affection, and belongingness.* Given the arousal of these needs, a person will feel keenly the absence of friends or loved ones and will desire to be in a social setting to which there is a feeling of attachment.

Next in the hierarchy are *esteem needs.* These involve a person's desire for a stable, firmly based, usually high evaluation of themselves, for self-respect, and for the respect and esteem of others. Esteem needs are subdivided by Maslow into two sets. One is the desire for achievement, mastery, and competence. The other is the desire for reputation or prestige. Satisfaction of the **self-esteem** need leads to feelings of self-confidence, capability, and adequacy. Finally, at the peak of the hierarchy there is the need for self-actualization. When all other needs are fulfilled, a person seeks to develop his or her individual capabilities. Maslow viewed this hierarchy as applicable to everyone.

A somewhat different perspective, proposed by Murray, indicates that individuals have, in differing degrees, 20 needs.[3] Included are the need for achievement, i.e. to accomplish something significant; the need for affiliation (i.e., to draw near and enjoy cooperation with others), the need for dominance (i.e., to control one's human environment), the need for nurturance (i.e., to give sympathy and to gratify the needs of helpless other), and the need for understanding (i.e., to ask or answer general questions).

Murray agrees with Maslow in viewing individual needs as hierarchically ordered. They also agree on the overarching importance of physiological needs, safety needs, and the need for belongingness. However, for Murray the hierarchy of needs associated with esteem and self-actualization differs from individual to individual. For example, individuals high in the need for achievement will seek out and perform in achievement-oriented situations. Those high in the need for affiliation will seek situations where they can interact with other people. Individuals high in both needs will seek situations where they can both work to achieve while at the same time interacting with others.

Differences in motivational hierarchies between team members help to explain why some members find some activities more satisfying than others. These motivational differences, while adding complexity to a team's interactions, also offer a wider range of resources to a team. As team members become better acquainted, they learn each member's more dominant needs. While

> *"When the organism needs food, all other capacities are put into the service of obtaining food."*

> *"When all other needs are fulfilled, a person seeks to develop his or her individual capabilities."*

"As team members become better acquainted, they learn each member's more dominant needs."

assessment procedures can systematically identify an individual's need hierarchy, these generally depend on what an individual describes about his or her pattern of needs and interests. This assumes that individuals know their interests and what they find satisfying or unsatisfying. In a context of trust, this information can be shared with other team members. When team tasks can be distributed in accord with member interests, the likelihood is increased that members will perform tasks well and experience satisfaction in doing so.

This latter applies to Sami, the dissatisfied member of the environmental awareness team. In a relaxed and open discussion with other team members, Sami describes his sense of frustration. Other team members are truly interested for Sami to continue as a member and in their discussions discover that what is most interesting to him is to achieve something distinctive in the area of environmental awareness. After further discussion, it becomes clear that developing a new type of environmental awareness workshop really captures his interest. The team and Sami decide that this is how Sami will proceed.

SOURCES OF SATISFACTION OR DISSATISFACTION

"Teamwork offers many sources of satisfaction and of dissatisfaction."

Teamwork offers many sources of satisfaction and of dissatisfaction. It is important for team members to understand the variety of sources of **satisfaction** and how to realize them while also being able to identify and to avoid the dissatisfactions.

Satisfactions from Performing Tasks and Roles

Individual Skill Utilization and Development.   Individual members' use of their skills to benefit the team's goal achievement can be satisfying. The opportunity to develop higher level or new skills can also be satisfying. Without renewed challenges to individuals, however, this source of incentive can be reduced or removed altogether.[4]

The tasks a team performs (see Chapter 8) can be specified by someone outside the team or left to the team to decide. For example, a team with the goal of designing a new product and submitting a report that includes the design, a cost analysis, and a marketing plan has at least three subtasks already specified. What remains to determine is who will do the different tasks. When a team is free to devise its own tasks and to define its roles, the opportunities for member involvement and satisfaction are increased. Placing responsibility on a team to arrive at a task design that both optimizes the opportunities for goal achievement and optimizes the opportunities for member satisfaction is a challenge.

An important consideration is assigning to a task or role a member who has the necessary skills or has access to training to develop the skills. Lacking these creates frustration, dissatisfaction, and eventually reduced motivation. Another consideration is whether a member will find a task or role satisfying. Because varied paths exist by which a team can achieve its goal, a team with the discretion to choose its path has more latitude to find a path that accommodates members' needs and interests. Members' satisfaction with their tasks and roles should be revisited regularly as progress toward the goal occurs and as team members become better known to, and comfortable with, each other.

Facilitating Progress.   A major source of satisfaction or dissatisfaction for team members is whether they feel that the team is making progress. Members make progress when they have similar work styles or adjust their styles to be similar, relate easily, understand how to identify relevant compatible behaviors, and pursue their tasks to completion. Discussion moves freely. Suggestions from one member are heard by others and thoughtfully evaluated. Under these circumstances each member experiences reduced effort because of the ease with which the task performance process proceeds, even when the work is hard and difficult decisions must be made. A result can be that more is accomplished jointly than would have been accomplished had the individuals worked independently. Such behaviors facilitate the process.[5]

"Suggestions from one member are heard by others and thoughtfully evaluated."

Behaviors that interfere with progress add effort and reduce satisfaction. They can also take a psychological toll in the form of annoyance, embarrassment, or anxiety. For example, team members are working on a report. Two insist on listening to music while the others prefer quiet. Having music playing requires greater effort to concentrate by the quiet-preferring members. After a time, additional interference arises because those who prefer quiet become annoyed. This irritation requires even more effort to remain focused on the task. Effort to produce the report increases, performance deteriorates, and everyone's satisfaction disappears.

Interference can also occur when the behavior of one or more team members causes other members to react in ways that reduce team effectiveness. For example, a team is preparing a report, using an earlier report as a model. One member repeatedly describes as "dumb" parts of the earlier report. The effect is to raise other members' anxieties about how their own performance is perceived. As a result, some members are more reserved in their efforts and less forthcoming with ideas for improvement. Another type of interference occurs when one team member so dominates discussions that other members simply cease to make suggestions. In both cases, members' knowledge and experience are lost to the undertaking and progress slows.

"Interference can also occur when the behavior of one or more team members causes other members to react in ways that reduce team effectiveness."

Satisfactions of Team Membership

Open Communication.   Communication among team members can be a source of satisfaction or dissatisfaction. We discuss several reasons why next.[6]

Team members who *express their views* are likely to be more satisfied than those who do not. Some may feel discomfort expressing what they think, especially if this differs from the majority. Reticence can be overcome if other team members ask "quiet" members for their views and encourage them to join in discussions. By contrast, some members may tend to dominate discussions, effectively talking over anyone else. When this occurs, the persons being talked over should insist on completing what they have to say and others may need to intervene to achieve this end.

"Persons who express their views need to feel heard."

Persons who express their views need to feel heard. Having said something one believes is relevant to a discussion and having others act as if nothing has been said, or at least nothing important, can be painful. One reaction is to withdraw from the exchange. With careful monitoring team members can identify when this occurs and take steps, by asking questions, to provide the persons who feel unheard an opportunity to elaborate and to feel that their contribution is acknowledged.

Individuals also *need to be taken seriously*. Being heard and being taken seriously are not necessarily the same. A person's comments may be acknowledged but may not be taken seriously when, for example, one member does not consider another member competent to make relevant comments or suggestions. When this occurs it is important to remember that each member is on the team because he or she can contribute to achieving the team's goal. To act otherwise is to engender dissatisfaction and lose team resources.

A team needs to *resolve misunderstandings constructively*. Misunderstandings create barriers. A team member who feels misunderstood will feel dissatisfied and will reduce his or her effort. When differences are identified, it is important to address them in a way that does not leave anyone feeling diminished. Focusing on the team's progress, rather than on winning an argument, is crucial for individual satisfaction and for effective team performance.

Being *kept out of the loop* also generates dissatisfaction. Each team member needs to feel "included." Feeling that some members have information that has been denied to others results in dissatisfaction. A member who occupies a central position in a communication network usually has more information and is more satisfied with the group's work. Members on the fringe have less information and are usually less satisfied. Keeping communication inclusive is important for member satisfaction.[7]

"Social support is an important source of satisfaction."

Social support is an important source of satisfaction.[8] It involves the exchange of resources intended to enhance mutual well-being. It derives from the availability of people on whom one can rely for assistance, encouragement, acceptance, and caring. A team's social support system consists of respected team members who collaboratively share tasks and goals, and who provide to team members resources, such as materials, tools, skills, information, and advice, and even attentive, concerned listening. The presence of such a system enhances members' sense of well-being and is especially helpful in dealing with stressful situations.

A team's social support system generates in each team member a feeling of being able to rely on other team members. Having supportive associates promotes several outcomes. They can provide emotional support, such as expressions of concern; instrumental aid, such as goods or services; informational aid, such as facts or advice about how to solve a problem; and appraisal support, such as feedback needed for self-evaluation or for determining whether certain behavioral standards are being met or for understanding others' reactions.[9] Social support also helps to maintain a sense of interdependence. As a result, members' sense of psychological well-being is improved. Performance is enhanced.

Personal and Interpersonal Appraisal.   When a team member performs, that performance is appraised and appreciated by the performer (**personal appraisal**). Appreciation partly refers to the reward value of the behavior for the performer. For example, Juan is preparing a report. He values quality work and begins by expecting of himself the best performance. He will not be satisfied until the report is clear and covers relevant issues. When the report meets his personal standards, he feels satisfaction.

"When a team member performs, that performance is appraised and appreciated by the performer."

A second source of a person's appreciation depends on others' appraisal of an individual's effort or activity (**interpersonal appraisal**).[10] For example, if Sara feels that Juan's report does not address certain issues, Juan is likely to be less confident of his appraisal. This will reduce the reward value of the report. This difference means not only that Juan and Sara have additional work to do to prepare a report that both accept, but they also need to reduce the differences in their appraisal standards. While Sara's negative evaluation introduces interference, even some conflict, to the process of working together, it can bring Juan and Sara into closer accord on their evaluation standard. After an open and constructive discussion, they may decide on a standard that is higher than Juan's original standard but lower than Sara's, although Sara may have difficulty lowering her standards. What they should seek is a mutually acceptable standard that is both appropriately challenging and realistic and will give satisfaction to both Sara and Juan.

A third source of appraisal and appreciation is **comparative self-appraisal.**[11] This is a person's estimate of how positively his or her performance (or other attributes) compares with those of peers. If a person perceives peers to be exceptionally skilled, this may result in a person's feeling less self-confident initially, although the person may feel honored to be with such talented or capable people. If a person perceives him- or herself to be equal to or superior to peers, the result is usually a feeling of greater self-confidence, although, within limits, more capable peers may challenge the person.

"If a person perceives peers to be exceptionally skilled, this may result in a person's feeling less self-confident initially."

Of these processes, one may be more dominant at some times and in some situations than others. Which is dominant depends on the individual's own experience and the social setting. For example, a person working alone will need to depend more on self-appraisal. In a team setting, comparison with the performance of other team members and members who offer suggestions for improving performance can result in both improved performance and increased satisfaction.

Enjoyment of Productive Interaction

Successful teams make the team's work fun for members.[12] Humor can be an important feature of team functioning. It can calm or anger, ease or embarrass,

"Successful teams make the team's work fun for members."

"Humor can defuse a negative event or resolve a conflict among group members."

relax tensions or create them, reduce boredom, dissolve fears, establish rapport with strangers, and dramatically build more positive relationships. Humor, used appropriately in a team, can redirect members away from potentially hostile, aggressive, or tense situations. Humor can defuse a negative event or resolve a conflict among group members. It can energize, freeing one from anger, resentment, and disappointment, so that more energy is available to work productively. For example, in the environmental awareness team's discussion of Sami's desire for leadership, Sami might easily feel offended, especially discussing his remaining on the team. A humorous comment (not a putdown) could lighten the discussion and make it move smoothly. Conversely, were something said jokingly that minimized Sami's contribution, the effect would be hurtful emotionally.

SATISFACTIONS FROM REWARDS AND RECOGNITION

Rewards and recognition are important sources of team member satisfaction.[13] Their lack can be significant sources of dissatisfaction. Rewards and recognition are intended not only to acknowledge past performance but to encourage high-level future performance. This is not easy to accomplish because there are many types of rewards, including recognition, and individuals can react differently to the same reward.

Rewards and recognition are difficult to differentiate. One reason is that they both directly influence an individual's esteem motive. The way in which rewards and recognition are distributed can have a marked effect on an individual's effectiveness, on members' behavior toward one another, and on how effective the team is overall.[14]

"Rewards are compensation for performance."

Rewards are compensation for performance. In a work situation the reward for work is primarily monetary, a wage. This is motivating because it is how the needs for food, shelter, safety, and status are satisfied. In an academic classroom situation, a grade is a reward a team receives for its work preparing a report. In either context, work or class, recognition is generally given for exceptional performance. Certain members of the team may be singled out for special recognition for their contribution. The discussion that follows considers different forms of reward and recognition.[15]

How are rewards to be given? Broadly, there are three answers to this question. One is to distribute rewards according to an individual's level of performance. Another is to reward the performance of an organizational subdivision such as a team. Finally, a third is to reward the performance of the organization of which the team is a part. Once a unit of performance is determined, there are different ways to determine the amount of the reward.[16]

Equity or merit strategies distribute rewards[17] in proportion to an individual's contribution. Their attraction is their apparent "fairness." Being rewarded in proportion to one's contribution is assumed to motivate individuals to achieve and maintain a high level of performance. A key question is how to define and identify "contribution." How many dimensions are involved? Is it effort (i.e., units produced), quality (i.e., number of defects), or simply hours on the job? When an individual's job is clearly defined and clearly distinguishable from the jobs of fellow workers, an individual's contribution can be readily identified. When, however, an individual's contribution is intermingled with others' contributions, as it is with a team, an individual's contribution is more difficult to define.

> *"Equity or merit strategies distribute rewards in proportion to an individual's contribution."*

The merit strategy can also have unfortunate effects on team members' views of themselves, of each other, of their relationships, and of how much each contributes. One reason is that those with the most talent and skill, including interpersonal skill, regardless of effort, often receive a disproportionately large part of a reward package. Those who work hardest, but have less talent, are perceived as contributing less. This person often receives a smaller proportion of the reward and she interprets this as meaning that she is less worthy.[18] Another result is that both misunderstand the basis for their reward level. For example, a person whose winning personality makes it relatively easy to make sales interprets this as reflecting superior effort, whereas a person with a less attractive personality, who must work extra hard to make sales, interprets this as a lack of capability and self-worth, especially when he earns less.

The merit strategy is also inherently competitive because it assumes a finite set of rewards. This tends to undermine mutuality that can, in turn, reduce group cohesiveness, cause morale problems, and undermine trust and cooperation. Another question is whether a person who makes exceptional contributions to a poor team should be rewarded at the same level as a person who makes the same level of contribution to a good team.[19]

An **equality system** specifies that all members of a team receive the same reward. Such an equality system focuses on team performance rather than individual performance and rewards all members equally. An equality system is assumed to result in mutual esteem, equal status, and mutual respect among members and to encourage interdependence. Some see an equality distribution as fostering enjoyable, personal relationships, group loyalty, and cooperation. Others, however, contend that receiving the same wage will not motivate workers to perform at as high a level and will result in mediocre performance.[20]

> *"an equality system focuses on team performance rather than individual performance and rewards all members equally"*

An equality system addresses the problem of how to attribute members' contributions when their behaviors are highly interrelated and coordinated into a single activity. Members of winning amateur athletic teams generally are given the same reward for their team's outstanding performance. The key to members accepting and being motivated by such rewards (and the associated recognition) is that the "rules" say that rewards are to be distributed equally to each member. Such a rule tends to encourage interdependence.[21]

Hybrid reward systems combine features of two or more reward systems. For example, a reward system can be designed such that the team's level of performance and the individual's level of performance are both determined. The latter need not reflect only team performance. For example, it could include a determination and assessment of an individual's skill or knowledge level. With a performance score for the team and a contribution score for individual team members, the individual's final performance level is a weighted combination of the two.[22]

Organizational-based reward systems reward employees based in part or totally on an organization's performance. This system (e.g., gain-sharing)[23] aims to develop employees' commitment to the overall activities of the organization. The rule is that when the organization does well, the reward for employees will be larger than when the organization does poorly.

Overall, for a reward system to be perceived by team members as just, the "rules" for distributing rewards must at least be clear. When the rules are unclear or are viewed as unjust, the result is likely to be lowered morale, increased interpersonal conflict, and lowered performance.

"Recognition is closely related to the esteem need."

Recognition is a special type of reward. It is social in nature. It involves being singled out and having an accomplishment given special notice. Recognition can also involve receiving some reward, such as a cash prize. Recognition is closely related to the esteem need. Self-esteem reflects a person's judgment about self-worth. It is a judgment about one's competence or value, based on the information one gathers and organizes about oneself and one's experiences. Recognition addresses both one's sense of mastery and self-acceptance and one's reputation or comparative self-worth.[24]

Many companies, in addition to the recognition that occurs among team members, recognize high-quality performance either by individuals or by teams. Recognition programs include announcements in company publications of meritorious performance, company-funded celebrations for meritorious teams, and symbolic awards such as caps, cups, or t-shirts. Although such recognition is more symbolic than material, individuals or groups are singled out for recognition of significant accomplishments. This enhances the self-esteem of individuals either singly or as members of groups and is likely to have a positive effect on their sense of satisfaction and their level of performance.

"An important source of recognition for a team member is from fellow team members."

Recognition by One's Team.   An important source of recognition for a team member is from fellow team members. Just as a team knows how best to perform tasks to achieve its goal, team members know who among them has made a special contribution to the goal's achievement. As team members develop trust and respect for each other, they also become sensitive to how members appraise each other's contributions. A part of a team's improving its performance is through members voicing these appraisals in ways that help the team to achieve its goal and improve its performance.

Team recognition is important for member self-esteem and member self-esteem is important for team functioning. Members who feel that their contributions are not acknowledged will not feel highly regarded (esteemed) by fellow team members. Dissatisfaction and deteriorating performance are likely to result. This is especially true for members who have low self-esteem to begin with. They may need more recognition from the team, even when their contribution has not been exceptional.

The Role of a Team Leader in Member Satisfaction.   A team's leader has an important role in helping members to find and maintain satisfaction in performing their team's activities. Initially, this involves the leader working with members to identify and undertake performance of attractive activities and roles. As the team proceeds, the leader looks for and addresses indications of member dissatisfaction. The leader also creates an environment in which member contributions are readily acknowledged. This can include evaluating both members' accomplishments and the amount of recognition appropriate for each and devising ways to provide recognition of members for their accomplishments.[25]

The Challenge Revisited
Team Member Satisfaction

1. Experiencing satisfaction is crucial for team member involvement.

2. Satisfaction derives from feeling that one is a part of something important, from enjoying interpersonal interactions, from being recognized for one's contributions to the team's activities, and from sharing in the recognitions and rewards given the team.

3. Members who do not contribute experience reduced satisfaction. Members who do not experience satisfaction lose interest and reduce their contributions.

4. Communication is at the heart of satisfaction. Members need to express their views, feel that they are heard, and feel that they are taken seriously.

5. A team's leaders and its members are responsible for assuring that every member experiences satisfaction.

EXERCISE 9.1 • *Facilitating Problem Resolution*

As a team, discuss the following two short scenarios; then answer the accompanying questions. Be prepared to present your findings to the class.

> A very task-oriented individual finds herself on a team with two other members who periodically argue about the steps needed to achieve the team's goal. When this happens the team spends considerable time resolving the conflict. As a result, the task-oriented individual becomes bored and withdraws from any further discussion.

1. What can the task-oriented team member do to facilitate the process of being more focused on the team's goal?

> A member of a team misses team meetings. Other members would like to discuss the absences but are hesitant to do so.

2. How can the members go about creating a positive context for such a discussion? What do they say in the discussion?

EXERCISE 9.2 • *Interpersonal Feedback*

This is an exercise in peer evaluation. The task involves each team member providing feedback to other members of the team.

1. Read the labels of the parts on the sailboat diagram that follows and then assign the names of your team's members to one or more boat parts on the accompanying chart. Each member must be assigned to at least one boat part. More than one team member can be assigned to the same part and one member can be assigned to more than one part.

2. When the boat part assignments have been made, turn to page 231 and find the forms labeled "Individual Feedback Notes." Prepare one feedback note for each of the your team's members.

3. When all of your team's members have completed their sets of feedback notes, do the following:

   a. Team members read their feedback to the named team member.

   b. After reading the feedback, hand your notes to that person.

   c. Repeat steps a and b until every member of your team has given feedback to every other member.

4. When the task is complete, discuss why this task was difficult.

   a. What did you expect when you started?

   b. Was the result different from what you expected? How was it the same or different?

   c. Were reactions the same or different? How were they the same? How different?

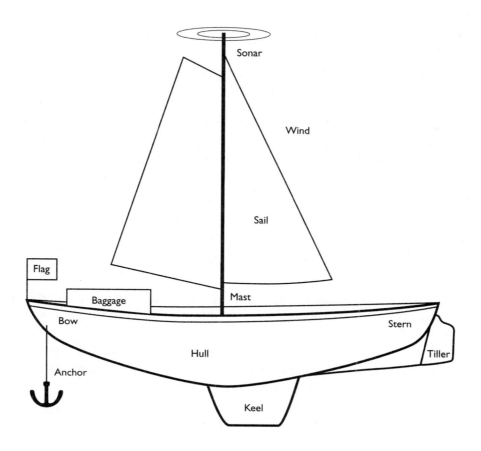

SAILBOAT PART DESCRIPTIONS

PARTS   Team Member

Anchor: keeps the boat from moving   _____ _____ _____

Baggage: is weight to carry   _____ _____ _____

Bow: is always out in front   _____ _____ _____

Flag: indicates the direction of the wind   _____ _____ _____

Hull: provides support and buoyancy   _____ _____ _____

Keel: gives the boat stability   _____ _____ _____

Mast: supports the boat's sail and sonar   _____ _____ _____

Sail: catches the wind to power the boat   _____ _____ _____

Sonar: locates barriers to the boat's progress _____ _____ _____

Stern: always behind   _____ _____ _____

Tiller: controls the boat's direction   _____ _____ _____

Wind: fills the sail to power the boat   _____ _____ _____

QUESTIONS FOR REVIEW AND DISCUSSION

1. What is *team member cohesion*? How does its presence or absence affect team performance?

2. What is Maslow's perspective on human motivation? According to Maslow, how does motivation function in humans?

3. What is Murray's perspective on human motivation? In what ways is it similar to Maslow's view? In what ways is it different? What is the significance of individual motivation hierarchies for team functioning?

4. Why do team members find using their skills to assist their team satisfying? Why can a member who agrees to perform a task, but finds that he or she lacks the relevant skills, lose interest in performing the task?

5. How can the work of other members interfere with or facilitate a team member's task performance? How can interference be avoided and facilitation encouraged?

6. List several sources of satisfaction that can derive from team membership. Why does each provide satisfaction? How can each become a source of dissatisfaction?

7. What is *social support*? Why is it important for team members' satisfaction?

8. What is the difference between personal and interpersonal appraisal? What is the role of each in a team member's experience of satisfaction?

9. What is the difference for a team between *reward* and *recognition*? Which is more important for a team member's satisfaction? Why?

10. What is the difference between an equity (merit) strategy of reward and an equality strategy? For a team, what are the strengths and weaknesses of each strategy?

11. What is the role of a team's leader in members' experience of satisfaction?

NOTES

1. See J. E. Driskell & E. Salas (1992), Can you study real teams in contrived settings? The value of small group research in understanding teams, in R. Swezy & E. Salas (Eds.), *Teams, Their Training and Performance*, Norwood, NJ: Ablex Publishing, pp. 117–119; K. L. Dion (2000), Group cohesion: From "field of forces" to multidimensional construct, *Group Dynamics*, 4, 7–26; and F. Gammage, A. Carron, & P. Estabrooks (2001), Team cohesion and individual productivity, *Small Group Research*, 32, 3–18.

2. A. H. Maslow (1970), *Motivation and Personality* (2nd ed.), New York: Harper & Row.

3. H. A. Murray (1938), *Explorations in Personality*, New York: Oxford.

4. For more on satisfactions from performing tasks and task roles, see D. E. Yeatts & C. Hyten (1998), *High-Performing Self-Managed Work Teams*,

Thousand Oaks, CA: Sage; also H. Arrow, J. McGrath, & J. Berdahl (2000), *Small Groups as Complex Systems,* Thousand Oaks, CA: Sage.

5. On facilitation and interference, see J. W. Thibaut & H. H. Kelly (1959), *The Social Psychology of Groups,* New York: John Wiley, pp. 51–63.

6. On reasons open communication provides satisfaction, see Yeatts & Hyten, op. cit., pp. 79–86.

7. Feeling included also holds for those who are infrequent communicators.

8. For more on social support as a source of satisfaction, see J. S. House (1981), *Work, Stress and Social Support,* Reading, MA: Addison-Wesley, which cites four dimensions: emotional support, instrumental support, informational support, and appraisal support.

9. On functions of social support, see S. Cohen, R. Mermelstein, T. Kamarck, & H. M. Hoberman (1985), Measuring functional components of social support, in I. G. Sarason & B. R. Sarason (Eds.), *Social Support: Theory, Research and Applications,* The Hague, The Netherlands: Martimes Nijhoof, pp. 73–94. Also House, op. cit.

10. On interpersonal appraisal, see M. Argyle (1969), *Social Interaction,* Chicago: Aldine, chap. II.

11. On social comparison processes, see J. Suls, R. Martin, & L. Wheeler (2002), Social comparison: Why, with whom, and with what effect? *Current Directions in Psychological Science,* 11, 159–163.

12. On the role of humor, see D. Johnson & F. Johnson (1987), *Joining Together: Group Theory and Group Skills,* Englewood Cliffs, NJ: Prentice-Hall, 439–443.

13. See Yeatts & Hyten, op. cit., pp. 142–156.

14. M. Deutsch (1975), Equity, equality, and need: What determines which value will be used as a basis of distributive justice? *Journal of Social Issues,* 31, 137–149; and M. Deutsch (1979), Education and distributive justice: Some reflections on grading systems, *American Psychologist,* 34, 391–401.

15. On the general role of reward and recognition, see Yeatts & Hyten, op. cit., chap. 14 and 15.

16. For more on different ways to reward, see Yeatts & Hyten, op. cit., chap. 15; also L. Thompson (2000), *Making the Team: A Guide for Managers,* Upper Saddle River, NJ: Prentice-Hall, pp. 35–43.

17. On equity or merit reward, see G. Homans (1961), *Social Behavior: Its Elementary Forms,* New York: Harcourt Brace.

18. For more on an individual's interpretation of receiving a smaller reward, see P. Diesing (1962), *Reason in Society,* Urbana: University of Illinois Press, cited in Johnson & Johnson, op. cit., p. 160.

19. On the merit system being competitive, see D. Levi (2001), *Group Dynamics for Teams,* Thousand Oaks, CA: Sage, pp. 70–82.

20. On the advantages and drawbacks of an equality system, see Yeatts & Hyten, op. cit., pp. 164–166.

21. On interdependence, see R. Wageman (1995), Interdependence and group effectiveness, *Administrative Science Quarterly*, 40, 145–180; and R. Wageman (2001), The meaning of interdependence, in M. E. Turner (Ed.), *Groups at Work*, Mahwah, NJ: Erlbaum, pp. 197–217.

22. On hybrid systems, see E. Lawler, S. Mohrman, & G. Ledford (1995), *Creating High Performance Organizations: Practices and Results of Employee Involvement and Total Quality Management in Fortune 1000 Companies.* San Francisco: Jossey-Bass.

23. On organizational rewards, see Levi, op. cit., pp. 319–320; Yeatts & Hyten, op. cit., pp. 166–171; and L. Thompson, op. cit., pp. 42–43.

24. On the role of recognition as a special reward, see Yeatts & Hyten, op. cit., pp. 157–159. Social comparison processes also play a role in this; see Suls et al., op. cit.

25. On the role of leadership, see R. Foels, J. Driskell, B. Mullen, & E. Salas (2000), The effects of democratic leadership in group member satisfaction, *Small Group Research*, 31, 676–701.

26. This type of peer evaluation was participated in by the author in a team building workshop conducted by David Miller Associates.

The Challenge

The Team in an Organizational Environment

A team operates within an organization that influences the team's functioning. This derives from the environment created primarily by the style of managing the organization. This environment influences how readily a team can develop working relationships, provide social support for its members, interpret organizational realities such as expectations, regulate performance-related behaviors, and provide members with a voice in organizational decisions. Relationships among teams in an organization can easily become conflicted due to differing priorities. Finding ways to resolve these conflicts is important for a team and for the organization. A variety of organizational barriers, such as communication difficulties and inadequate leadership, can also effect member commitment and team performance and must be addressed.

chapter 10

The Team in an Organizational Environment

Teams are small organizational systems set inside larger organizational systems and each influences the other. Football or basketball teams are part of and are supported by the academic institutions or communities of which they are a part. Emergency medical teams are part of larger, more complex medical service organizations, such as hospitals. A team manufacturing computer chips is part of a larger manufacturing organization. Consider the following examples:

Miguel, Eva, Betsy, Alice, and Bert are employees of a large supermarket owned by a national chain. Their job is to maintain the produce area of the store. Sam, their supervisor, has worked for the chain for four years in two different stores. Miguel, Betsy, and Bert have worked at the present store for two years and Eva and Alice have worked there for less than three months. Sam gives very specific instructions to each employee, indicating adjustments to displays, when and how to dispose of damaged produce, and when to replenish supplies. He is also strict about their talking while working, insisting that they talk only on their breaks. Breaks have become a problem recently. Betsy and Bert often return from breaks late and Sam reprimands them for it. The five employees resent the control, although they recognize that the store manager regularly tells Sam in a rather critical way about changes needed in the produce area. The five employees are not enthusiastic about their work.

Carla, Kevin, Roberta, Aneesha, and Tom are employees in the produce section of a different supermarket owned by a different chain. In their store, employees are organized in teams. Aneesha, the team leader, has worked in this market for two years. The others have worked there for less time. Each day before the team begins work, Aneesha leads a meeting to set objectives for the day, to discuss specific tasks by which to achieve the objectives, and to decide who will be responsible for them. Throughout the day, team members discuss ways to improve their original plan. Every two or three days, Jim, their supervisor, joins the meeting to discuss plans for special promotional activities and to listen to members' suggestions. Frequently, he compliments the team on their work. The team members are proud of their work and enjoy doing it.

These examples illustrate different **social environments.** The "atmosphere" associated with each environment reflects how employees relate to each other and to the organization's supervision.[1] The following discussion examines these issues.

AN ORGANIZATION'S SOCIAL ENVIRONMENT

A team system (described in Chapter 1) is open to its environment, which is the larger organization of which the team is a part. This means that it interacts with and is dependent on the organization. The organization specifies its goal, provides the resources (personnel, material, etc.) it needs to pursue the goal, and is the recipient of the team's product when it is completed. In the period between goal specification and goal accomplishment, the organization can also influence a team in different ways, some more supportive of a team's activities than others. An important feature of an organization is its *social environment,* sometimes referred to as its *social architecture*[2] or as its *culture.* This is created and maintained by an organization's leadership (including the team's leadership) who manage the activities of the organization.

> *"A traditional management strategy or style is to control employee activities in the interest of achieving efficiency."*

A traditional management strategy or style is to control employee activities in the interest of achieving efficiency. This strategy originated in large blue-collar and clerical organizations where large quantities of routine work needed to be done. Although management in a **control-oriented organization** welcomes employee commitment to its goals, the organization is designed to function adequately even if employee commitment is relatively low. As a consequence, control-oriented organizations have few means (other than by increasing effort) by which to improve organizational effectiveness.[3] In this style of management, work is divided into small, well-defined tasks that minimize the skill and judgment required. This keeps the training investment in individuals low and in turn minimizes the organization's dependence on specific individuals for specific tasks.

In control-oriented organizations, performance is managed by reference to explicit standards that define minimal acceptable performance levels and puts maximum pressure on the individual to meet standard expectations. Pay is based on individual performance or job classification, sometimes with added incentive compensation for above-standard performance. Individualized incentives are designed to induce workers to act in their own short-term interests and in ways that serve management's interests in the longer term.[4] Management prerogatives and positional authority are emphasized, consistent with the general strategy of top-down control. These organizations typically have many hierarchical levels, and status symbols reinforce hierarchical differences. Employees are expected to follow orders, not make suggestions. There are many rules to make sure people know what they are supposed to do, and formal sanctions are designed to ensure compliance.

"Employees are expected to follow orders, not make suggestions."

A contrasting management strategy is goal oriented and seeks to foster in employees commitment to the organization's goals. **Goal-oriented organizations** value competence, encourage interpersonal support for both technical and social activities, and create an atmosphere that encourages problem solving and continuous learning. This employee commitment model was explored initially in organizations with high levels of employee dissatisfaction, as indicated by worker absenteeism and disordered behavior.[5] Challenges from competing organizations resulted in efforts to increase employees' motivation and to improve utilization of their skills. Rising employee expectations for participation and fairness led managers to establish policies and practices to meet these expectations and simultaneously improve organizational effectiveness.

The commitment management model seeks to increase employee self-management and to achieve organizational effectiveness and efficiency.[6] The model was initiated most recently in high-technology engineering companies. Employees are expected to manage themselves to a considerable extent, making adjustments in what they do or how they do it when circumstances change. Self-managing teams, rather than individuals, are often accountable for performance. Rather than minimum standards of acceptable performance, **commitment-oriented organizations** set *stretch objectives* intended to motivate employees to seek the highest level of performance possible. These objectives emphasize continuous improvement and often change in response to changing market conditions.

"The commitment management model seeks to increase employee self-management and to achieve organizational effectiveness and efficiency."

Commitment organizations tend to be less hierarchical and offer relatively few management perks and status symbols. Employee ideas are actively sought to provide means for upward influence by rank-and-file organization members. Instead of rules, coordination and control are handled through shared philosophy, goals held in common, and group meetings of various kinds. Probably the most pervasive and powerful influence on employee compliance originates between coworkers.

One further reason for the shift from control to commitment models of management is that well-managed control organizations tend to reach a ceiling in their performance that is lower than that presumed to exist for commitment-based, teamwork-oriented organizations. Few commitment organizations achieve that potential, however. Most have a mix of control by management and of self-management by teams.

Does the trend from control to commitment strategies suggest that the latter is inherently more effective? Not necessarily. A well-managed control-oriented organization can easily outperform a poorly managed commitment-oriented organization. If a commitment-oriented strategy is to be successful, it requires a supportive organizational environment. What this means is discussed later in this chapter.

THE FUNCTIONS OF TEAMS IN ORGANIZATIONS

"Teams in organizations serve several important functions in addition to performing work-related tasks."

Teams in organizations serve several important functions in addition to performing work-related tasks. It is their ability to perform these functions that gives them power with respect to both individual members and the organization in which they perform. There is a need for these functions in any organization, whether they use the control or commitment types of management strategies. A team-based management strategy provides more latitude for these functions to be fulfilled, however.

Social Function

Individuals' needs for social relationships are universal and not easily set aside. Control-oriented organizations often seek to minimize their presence, although informal groups tend to develop anyway. Their function is to provide social support that helps employees to cope with restrictive policies. By instituting teams, commitment-oriented organizations enable **social support** to help members to deal with stress, responsibility, and the challenges that pervade most organizations.

"A good supervisor can provide emotional, informational, instrumental, and evaluative support."

Both supervisors and fellow workers can be sources of work-related support.[7] A good supervisor can provide emotional, informational, instrumental, and evaluative support. Individuals can be trained in these skills although broad organizational support for using and maintaining the skills is required for their continuance. Furthermore, a supervisor's ability to provide social support depends on the number of employees supervised, the nature of the supervisory task, and the relationships among supervised employees. A key attribute of a supportive organization is that each person is a member of one or more supportive, effective work teams. Coworker support reflects the supervisor's modeling of supportive behavior and use of participative, group-oriented methods of supervision.[8]

Interpretation of Reality

Teams help their members to create and interpret social reality. Any action can have a variety of interpretations. Inevitably, individuals turn to others in their work teams for help in making sense of what is going on. Teams transmit to their members the **social reality** of their organizational environment by making sure that all members comprehend "how things are here." Special attention is given to organizational expectations about what is (and is not) appropriate behavior at work, to determinations about what is fair and just, and to assessments of the intentions and competencies of management. Members can firm up their own self-perceptions by comparing their attitudes and behavior with those of other members.[9] Once an interpretation is established, members convey this meaning to others. This process provides employees with a sense of the organizational reality in which they work. This reality is often difficult to determine in new and often changing organizational environments.

These matters are close to the core of the difference between control-oriented and commitment-oriented organizations. In control organizations, major organizational policies assume a conflict of interest between managers and rank-and-file employees. In commitment organizations, policies send strong signals, suggesting an alignment of interests between the organization and its employees. In commitment organizations, teams provide a means to transmit and support core organizational values, to the benefit of both team members and the organization.

Internal Regulation

The **internal regulation** function involves generating and enforcing standards (norms) that govern member behavior. By regulating the workplace behavior of their members, teams provide social control that is both efficient and powerful.[10] It is efficient because regulators and those being regulated are in frequent and close contact and can address the special circumstances that may be affecting a member's behavior. Social control is powerful because peer approval or disapproval is a strong incentive for compliance.

"By regulating the workplace behavior of their members, teams provide social control that is both efficient and powerful."

In control organizations, the norms of self-enacted (informal) groups often run counter to management-specified rules and policies that members view as unfair or oppressive. In commitment organizations, norms provide readily available, powerful ways to direct the work of individuals toward achieving a common goal. Self-regulation within teams means that less supervision is needed. However, a committed team can influence its members' behavior more effectively than most supervisors can.

Agency and Voice

Teams amplify members' voices and provide them with a way to influence the organization's views and actions. When most members hold the same view on some matter, their collective voice can have greater impact than any individual can. When an expression of opinion is accompanied by group power, for example, by withholding cooperation, the team becomes especially effective in representing the interests of its members.

"Teams amplify members' voices and provide them with a way to influence the organization's views and actions."

Task Management

Another function of teams in organizations is coordinating resources to perform organizationally assigned tasks. Teams provide a means for concerted, coordinated action to accomplish the work of the organization. Teams can accomplish certain kinds of tasks more efficiently and effectively than individuals can, even when managers have carefully choreographed and supervised individual behavior.

RELATIONSHIPS AMONG TEAMS IN AN ORGANIZATION

"Coordination between teams is essential."

Within a larger organization, a team can be recognized by both its members and nonmembers. Teams are further distinguished by specific work tasks, by the technologies they use, and by their goals and values. If each team were producing its own product or service without reference to other teams, there would be little need for inter-team coordination. In organizations, however, teams produce specialized segments of the organization's product or service. Coordination between teams is essential.[11]

Coordination is necessary because each team depends on receiving resources from another team (or teams) to achieve its goal.[12] The degree of dependency depends on the availability of needed resources from other teams. For example, a marketing team is dependent on receiving its plan for a new product from the organization's new product design team. There is only one plan and the marketing team's success depends on receiving it. The design team has considerable power over the marketing team because it controls a scarce resource, the new product design. As a result the marketing team is under considerable pressure to coordinate closely with the design team.

Factors do exist, however, that inhibit such coordination. One factor is the presence of differences between teams. Teams are differentiated by task performed, by technology used in performing tasks, by goals, by reward systems, and by member characteristics.[13] For example, the design team just mentioned is made up of creative individuals who follow unusual work patterns. They wait for inspiration and then meet at odd hours of the day and night and even on weekends. This makes arranging meetings between representatives of the two teams difficult. Each tends to protect its "style," the one the more creative and less structured, the other the more structured and business-like. Because the marketing team is so dependent on the design team's plan, they might negotiate to adjust their schedule, agreeing to meet in the evenings, but not on weekends.

"Conflict among teams is frequent in organizations."

Conflict among teams is frequent in organizations. It occurs when two interdependent teams disagree about one or more aspects of their relationship. Scarce resources can intensify the conflict, whereas excess resources (say, when multiple teams produce the same resource) can reduce conflict. It is often the case that the scarcity of resources cannot be changed. When conflict occurs, efforts at resolution take place among individuals (leaders or appointed representatives) who represent the teams. Several possible **conflict resolution** strategies are discussed next.

One model (*hierarchical decisions*) calls for the teams to appeal to a common superior,[14] that is, someone more senior in the organization's hierarchy. Doing this can, however, overload the hierarchy, especially in organizations undergoing change or when decision making is centralized with top management. Overloaded hierarchies are slow to respond to situations that require quick decisions. Decisions from this model can also be of poor quality in the sense that they do not support or facilitate interteam coordination.

Hierarchical decisions may be poor for other reasons as well. Hierarchical leaders may understand the organization's goals but lack detailed knowledge and understanding of each team's goals and how these relate to the matter in conflict. Hierarchical managers, either because they are already overloaded or because they perceive their role in conflict management as making decisions, fail to investigate conflict issues thoroughly.[15] They ask what they perceive to be relevant questions, then impose what they perceive to be a solution. This approach can result in inadequate decisions and create dependency on the superior that limits a team's ability to deal with future conflict.

Other conflict resolution models[16] have been proposed as better than hierarchical decisions. In one model (*the manager as judge*), a supervisor or manager acts as judge and requires each team to make a presentation outlining its position, interests, and potential settlements. This enables the manager to become better informed about both teams' positions and as a result to make a better decision. It can, however, result in imposing a settlement that neither side is committed to upholding.

In a second model (*manager as mediator*), the manager mediates to an agreement between conflicting teams. Relevant techniques include (1) getting the team representatives to identify their own team's and the other team's interests with respect to the issues in contention, (2) getting the teams to generate proposals that meet some of each team's interests, and (3) suggesting that a particular proposal be tried on an experimental basis.[17]

A third model (*direct lateral negotiation*) is presumed to be effective in high-conflict situations in which disputing parties are also highly interdependent.[18] It also assumes that disputing parties can learn negotiating skills, but there is mixed evidence to support this. In this strategy, the manager pushes the conflict back to the contending teams, refusing to resolve the conflict but instead making it clear to team representatives that they are the best ones to resolve the matter and must do so.

The effectiveness of this approach depends on the group representatives' **negotiation** skills. Direct lateral negotiation may be particularly difficult when power is unequally distributed between teams. For example, the design team, described earlier, possesses more power (they "own" the design) than the marketing team. The more powerful team may force an unequal settlement that does not survive. There is also the possibility that teams may negotiate exchanges that are optimal for them but distinctly suboptimal for the organization as a whole.[19] Teams in organizations seldom have the formal authority necessary to successfully formalize a negotiation. Without means to reward successful interteam coordination, conflict resolution by direct lateral negotiations can be difficult to achieve.

> *"Direct lateral negotiation may be particularly difficult when power is unequally distributed between teams."*

A problem-solving model is an alternative in such situations. This type of negotiation uses five steps.[20] First, focus on interests, not positions, anticipating that the conflict is likely to concern interteam coordination issues. Second, distinguish the people from the problem and think through the reasons underlying the conflicting positions. Consider possible hidden agendas (underlying reasons) called "interests." Third, invent options that represent gains for both sides. Fourth, invent objective criteria to indicate accomplishment of the options. Finally, identify the best alternative to a negotiated agreement. Consider what will happen if no settlement is reached. Will the status quo remain? Will the conflict escalate? This analysis is really an assessment of each team's power. The search is for areas of likely agreement and for alternative settlements that maximize both of the teams' interests, regardless of their original positions. A problem-solving negotiation should be a serious joint attempt to reach a mutually beneficial settlement.

Which of these models is best? The answer depends on the cost (efficiency) and the durability (quality) of solutions generated by each approach. Results depend on the skills of the parties, the power distribution between groups, and the organization's culture. The mediation and judicial models may be superior to the hierarchical decision model because they generate higher quality exchanges. When parties are not skilled negotiators, third-party modes of dispute resolution may be more effective than direct lateral negotiation, especially when one team has more power than another. When negotiation skills are more developed and power differentials are small, lateral negotiation may be effective. This model may result in solutions that are optimal for the two groups but are suboptimal for the organization as a whole.

Negotiation by problem solving can be effective when teams are committed to reaching a solution and when negotiation skills are reasonably developed. This approach may prove to be especially useful in dynamic organizations. Teams in these organizations will have to negotiate more frequently and their solutions will be less enduring than those of groups in organizations characterized by stable environments. When evaluating the effectiveness of a resolution to an interteam conflict, it is essential that the rate of organizational change be considered.

ORGANIZATIONAL BARRIERS TO EFFECTIVE TEAMWORK

Organizations, having chosen team-based management, can still experience a variety of barriers to effective teamwork.[21] The following are frequently described.

Communication Difficulties

Communication, more than any other single issue, is noted as a potential barrier. This is revealed in several ways.

Communication of expectations poses problems at all levels, management to employees, and team leaders to team members. There is a need for a clear and unequivocal expression of expectations by those whose role it is to formulate them. For example, there may be a need for clearer job definitions or clearer statements of who is responsible for a specific problem. Related to this is the need for an unequivocal strategy for tracking the accomplishment of those expectations. Although it might seem that a clear statement would be enough, in fact, obtaining feedback about the accomplishment of expectations often helps to clarify them.

Some employees see management as unclear about the organization's *vision*. It is out of focus and difficult to relate to team goals. Vision refers to where or to what end the process in which the team is involved is headed. If the vision is clear, forward looking, and realistic in a business sense, it inspires workers to expend effort to achieve it. It is important that each team and each team member have a clear sense of the organization's vision and their role in achieving it.

How frequently *top management interacts with employees* is a related issue. The periodic presence of upper management in different work areas makes management real and less distant, manifests a concern for and valuation of the work teams are performing, and lends credibility to values statements which claim that people are first. Put another way, it shortens the perceived distance between the work areas and executive offices. Even after layers of middle management are removed, that distance can still be considerable.

Team meetings are a time when team members address and agree on a variety of issues. Meetings often are felt to be too short, to occur irregularly, to be unproductive, and to have unclear objectives. In one setting, meetings were changed from being held at a set time to being held whenever a crisis arose. This focus on resolving crises and disputes can resolve one set of problems, but allows little time for planning and for identifying ways to improve performance. Some managers also worried that if more time were allotted for team meetings, the time might not be used productively. Learning how to run productive meetings is essential. Such meetings result from a small number of team members identifying important meeting objectives beforehand and having a leader who can maintain the team's focus and lead effective problem solving and decision making to achieve the objectives.

Failure to Understand Interrelationships

Team members' failure to understand how their own performance relates to and affects the performance of other team members, the performance of the team as a whole, and the performance of the entire organization is often cited as a problem. Managers who note this with reference to employees indicate that workers tend not to see beyond their own immediate jobs to the overall performance of the plant, nor do they understand how their performance has implications for the plant's performance. This includes team members lacking a clear image of how their work makes the organization's product or service

"There is a need for a clear and unequivocal expression of expectations by those whose role it is to formulate them."

"If the vision is clear, forward looking, and realistic in a business sense, it inspires workers to expend effort to achieve it."

> *"Perceiving their stake in accomplishing the organization's vision and participating in the rewards of that accomplishment can be a powerful motivator."*

> *"A customer may be another team, a supervisor, the organization's management, or a group external to the organization."*

possible. It means, for example, learning enough about a car or truck to understand how the electronic control system a team produces contributes to the vehicle's operation. Perceiving their stake in accomplishing the organization's vision and participating in the rewards of that accomplishment can be a powerful motivator.

Several years ago the Boeing Company, as a final stage in winning approval for their B777, had to demonstrate the point at which the wings would fail (i.e., break). The test was conducted in a large construction hanger with the several hundred employees who worked on the plane present to witness the test. The wings were stressed (i.e., bent) to a point where they broke. This point was, however, considerably beyond the point required for safety in a powerful storm. Not only did the workers understand more about the company's vision for safe travel, but they also shared in the pride of a superior accomplishment to which they had contributed.[22]

Focusing on a team's *customer* also helps team members to understand interrelationships. A team's customer is the recipient of the team's product. A customer may be another team, a supervisor, the organization's management, or a group external to the organization. Putting emphasis on a team's customer is a strategy for getting workers to broaden their views from simply doing their own, segmented task to understanding how their task links to the work of others and to the eventual recipient of the product of which their work is a part.

Failure to Gain Employee Commitment

Commitment is the willingness to expend effort and to persevere in working toward a goal and its associated vision, even in the face of difficulties. Commitment develops, fails to develop, or deteriorates, according to the employees, for one or a combination of reasons.

The *inequitable treatment of workers* is a concern. Team members and managers alike note that failing to sanction unacceptable behavior undercuts motivation. Particularly difficult are nonperformers who simply "don't care." For employees, a lack of caring is revealed by those who, for example, fail to return from breaks on time. Team members resent other members who do not work as hard as they do. Managers resent other managers who fail to address unacceptable behaviors of team members they supervise. Some team managers note another source of inequity—that of repeatedly calling on willing workers to do tasks that others are supposed to do. The willing workers do what they are asked to do, but resent taking up the slack created by less willing workers.[23]

The *reward and recognition system*, discussed in Chapter 9, can either enhance or detract from team members' commitment. The most effective reward system is likely to be a combination of team rewards and individual recognition. Inequities occur when a team leader takes the credit for a team's work or a more talented team member receives all of the recognition while team members who do most of the work receive none.

Peer influence or peer pressure can also affect commitment and influence performance. This occurs when team members encourage each other to achieve higher levels of performance. It can also serve to reduce performance, as occurs when some team members pressure other team members to moderate their efforts so as not to create higher standards for their performance. This is a situation in which employee commitment goes to a certain point but no farther. At the root of this resistance to higher performance is a fear of being exploited that must be addressed by all involved.[24]

Change characterizes many organizations. A team changes because its environment changes. An effective team also changes in the process of improving its performance. Team members enhance existing capabilities, develop new ones, and make other changes to improve performance. One reason companies encourage teamwork is to allow its teams to identify, within this changing context, the best way to perform its work. This gives team members control over the changes they make.[25] When a team has control over selecting and implementing strategies for achieving its goal, it must also have a sense that it can successfully carry out the strategies. This sense arises from having relevant capabilities and from having leadership that supports and facilitates the team's activities.

There are other changes a team has less control over. One is "churning" of team members. When reductions in a workforce are necessary, more senior employees may opt for positions opened by the downsizing. A result can be not only the loss of some team members, but also shifting of others to fill vacant openings. Leadership also changes but for different reasons. Team managers are often relatively young employees who aspire to management positions. Their goal is often to move up as quickly as possible into the ranks of management. Thus, good team managers move readily and team members experience destabilization.

In spite of the pervasiveness of changes in organizations, some members and even whole teams may resist changes largely because they fear a lack of control. Some feel that they have worked hard to maintain a "system" and now are being told that it must be changed. They may feel betrayed. This can be especially difficult if changes are presented as being "for the good of the organization." Some will see maintaining the "system" as making better sense and will therefore experience reduced commitment to the changed organization.

> *"The most effective reward system is likely to be a combination of team rewards and individual recognition."*

> *"Team managers are often relatively young employees who aspire to management positions."*

Leadership Inadequacies

The *leadership role* can be problematic in several ways. In organizations where the idea of working in teams is new, questions are likely to come up about whether team leadership is one person's responsibility or a responsibility to be shared and rotated. There are also questions about the amount of responsibility managers (or supervisors) and team leaders have. Ideally, as a team leader gains experience and can take more responsibility, a team's manager will have less responsibility. There are also questions about leadership style. Do leaders give orders, suggest, facilitate, or coach? An organization must address these issues for its leadership to be effective.

A *divided management perspective on teamwork* is another barrier to employee commitment. Some managers might question whether teamwork can improve employee performance, whereas others strongly support teamwork. This split opinion creates several problems for team members. First, awareness that managers are divided raises doubts in team members about the strategy and undermines learning in a situation that requires commitment to the strategy and learning new ways to perform. Second, when team managers change responsibilities, team members must change styles to meet managers' views about the ability of teams. This creates disruption and can even lower morale. Third, relationships between teams in the same organization become difficult because of different managers' perspectives on the effectiveness of teams. For example, decisions made in one team must be referred to the manager of another who may not agree. In essence, managers need to be moving in a singular direction to give credibility to the expectation that workers develop competencies and apply them as team members.

"This "do as I say, not as I do" message inhibits effective teamwork."

A related issue arises with executives who expect the organization's lower level employees to work effectively in teams but cannot themselves work with other executives as a team. This "do as I say, not as I do" message inhibits effective teamwork.

Management's distrust and lack of respect for workers is also considered a barrier to effective teamwork. In some instances, this is traceable to suspicion between management and an employees' union. In other instances, it is individualized. In either case distrust and lack of respect in a team's environment can undercut the objective of having a team take increased responsibility for the work it does and performing that work effectively.

Insufficient Education/Training

Lack of education and training is also cited as a barrier to effective team functioning. Adequate procedures are needed for giving additional training to workers who do not do well. Adequate procedures are also needed for assessing leaders' and manager-leaders' skills and for providing further training. Criteria for identifying potential leaders are also needed. Questions about how a team's leader is to be chosen need to be answered. Should the choice be made by team vote or by who volunteers, or should management appoint the leader? This issue must be addressed to the satisfaction of team members for a leader to be effective. Finally, a general leadership training program for all is needed with specific training for those who show the greatest potential for leadership.

The Challenge Revisited
The Team in an Organizational Environment

1. A team's relationship to the organization in which it operates is influenced by the quality of the organizational environment.

2. A supportive organizational environment encourages a team to develop close working relationships among its members and to regulate member behavior in the interests of achieving the team's goal.

3. A supportive environment communicates clear expectations for a team and, when those expectations are met, recognizes and rewards the accomplishment.

4. A supportive organizational environment facilitates productive working relationships among different teams in an organization.

5. An organization can create barriers to effective team functioning through unclear communication by the organization's leadership, through leadership that is ambivalent about team-based management, and through failure to gain team commitment to organizational goals.

EXERCISE 10.1 • *Barriers to High Performance*

1. As a team, identify the most significant barrier(s) to high performance that originate in the organizational environment in which your team is performing.

2. List and discuss the barrier(s) and identify ways to reduce or resolve it/them.

3. Develop a short report on your team's deliberations.

EXERCISE 10.2 • *Selecting a President of Bewise College*[26]

The purpose of this exercise is to see how relevant information is shared within a team and to explore how this affects team problem solving. The materials to be used in the exercise are a briefing and data sheet and a candidate summary sheet. The exercise takes approximately an hour.

1. Assign each team member a briefing and data sheet number, either I, II, III, IV, or V. Then without reading the briefs assigned to others, retrieve and read your assigned brief pages 243–247.

2. Begin deliberating to choose the correct president for Bewise College based on the briefs provided. There is one correct solution to the problem. No collusion is allowed. Teams must reach their solutions independent of other teams.

3. Consult the candidate summary sheet page 248 as required.

4. Keep a record of the time required to reach a decision. A decision must be reached before the one-hour time limit expires.

5. Be prepared to discuss your experience by having one member keep notes of the discussion. Consider the following questions:

    a. *Communication:* Who spoke? Who did not speak? Why the difference? How do members feel about the amount of communication? How well did members listen to each other? Would wider participation have helped to improve the process?

    b. *Information:* Was the needed information available to each member? Was the needed information readily available to other members? If yes, why? If no, why not? Were conditions in the sessions such that information could be readily shared? What would have improved conditions for sharing?

    c. *Problem solving:* How effective was the team's problem solving and decision making? Were there barriers to high performance in these processes? How might the team's problem solving be improved?

6. When the teams meet as a whole to discuss their experiences, be prepared to examine the similarities and differences among teams. Why might some teams have reached a decision sooner than others?

QUESTIONS FOR REVIEW AND DISCUSSION

1. What is the relationship of a team to the organization of which the team is a part? What are the implications of the team being "open" to its organizational environment?

2. How is an organization's social environment created? Describe three different management styles and the social environment each creates.

3. With reference to its organization, what are the functions a team can perform? Why is each function important for the organization?

4. Why are the relationships between teams in an organization important? Why is conflict among such teams a frequent occurrence?

5. What are the different strategies for resolving conflicts between teams? What are the strengths and weaknesses of each strategy?

6. Which model (or strategy) of interteam conflict resolution is best? How does a team or a team's supervisor select a strategy?

7. Communication difficulties between the organization and the team are often a barrier to effective teamwork in the organization. What are the contexts or sources of these difficulties? How can they be addressed?

8. How do team members' (or employees' generally) failure to understand the relationship between their activities and the performance of the organization create a barrier to high performance? What strategies can be used to remove this barrier?

9. Why does employee commitment develop, fail to develop, or deteriorate? How can each of these reasons be addressed in a way that enhances commitment?

10. What are the reasons for leadership inadequacy as it relates to teams in organizations? How can each of these inadequacies be addressed?

NOTES

1. See C. Fishman (1996, April/May), Whole Foods is all teams, *Fast Company,* pp. 103ff, for a description of teams in a retail company.

2. Social architecture is discussed in Chapter 6 and in W. Bennis & B. Nanus (1985), *Leaders: The Strategies for Taking Charge,* New York: Harper & Row, pp. 110–111.

3. See H. Leonard & A. Freedman (2000), From scientific management through fun and games to high-performing teams: A historical perspective on consulting in team-based organization, *Consulting Psychology Journal,* 52, 3–19.

4. This style of scientific management is often attributed to F. W. Taylor; see R. Kanigel (1997), *The One Best Way: Frederick Winslow Taylor and the Enigma of Efficiency,* New York: Viking.

5. L. Ketchum & E. Trist (1992), *All Teams Are Not Created Equal,* Thousand Oaks, CA: Sage.

6. R. E. Walton (1980), Establishing and maintaining high commitment work systems, in J. R. Kimberly, R. H. Miles, and Associates (Eds.), *The Organizational Life Cycle: Issues in the Creation, Transformation, and Decline of Organizations,* San Francisco: Jossey-Bass.

7. As used here the term *supervisor* (or *manager*) refers to a person who is not a member of a team but is in the management hierarchy to whom the team reports. *Team leader* refers to a team member who is the chosen or appointed leader.

8. R. Likert (1961), *New Patterns of Management,* New York: McGraw-Hill.

9. See J. Suls, R. Martin, & L. Wheeler (2002), Social comparison: Why, with whom, and with what effect? *Current Directions in Psychological Science,* 11, 159–163.

10. R. Hackman (1983), Group influences on individuals, in M. Dunnett (Ed.), *Handbook of Industrial and Organizational Psychology,* Chicago: Rand-McNally.

11. The discussion of relationships between groups in organizations is summarized from J. Brett & J. Rognes (1986), Intergroup relations in organizations, in P. S. Goodman and Associates (Eds.), *Designing Effective Work Groups,* San Francisco: Jossey-Bass.

12. M. Aiken & J. Hage (1968), Organizational independence and intra-organizational structure, *American Sociological Review*, 33, 912–930; also R. Emerson (1962), Power dependence relations, *American Sociological Review*, 27, 31–41.

13. P. Lawrence and J. Lorsch (1967), *Organization and Environment*, Boston: Graduate School of Business Administration, Harvard University; and J. March & H. Simon (1958), *Organizations*, New York: Wiley.

14. J. McCann & J. Galbraith (1981), Interdepartmental relations, in P. C. Nystrom & W. H. Starbuck (Eds.), *Handbook of Organizational Design*, New York: Oxford University Press.

15. B. Sheppard (1983), Managers as inquisitors: Some lessons from the law, in M. H. Bazerman & R. J. Lewicki (Eds.), *Negotiating in Organizations*, Beverly Hills, CA: Sage.

16. Brett & Rognes, op. cit.

17. See P. Carnevale (1986), Strategic choices by third parties: A theory of dispute resolution, in R. J. Lewicki, B. H. Sheppard, and M. H. Bazerman (Eds.), *Research on Negotiations in Organizations*, Greenwich, CT: JAI Press; also D. Shapiro, R. Drieghe, and J. Brett (1985), Mediator behavior and the outcome of mediation, *Journal of Social Issues*, 41, 101–114.

18. See J. Brett & S. Goldberg (1983), Wildcat strikes in the bituminous coal mining industry, *Industrial and Labor Relations Review*, 32, 467–483.

19. J. Hage (1983), Communication and coordination, in S. M. Shortell & A. K. Kalunzy (Eds.), *Health Care Management*, New York: Wiley.

20. Steps described in R. Fisher & W. Ury (1981), *Getting to Yes*, New York: Penguin.

21. The author conducted a series of interviews during 1996–1997 in companies using team-based management to identify barriers to effective teamwork. Employees ranging from plant managers to hourly assembly-line workers were surveyed. Although responses varied, they could be grouped in a limited set of broad categories.

22. Public Television presentation of the testing of the B777.

23. Social loafing has been studied extensively. See D. Johnson & F. Johnson (1987), *Joining Together: Group Theory and Group Skills*, Englewood Cliffs, NJ: Prentice Hall, p. 401. See also B. Latane, K. Williams, & S. Harkins (1979), Many hands make light the work: The causes and consequences of social loafing, *Journal of Personality and Social Psychology*, 37, 822–832.

24. A classic description of pressure to maintain a group established standard is the Bank Wiring Room; see G. Homans (1958), Group factors in worker productivity in E. Maccoby, T. Newcomb, & E. Hartley (Eds.), *Readings in Social Psychology*, New York: Holt, Rinehart and Winston, pp. 583–595.

25. The stress created by change has long been studied; see D. Glass & J. Singer (1972), *Urban Stress*, New York: Academic Press.

26. Adapted from Johnson & Johnson, op. cit., pp. 182–188, 465. Used with permission.

The Challenge
Evaluating Products and Processes

A team depends on its evaluation process to keep it informed about progress toward its goal, about the functioning of its throughput subprocesses as it proceeds, and about how well its product meets the standards set for it. It is important, as part of the team's planning process, to specify the criteria by which to determine progress, subprocess functioning, and product status and quality. Examining a member's own and the member's team performance can be difficult. It requires putting aside defensiveness about inadequacies and devising a strategy for improvement that is both effective and efficient and applying that strategy with consistency and perseverance.

chapter 11

Evaluating Products and Processes

EVALUATION

An important team activity is evaluating its product and the performance that produces the product. Although some type of **evaluation** exists for all teams, its form can vary widely. For pick-up basketball teams, most team members will keep track of the score "in their head" and differences can arise over whose memory is correct. More formal athletic events involve scorekeepers and a scoreboard to keep track of each team's goal achievement and one or more referees to ensure that each team plays (performs) by the rules, assessing penalties if they do not. There is, in other words, a dual evaluation. One is keeping track of the team goals, that is, the team product. The other is keeping track of the quality of team functioning. For football, this latter is reflected in yards gained, passes completed, and the number of penalties (defects).

In nonathletic settings, such as businesses, human services, and academic organizations, team activities are also evaluated. A team's product may be evaluated in terms of the number of sales made, the number of clients served, or the number of students taught. Quality and timeliness may also be assessed. A team's performance process is reflected in the quality of its planning, the ease of its communication, and the coordination of its activities. Evaluating a team's performance process enables it to produce more of a better product. The following illustrates the role of evaluation.

Earle, Jane, Sam, Beatrice, and Melody are the customer service team for a large manufacturing company. Their responsibility is to follow up on product returns under warranty and to determine the reason for the return. They obtain two types of information: why the customer was dissatisfied and what defects existed in the product. Recently, they discovered that some customers who had returned a product had received calls from two team members. Some of these customers were upset at the double inquiry, and the team was concerned that they were not using their resources efficiently. At a team meeting, Beatrice proposed a review of their tracking process to reduce duplication. Better coordination among team members was needed.

This team is conducting evaluation on three levels. First, the team is the evaluation unit for its organization. Its product enables the organization to adjust its manufacturing processes to reduce the number of defective products and, as a result, to improve customer satisfaction. Second, the team's goal is to produce clear analyses of reasons for the returns. The number and quality of these analyses represent the team's product. On a third level, the team evaluates its own performance to determine whether improvements are needed. This team has discovered through its evaluation that duplication of effort has occurred. Improved coordination will remove the duplication, making the team more efficient, remove the added customer dissatisfaction, and increase the number of analyses the team produces. This will provide the organization with more information on which to base its decisions.

"Feedback is a team's guidance system."

Evaluation results, or **feedback** as they are sometimes called, enable a team to assess the quality of its product when its goal is reached and to assess the process by which it proceeds toward its goal. Feedback is a team's guidance system. When a team's progress is below a desired standard, evaluation assists a team to identify barriers to improvement. When a barrier is identified, a team can use its problem-solving skills to define and implement a solution.

Evaluation enables a team to take responsibility for its activities in a manner that only those closest to the work can do. It reflects a team's strong commitment to achieving its goal and fulfilling its vision. Taking steps to improve its performance reflects a team's desire to become accountable for its own activities. This means that rather than waiting for others (e.g., a supervisor) to identify shortcomings, the team actively seeks to identify inadequacies and barriers and acts to remedy them in the interests of improved performance.

Evaluation is the responsibility of all team members; however, a team's leader is responsible for initiating the evaluation process and guiding the problem-solving activity when barriers are identified. In the excitement and sometimes in the tedium of team performance it can be easy to put off or overlook evaluation. It is the team leader's responsibility to insist on the added effort needed to evaluate what has been completed and seek to identify ways to improve the team's performance process and the quality of its product.

Mapping the Teamwork System

Evaluation encompasses each phase of the teamwork system process, that is, *input, throughput,* and *output*[1]. Evaluation determines if inputs are adequate or need to be adjusted to achieve the goal. Goals cannot be met if relevant inputs are not available. In the throughput phase, evaluation assesses the functioning of each subprocess to determine how well it is performing. If a subprocess is performing below standard, it is not contributing to goal achievement as it might. Evaluation also examines outputs to determine if they meet expectations. If outputs are not up to standard, relevant evaluation results can help to identify an explanation. Having identified a potential explanation for inadequate outputs, the objective is to improve the substandard process(es) or subprocess(es). Team system subprocesses are depicted in Table 11.1.[2]

"Goals cannot be met if relevant inputs are not available."

The following discussion examines the performance of a team's system from several perspectives. One is to define and make operational the **evaluation criteria** for the different team subsystems (listed in Table 11.1). The second is to apply the criteria to the team's *performance process.* How well does the team progress from input to throughput to output? The third is to ask "How do the subsystems *influence a team's progress and output?*" Are there points at which performance can be improved and, if so, how?

Developing and Using Evaluation Criteria

Team evaluation involves identifying criteria that reflect some aspect of a team's performance. For example, communication is related to coordination. Are team members sharing (or being

"Team evaluation involves identifying criteria that reflect some aspect of a team's performance."

TABLE 11.1
Team System Subprocesses

Input	Process Throughput	Output
Goals/vision/values	Planning/communication	Products
Skills/styles	Leading	Development and learning
	Performing	Effectiveness
	Coordinating and structuring	
	Satisfying	
	Relating to organization	
	Evaluating	

provided) relevant information? The coordination problem experienced by the customer service team discussed earlier may require them to develop a better method for keeping each other informed about which customers have been contacted.

Gathering relevant information involves developing procedures by which to obtain the needed information accurately, systematically, and efficiently. For example, if our customer service team were to establish an electronic customer complaint list, would members use it to coordinate their calls to customers? When they use it, does coordination improve (i.e., are fewer duplicate calls made)? Furthermore, if coordination improves, will the team's overall performance improve? **Improvement** is measured as both reduced customer dissatisfaction from duplicate calls and an increase in the total number of follow-up contacts made.

Evaluation is an iterative process. This means that a team defines or *sets an objective*. It then *plans a strategy* to achieve the objective. This often involves problem solving. Next, it *executes the strategy* that *produces a result*. This *result is evaluated* to determine how well it meets the objective. If the objective is met, the team moves on to the next objective (or step) in the process. If it is not met, the process is repeated, using what has been learned to make appropriate adjustments.

For example, the customer service team has the objective of reducing duplicate customer calls. They decide to use a pencil-and-paper list to keep track of calls (their plan). They use such a list for two weeks (they execute). This results in a level of duplicate calls (result) that is lower than before, but still unacceptably high (they evaluate). They repeat the cycle. In discussions among themselves, the team learns that the paper list is difficult to pass back and forth between their cubicles. They decide to develop an electronic system. When it is in place, they repeat the evaluation process and find that the number of duplications is zero. They consider the objective met. Figure 11.1 depicts this process.

EVALUATION TASKS

The evaluation task is to develop objective criteria that specify the level of functioning of each subsystem of a team's system. Developing such criteria is

FIGURE 1 1 . 1
Evaluating for High Performance

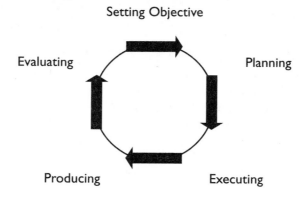

Setting Objective

Evaluating

Planning

Producing

Executing

referred to as *making the subsystem operational,* that is, developing one or more objective criteria that reflect the subsystems' level of performance. These criteria, in addition to providing information about level of performance, also guide efforts to improve performance. This latter is accomplished by focusing team problem solving on identifying and removing barriers that reduce a team's level of performance. Evaluation of these subsystems can be examined under several broad headings.

Making a Team's Goal, Vision, and Values Operational

Evaluation translates the image of successful goal achievement into objective terms. For example, for a team with a goal of raising funds for college scholarships, the criterion of success is to raise $600,000. This criterion translates an abstraction, raising scholarship funds, into a specific, concrete state. This criterion enables a team to judge its current performance relative to its goal. Another example of a criterion could be for a manufacturing team to produce 60 units per hour with fewer than 6 defects per 1000 units. This specifies both quantity and quality levels.

"Evaluation translates the image of successful goal achievement into objective terms."

A goal for a planning team could be to develop an innovative strategy for launching a new product. The criteria for judging the outcome involve first, that the team provide a coherent strategy and, second, that the strategy be innovative. These criteria are less objective than the manufacturing team criteria and require that the team develop more precise indicators of "coherent" and "innovative." To develop both would require one or more team members who are versed in existing strategies for launching a new product. Once specified, each can be further subjected to the criterion development process depicted in Figure 11.1.

Criteria, such as being "best," selling the most, or making the highest grade are inadequate for two reasons. First, a team does not control the criterion. Being best depends on the performance of other teams or individuals. Second, who reaches the criterion cannot be determined until the conclusion of a game or other performance cycle. Consequently, determining during the performance process whether improvement is needed is difficult to do before the goal is reached. An adequate criterion is one that is objective and indicates a team's status at any time in the performance process. For example, in a journalism class a team's report on a current event is not only on time and of the prescribed length, but is accurate, well written, and engaging to the reader. If team members have sufficient expertise, each of these characteristics can be judged, even before the report is submitted.

An operational goal enables a team to know where it is relative to its goal. Some teams may prefer to avoid what they perceive to be added pressure imposed by knowing where they are relative to their goal. A realistic appraisal of the team's current level of performance provides greater assurance that the team's goal and the associated vision will be achieved. Commitment to achieving that goal makes a team's understanding where it is relative to its goal crucial.

"An operational goal enables a team to know where it is relative to its goal."

Making the Steps to Achieve the Goal Operational

Evaluation also addresses the steps by which a team's goal is achieved. These steps are determined during a team's planning activity (see Chapter 5). The role of evaluation is to specify what represents the accomplishment of each step. For example, the plan of a team seeking to raise money for scholarships includes several steps: to develop a rationale that presents the need for the scholarships, to develop a list of potential donors, to present the rationale to the donors, and to solicit their financial support.

"The evaluation process clarifies the steps to the goal and monitors their accomplishment."

The evaluation process clarifies the steps to the goal and monitors their accomplishment. Members can have different views of what accomplishing the different steps will mean, so specifying the criteria by which to judge their accomplishment, including quality standards for each, makes it possible to identify any differences in members' expectations. Making explicit the criteria for both goal achievement and the steps needed to achieve it enables members to develop clear, mutual expectations about the process.

The desired result of this process is for team members to develop the same mental image or cognitive map of where the team is going and the steps required to get there.[3] To use the scholarship fund-raising example again, members need to agree on how polished the rationale for raising the funds is to be, what the size and characteristics of the donor list are to be, and how the solicitation is to be conducted. Furthermore, team members should reach agreement about whether each step is in accord with the team's core values. Criteria indicate specifically what will be done. For example, if a team's plan for raising scholarship funds calls for a part of the rationale to include negative statements about other institutions, it would be seen as contrary to the team's expressed value of not promoting its efforts at the expense of other institutions. This would not conform to the team's core values and would need to be changed.

Making Progress Operational

Evaluation also monitors a team's progress toward its goal. This can be viewed from two perspectives. One is to determine how much progress has occurred from the starting point, and the other is to determine the distance yet to be covered to reach the goal. For the fund-raising team, the amount raised at any point in time represents its progress. If it has raised $200,000, it is one-third of the way toward its goal of $600,000. A second perspective is to determine, at a particular point in time, which steps have been accomplished and which remain to be completed. Completed steps represent progress. After a period of time, if no steps have been completed, the team's performance should be examined.

Making Inputs Operational

Evaluation establishes criteria to indicate both the resources a team has available to reach its goal and the resources that will be needed. For example, the team planning to raise money for scholarships must have personnel skilled in developing polished presentations, in developing and maintaining a list of potential donors, and in making engaging personal solicitations. Lacking any one of these can jeopardize the team's success. Two broad types of inputs are to be evaluated: a team's goal, vision, and values and its members' skills and behavior styles. The first of these, a team's goal, has already been examined. The other two are interrelated. Skills and styles have to do with the human resources a team has available.[4] Planning both specifies the skills that a team will need and lays out the path for their use.

Skills and Behavior Styles.   When a team's goal is made operational and the steps required to accomplish the goal specified, the skills needed by a team to accomplish the steps to its goal can be identified. This makes it possible to determine whether the skills available among a team's members are adequate to complete the steps. For experienced teams, matching available member skills to team tasks may be relatively easy. For less experienced teams, this matching process may be more difficult. Members may not recognize the relevance of their skills to performance of the team's tasks.

A student team, for example, is to develop a plan for revitalizing a one-block area of a local neighborhood. The team conceives of the plan in three steps. One is to identify relevant issues or dimensions for consideration (step 1). A second is to develop an up-to-date status report on the current status of each issue (step 2). The third is to develop a proposal for future action pertaining to each issue (step 3). Their problem is how to allocate their resources. They decide that they will need all available resources (i.e., all team members) to identify relevant issues. This will be a brainstorming and decision-making process. When the list of issues is decided, the team will assign members singly or in subgroups to take the remaining two steps for each issue specified in step 1. For each step, evaluation criteria are needed to make clear what represents a completed step at the desired level of quality.

Evaluating Throughput Subprocesses

Evaluation specifies criteria that indicate the status of each throughput subprocess. These criteria enable a team to understand which subprocesses are contributing to and which are detracting from the team's progress. The following considers criteria related to each of the throughput subprocesses outline in Table 11.1.

Planning and Communicating.   Evaluating the planning process involves two considerations. One is how well the steps a team takes conform to the steps it has laid out in its plan. One reason a team does not make progress toward its goal or, more narrowly, cannot complete one or more steps, is that it does not follow its plan. The evaluation procedure in this instance is to compare what the team is doing (or has done) to what its plan said it would do. A team that finds

"Planning both specifies the skills that a team will need and lays out the path for their use."

"For experienced teams, matching available member skills to team tasks may be relatively easy."

"Evaluation specifies criteria that indicate the status of each throughput subprocess."

"Reasons for the deviation may be the plan's lack of clarity at one or more points."

it has strayed from its plan should revisit its plan. Reasons for the deviation may be the plan's lack of clarity at one or more points. Team members may have different views of what the plan specifies. Some members may even feel that the plan is too restrictive. Team members must follow the team's plan and adjustments must be made, if necessary, to enable them to do so.

The second consideration for planning is the adequacy of the plan. If a team is following its plan and making progress, there is generally no reason to reconsider it. If, however, a team is following its plan and there is no progress, the plan may be inadequate. Revising the plan may seem radical and in some ways it is, however, success is more readily achievable with an adequate plan than an inadequate one. Since there are always multiple paths to a team's goal, a team's initial decision about which path to take can be wrong. If it is, the plan should be corrected.

Team planning and team performance require effective communication among members. Evaluation must pay attention to all aspects of the communication process. Several questions are relevant. Is communication open? Do all team members participate in and feel comfortable with communication? If there are breakdowns in communication or a lack of participation, especially around significant issues pertaining to the performance process, are these problems addressed? Is requisite information available to the members? Does the leadership facilitate and support communication among members? Is communication appropriately balanced between task-oriented and group maintenance activities?

"Team planning and team performance require effective communication among members."

Leading.   These criteria concern how well the leadership role is performed and involve several questions: How well does the team's leader facilitate the team's planning process? How well does the leader assist the team to follow its plan, to keep focused on its goal, and to maintain a clear sense of the steps to its goal? Does the team leader attend to group maintenance activities? Does the leader assist the team to establish and maintain interdependence? Does the leader give sufficient attention to member satisfaction and encourage recognition of significant member contributions? How well does the leader keep the team defining, gathering, and utilizing relevant evaluative information?

Performing Tasks.   These criteria have to do with how well tasks are defined, whether appropriate members are assigned to the tasks, and how adequate performance of the tasks is. Several questions are involved: Are tasks being completed according to the team's plan? Are all members participating and using their skills and knowledge to perform relevant tasks? Is task performance making progress toward the team's goal?

Coordinating.   These criteria concern how well members work together in pursuit of the team's goal. Questions include how well coordinated or poorly coordinated members' activities are. Are there times when different members' activities fail to "mesh" or are not aligned? Are incompatible activities synchronized in ways that reduce or remove conflict? Is there evidence of cooperation? Is the team interdependent in its actions in ways that enhance its performance?

Structuring.   These criteria are concerned with how efficiently a team has structured its activities and how the structuring impacts the team's production of its outputs. Do team standards (norms) make clear to members the expectations for their performance? Are standards challenging, yet achievable? Has the team defined and assigned roles to its members that are both focused on the team's goal and utilize members' skills efficiently? Is the performance of roles effective and efficient?

> *"Are standards challenging, yet achievable?"*

Satisfying.   These criteria are indicators of member satisfaction and involvement. Do members find the tasks important and appropriately challenging? Is there evidence of member enjoyment and involvement, demonstrated by there being few absences or late arrivals? Member satisfaction is evaluated by gathering information about member reactions to all parts of the team system. Do team members find satisfaction in performing their roles? Do they find satisfaction in coordinating their activities with those of other team members? Do members take pride in the challenges that confront the team and in successfully addressing the challenges? Do team members recognize each other for their contributions?

Relationship to Organization.   These criteria involve the team's relationship to its organizational environment. The broad question is: how well does the relationship support the team's progress toward its goal? More specific questions concern the adequacy of inputs from the team's environment, the environment's support for the goal achievement process, the environment's evaluation of the team's product, and the environment's recognition and reward for effective team performance.

Evaluating.   This is evaluation of the evaluation subprocess. It involves how well the team gathers and uses information about the status of its goal achievement process and about improvements it can make in its performance. Questions include these: Are team members committed to regular evaluation of the team's activities? How relevant and usable is the evaluation information? Do members regularly examine the functioning of each subprocess? Do members use their understanding to improve their team's performance? Does the team's leader support and facilitate the evaluation process?

> *"How relevant and usable is the evaluation information?"*

Evaluation of Outputs

The evaluation subprocess also keeps track of the team system's outputs. While the image of a team's output is often that of winning a game, much more frequently a team's output is a product such as a computer chip, a report, a plan, a service, or a decision. Sometimes a team produces its output and disbands. Evaluation is important at such a time, although it is often overlooked. At other times, producing an output is a cyclic process. Once there is an output, the team proceeds to produce another, and so on. Evaluation of the output in this type of setting is more frequent. It is recognized that this is how a team learns and develops as a performing unit.

"When a team reaches its goal, the result is its product."

Product.   When a team reaches its goal, the result is its product. A central task of this aspect of evaluation is to determine the critical qualities of the product and to gather relevant information about them. Specifically, evaluation examines whether the product meets specification. Is it on time, within budget, and at the prescribed level of quality? How efficiently is the team able to produce its product? Efficiency is concerned with how well the team uses its resources, including its time, to produce its product. What is the product's quality; specifically, how many defects does it have? How satisfied are a team's customer(s)?

Teams that repeatedly produce a product (e.g., customer services, manufactured products, or airline flights crews) can address quality and efficiency issues on subsequent cycles. If any one or a combination of the indicators is below the level to which the team aspires, it is necessary to look at the system subprocesses to identify where adjustments are needed and to decide specifically what the adjustment should be.

Development and Learning.   In addition to producing a product, a team develops and learns to perform as a team. This process (discussed in Chapter 13) is important for the team's long-term viability. The evaluation process asks these questions: What have we as a team learned about producing this product? What have we learned about this team functioning and about teamwork in general? The answer to the first question reflects on a team's development and viability as a team. The answer to the second reflects on an understanding of teamwork in general and represents what individual members can carry away from the experience to apply in a future team activity.

Effectiveness.   A third output of a team is its effectiveness generally. This represents an overview of how well it functions in several senses: how well the team pursues its goal to produce its product, how satisfied the recipient of its product (its customer) is, how satisfied members are with their participation, and how well the team is maintaining its viability to produce the product. Members' awareness that their team is effective enhances their sense of team cohesiveness. This in turn supports team effectiveness.

MEASUREMENT IN EVALUATION

"Timeliness is defined as delivery on a specific date."

Consistent, effective evaluation requires commitment, discipline, and effort. It also requires an understanding of how to measure an abstraction. **Measurement** is a process of quantifying an abstraction. For example, weight (an abstraction) is measured by using a balance scale. Quality of a product is translated into the number of defects identified in the product. Timeliness is defined as delivery on a specific date.

Most of the evaluation criteria described earlier are questions that can be answered "yes" or "no" or placed on a scale: "always," "mostly," "sometimes," "rarely," or "never." Even more specifically these can be scaled: "always" (100% of the time), "mostly" (75% of the time), "sometimes"

(50% of the time), "rarely" (25% of the time), or "never" (0% of the time). Applying this scale, for example, can indicate how problematic a team's plan is and how much improvement is needed.

If a team focuses on its inadequate planning process, it can list a series of more specific questions. Questions like how clear the goal is, how clearly the steps to the goal are laid out, how fully members accept their responsibility for the steps, and how effective communication is among members in planning and carrying out the steps are directly related to a team's planning. Answers to these questions can help the team to identify a problem more specifically and then to devise a strategy to improve its planning. Knowing where the problem is requires a team problem-solving and decision-making process.

Essentially, the evaluation process involves team members becoming observers of their team's performance process. This means that a team member or the team leader takes note of and judges the level of functioning of a particular process or subsystem. The ability to make these types of judgments can be developed primarily by learning what to observe, how to make the observation, and how to interpret what is observed. To develop these skills, it is important for team members to practice observing their team's performance while at the same time being a part of that performance.

> *"Essentially, the evaluation process involves team members becoming observers of their team's performance process."*

The Challenge Revisited
Evaluating Products and Processes

1. Evaluation is a team's guidance system on the path to achieving its goal.

2. Evaluation is the basis for a team's improving its performance; without it, performance will deteriorate.

3. Obtaining a clear picture of progress toward the team goal, monitoring subprocess functioning that propels the team, and assessing the quality of the team product when the goal is reached are difficult but essential evaluation tasks.

4. A strategy for evaluation is developed in a team's planning process and refined as the team proceeds.

5. An objective evaluation of one's own and of one's team performance enables a team to improve its performance as it functions.

EXERCISE 11.1 • *Developing an Evaluation Plan*

1. As a team, develop an evaluation plan. In this plan specify what will be evaluated, how it will be evaluated, and who will do the evaluation.

2. Prepare a short report of the evaluation plan.

EXERCISE 11.2 • *Project Review and Evaluation*

1. For any three of the project exercises previously conducted by your team, list the project, its product, and two or three ways the product could be improved. What could your team do to improve each product? Be specific.
2. Using the relevant parts of the evaluation plan developed in Exercise 11.1, prepare short reports of your decisions and recommendations.

QUESTIONS FOR REVIEW AND DISCUSSION

1. What does team performance evaluation involve? Why is it important for a team?
2. How and why does evaluation enable a team to take responsibility for its own activities?
3. What is meant when evaluation is referred to as an iterative process? What are the steps in the process and what occurs at each step?
4. What are the evaluation tasks? What is involved in completing each task?
5. Why is evaluating each of the throughput subprocesses important?
6. What two evaluation issues must a team address in its planning process? When should a team consider revising its evaluation plan?
7. What is the team leader's role in the team's evaluation process?
8. What outputs does a team evaluate? What are the implications of evaluation results for a team's continued performance?
9. Why is it important for a team to evaluate its own development and learning? What issues need to be considered?
10. How are measurement issues related to the evaluation process? How can performance criteria be measured?

NOTES

1. On feedback, see E. Salas, T. Dickinson, S. Converse, & S. Tannenbaum (1992), Understanding team performance in R. Swezey & E. Salas (Eds.), *Teams: Their Training and Performance,* Norwood, NJ: Ablex Publishing, pp. 20–22; see also R. Swezey & E. Salas (1992), Guidelines for use in team training and development, in Swezey & Salas, op. cit., pp. 233–234; also, C. Prince, T. Chidester, C. Bowers, & J. Cannon-Bowers (1992), Aircrew coordination: Achieving teamwork in the cockpit, in Swezey & Salas, op. cit., pp. 340–342; and D. Yeats & C. Hyten (1998), *High-Performing Self-Managed Work Teams,* Thousand Oaks, CA: Sage, pp. 136–141.

2. A system subprocess refers to an identifiable feature of a system such as the system's inputs, coordination among member activities, or the process by which members experience satisfaction.

3. Cognitive map or mental image refers to how a team member "sees" the path to a team's goal laid out. See J. Cannon-Bowers, E. Salas, & C. Converse (1993), Shared mental models in expert team decision-making, in N. J. Castellan (Ed.), *Individual and Group Decision-Making*, Mahwah, NJ: Erlbaum, pp. 221–246.

4. A team's plan should specify the resources needed to achieve its goal.

The Products of Teamwork

section three

The teamwork process has three broad outcomes. First is the achievement of its goal—its product or service. These vary from team to team. For one team, winning a contest might be the goal; for another, making a decision; for yet others, developing a plan or manufacturing a product. For some teams, reaching its goal once marks the end of the process. For others, it is an iterative process; that is, once the team reaches its goal the first time, it returns to the beginning and repeats the process. Determining how a team can improve its product, especially as it repeats the performance process, is crucial. A second outcome concerns how well a team develops and learns to perform as a unit. A team's performance cannot remain at the same level from one production cycle to the next. If performance fails to improve, it deteriorates. Whether it improves depends on a team's ability to develop and learn. A third outcome is a team's overall effectiveness. Effectiveness involves four dimensions: how well a team achieves its goal, the effect of membership on team members, the consequences of team outcomes on those who depend on a team's performance, such as its customers, and a team's ability and desire to continue performing in the future. Each dimension has implications for a team's overall effectiveness.

The Challenge
Team Products

A team achieves its goal by producing a product for its customer. A team's vision establishes the expectations it has for its product. These include its acceptability to the customer and its broader significance. Few teams, especially those just beginning, accomplish their vision initially. The product falls short in some way. Only through repeated effort to improve does the vision become a reality. A team's evaluation process plays an important role in determining how fully the vision is achieved and what improvements are needed. Adjustments often involve changes in the way a team produces its product. A major challenge for a team is to move beyond simply producing a product to realizing its vision.

chapter 12

Team Products

A team's **product** generally refers to the results of the team's achieving its goal. This may be a completed report, plan, decision, or musical performance. This is a rather narrow view of what teamwork produces, however. A broader perspective considers not simply whether a team has produced its product, but how fully the product realizes the team's vision for its product. Consider, for example, the following team.

Tara, Samantha, Neil, Bill, and Leslie are members of a new financial review team. They perform internal audits and have just completed their first report. They are pleased to have the review completed and are ready to leave for the day. However, their team leader says that they should remain for a few minutes to develop a process for reviewing the quality of their performance. The objective of the process is to identify ways to improve their next report. After some discussion of why such a review is important, the group agrees to think about ways to improve their review process. They will compile the different possibilities at their next meeting.

This team is seeking to avoid a major pitfall for team performance—failing to evaluate their completed product—so that future products can be improved. This team knows about evaluation. They evaluate financial practices. They have begun to realize, however, that it is equally important to evaluate their own product and the performance that produces it. In doing so, this team can move closer to realizing its vision of providing financial reviews that help their organization to become a leader in their market segment.

The discussion in Chapter 11 focused on evaluating the performance process. The discussion that follows examines the quality of a team's product from the perspective of how well that completed product fulfills the team's vision for it. An assumption is that the team's vision expects the product to be exceptional in some way. To accomplish this, a team must examine the completed product to identify points for possible improvement.[1]

> *"An assumption is that the team's vision expects the product to be exceptional in some way."*

A Team's Products

Teams now produce many products. Teams in manufacturing produce everything from the design of a product to the product itself. Musical ensembles produce musical performances. Surgical teams produce heart bypass operations. Air crews produce airplane flights. Theater groups produce dramatic productions. The variety of work team types and products is notable. *Management teams* produce plans for new organizations, for new products, and for restructuring management. *Task forces* produce recommendations for new programs of activity or for new customer services. *Professional support teams* produce analyses of legislative issues, proposals for system revisions, or provide maintenance services for airlines. *Performing groups* provide musical performances, theatrical performances, or perform in athletic competitions. *Human service teams* conduct medical surgeries, guide the rehabilitation of prison inmates, or provide mental health treatment services. *Customer service teams* sell and deliver beverages, address customer questions and complaints, or provide services to airline passengers during flights. *Production teams* start up manufacturing production lines, fly airliners, or redesign manufacturing systems. This is just a sample of the many types of teams producing many different products.[2]

A team's production process, that is, its performance, involves a concert of activities, all focused on producing a product that represents achievement of its goal. The inputs are the basics needed to begin and sustain the process; the throughputs are the subprocesses that together produce a specified product, and the outputs are the results of the throughput process. Across teams, all the products are similar in the sense that they are the result of a team's performance and its progress toward its goal. A further similarity is that the different performance subprocesses, which optimally support that progress, can also slow and even undermine progress. How well these subprocesses support progress depends on the quality of a team's plan, especially in integrating the subprocesses, and on the team's performance in carrying out the plan.

A system perspective on team functioning suggests that human systems, such as teams, cannot maintain a steady-state performance. Performance varies because of openness to its environment, because of skill inadequacies or development, because of changes in member motivation and involvement, and because of adjustments in the performance process, such as changes in coordination. These do not remain the same. They either deteriorate or improve. Improving performance prevents performance deterioration and maintains the team's overall character. A team's *customer*, the recipient of its product, is the immediate reason a team attends to its product's quality.

A TEAM'S CUSTOMER

"A team's customer judges the usefulness of the product."

With regard to a team, the term customer refers broadly to the recipient of its product. A team's customer may be a part of the team's organization or outside it. Examples of customers inside an organization are another team, a supervisor, a teacher, or a coach. Customers outside the organization are those who purchase the product or otherwise use it. A team's customer judges the usefulness of the product. Sometimes this usefulness is referred to as the *value added* by the product.

When a team's customer judges its product, continued support for the team, even its existence, can be at stake. Resources in the form of time, material, and human effort are made available to the team in the expectation that the team's product will enable the customer to further its purposes. When the product is delivered, the team's customer makes a judgment about the value of the product. This judgment can be narrow, that is, simply being glad to have received the product, but often the customer makes a broader evaluation of both the product and the team that produced it.

This broader evaluation differs in several ways from evaluation(s) made by a team's members. First, the customer's view will be from outside the team. This means that the inner workings of the team may not be readily observable, only the results. Second, the evaluation is made of the team as a whole. Some members may be more visible than others to the customer, but the view is of the team as a whole. Third, the evaluation will be weighted toward the customer's intended use of the product. By contrast, team members are more likely to weight their evaluation toward the challenges posed by the tasks required to achieve the goal, to the progress the team has made toward achieving its goal, and to the satisfactions or dissatisfactions both engender.

"If a team is effective in its own internal evaluation, it is unlikely that the customer's evaluation will be a surprise."

If a team is effective in its own internal evaluation, it is unlikely that the customer's evaluation will be a surprise. In fact, initially the customer may make a more positive evaluation than a realistic team makes about itself. This is because poor internal functioning associated with poor performance has not yet become obvious to the outsider. If such a team does not, however, reduce its inadequacies over time, these failings will become evident to the customer. An unrealistic team, that is, one that does not realistically evaluate its internal functioning, may be startled to discover how poorly its performance is evaluated by its customer. A poor performance evaluation can act as a reality check that motivates a team to do a more realistic evaluation and to seek more accurate feedback. If this happens, the team will be taking a step in the direction of improved functioning and performance. A poor evaluation, however, can also demoralize a team and result in even poorer performance. A team's leadership is often the key to which reaction occurs.

Team products are often given a poor evaluation because they are not in accordance with an organization's goal(s). For example, consider a team established to develop a plan for a new product line. The team develops a good plan but the plan is rejected because the product's design is judged to be too "extreme" or too expensive to produce. In such a case, the product is judged by criteria imposed from outside the team by the organization. A major reason business organizations go to great lengths to make their goals clear to employees is to ensure that employees (and their teams) judge their activities both in terms of their quality and in terms of their relevance to achieving the organization's goals. Failing to support the organization's goals, a team may be disbanded.

EVALUATING A TEAM'S PRODUCT

Evaluation Criteria

What issues might a customer use to judge a team's product? Three general areas are proposed.

Product status refers to the degree to which the product meets customer expectations. There are three related criteria: Does the product as presented meet the customer's specifications? Is the product delivered on time or in a timely manner? Is the product of acceptable quality? Generally, a team's customer will expect all three to be met for the product to be acceptable. Superior performance, as far as product status is concerned, means exceeding customer expectations, not simply meeting them. For example, an additional service might be provided or a report might have useful material that was not specified. Superior performance can also mean delivering the product early and/or providing a product that has a higher than specified level of quality. Inferior performance means failure to meet one or more of the three status indicators.

"Superior performance, as far as product status is concerned, means exceeding customer expectations, not simply meeting them."

Resource use is a second area for external evaluation. This criterion is less frequently cited, but is of concern, especially to many businesses. It is relevant to athletic teams as well. Teams in poor physical condition are likely to experience more injuries, which results in poor resource use. A team's product may be acceptable, but if material resources were wasted in producing the product, unnecessary costs will be incurred. In one company, one evaluation criterion was whether electronic control panels were produced with a minimum of defects. Because a defective panel could not be repaired and, thus, had to be discarded, any defects resulted in wasted time and materials. Reducing the number of defective panels improved resource use. Other

"Team members who arrive late for team activities or return late from coffee and other breaks are wasting resources."

"If a team is learning and improving in each of the areas of its functioning, the overall direction of its performance is improvement and growth."

resource questions concern whether team member time, skills, and knowledge are used efficiently to further the team's progress. Team members who arrive late for team activities or return late from coffee and other breaks are wasting resources. Another example might be team meetings, such as those for planning. Are these run in a manner that maximizes accomplishment and minimizes the time and energy members expend? Meetings that are too long and too frequent reflect a team's inefficiency and result in a waste of resources.

The **team growth** criterion is concerned with whether a team's performance in repeatedly producing its product is becoming better or worse. As indicated earlier, performance does not simply stay the same. If a team learns from its mistakes and is able to replace inappropriate or mistaken actions with effective actions, and continues to practice the effective actions, the team is learning. If a team is learning and improving in each of the areas of its functioning, the overall direction of its performance is improvement and growth. If a team is not replacing mistakes with effective actions, and does not practice more effective actions, its performance will deteriorate.

Measuring the Criteria

Measuring (making operational) these three evaluation criteria will differ from situation to situation. The measurement question is this: Given these criteria in this situation, what indicators best reflect these criteria? For a manufacturing team that produces control panels, issues to measure could be number of panels delivered per eight-hour shift, the number of defective panels produced during that period (product status), the amount of waste material generated, the amount of time required for team meetings (resource use), the number of team members' absences, and production delays due to team members returning late from coffee breaks. Team growth is indicated by improved member coordination, fewer product defects, and improved resource use. By contrast, for a university student team working to produce a report for an accounting class, the issues to be evaluated could be whether the report is on time and of a specified level of quality (product status), the amount of time spent by the team on the report and how evenly distributed effort was among team members (resource use), and what and how much team members learned about accounting and about team functioning (team growth).[3]

To summarize, when evaluating a team's performance, product status is only part of the equation. Other aspects are also important. Resource use has direct implications for product cost. Growth has direct implications for future performance. Simply meeting specifications may mean a median or average level of performance. Exceeding the specifications and demonstrating above average use of resources and above average functioning and growth means above average performance. Failing to do these things means below average performance in the sense of high or escalating costs and generally deteriorating performance.

PRODUCT IMPROVEMENT

For a team to achieve its vision of delivering an extraordinary product, it must become a high-performing team. A **high-performing** team consistently meets or exceeds its customer's expectations. This should be the lens through which a team views all of its activities. Taking this perspective can be satisfying, if the focus is on improvement and experiencing satisfaction from the accomplishment. It also can be difficult and unsatisfying, especially if members take personally any evidence of personal shortcoming.

A consistent focus on improvement is important for several reasons. First, there is always something about a performance process that can be improved. In fact, if a process is not improving, as system theory indicates, it must be deteriorating. Second, as with other types of member contributions, identifying points for improvement and ways to achieve the improvements is every team member's responsibility. The presence of interdependence means that one member's inadequacy affects every other member. It also means that every member's contribution to improvement affects every other member. Third, commitment to continuous improvement reduces any threat posed when quality is reviewed. Improvement of the team system's performance is a central objective for the team and for each member and is not a reflection of personal failure.

"if a process is not improving, as system theory indicates, it must be deteriorating"

A further problem, raised by an emphasis on improvement, is that team members can become dissatisfied by constantly focusing on "problems." If identifying ways to improve performance is a team objective, team members should support each other and recognize each person's contribution to improvement rather than blame each other for shortcomings. Further, if problems are seen as "system" problems rather than specific individuals' problems, then the sense of personal blame is reduced or removed and the focus is kept on improving the system. Finally, if accomplishing improvement can be made a mark of distinction that merits recognition, then identifying and solving quality-related problems provides the grounds for achieving distinction and consequently becomes a reason for satisfaction.

A team's leader has a specific role in a team's efforts to improve. Although every team member has a responsibility to address ways to improve, the leader has the responsibility to be on the lookout for points that are overlooked or even avoided. Avoidance of specific areas that need improvement can become more pronounced as a team works together and members become friendly. Certain issues that pertain to the whole team are not looked at for fear of making the team look bad. Issues that pertain to one or a few individuals are avoided for fear of hurting other team members' feelings. The role of the leader is to enable the team to address such sensitive issues in a constructive manner.

"Certain issues that pertain to the whole team are not looked at for fear of making the team look bad."

A Strategy for Improvement

High performance depends on each team member's interdependent, coordinated, and goal-directed performance. When performance does not reach the desired standard, a team must address whatever barriers prevent its doing so. An important asset of a team is its ability to identify and remove such barriers. A team identifies these problems through the evaluation process and then uses problem-solving skills to resolve them.

Identifying the Presence of a Problem

At some point in its activities, one or more members of a team may sense that the team has a problem. A customer criticizes or rejects the team's product. A team's evaluation of its functioning identifies an area in which team functioning is faltering. A member feels that there is a problem, say, a lack of satisfaction in being a part of the team's activities. More generally, any team member may see or suspect that there is a barrier to developing high performance.

Several sources of resistance can prevent identification of barriers. One is when members' expectations for their team's performance are not very high. Another is when only one or two team members sense the presence of the barrier and hesitate to note it for fear of sounding negative or encountering the disfavor of the majority who are oblivious to or prefer not to acknowledge the difficulties. Another source of resistance results from the fear of bringing disfavor on the team if the presence of a barrier, often viewed as an inadequacy, were to become known outside the team to, for example, a customer or a supervisor.

The dilemma a team faces is that such short-term protectiveness is typically not effective in the long term. Unacknowledged barriers, for example, poor communication, inadequate coordination, poor leadership, and member dissatisfaction, eventually surface in the form of difficulty reaching the goal or, if it is reached, a defective product. At that point, a team's inadequate functioning becomes evident to the team's environment. This means that the inadequacy becomes "public" with an implied challenge, if not threat, to the team's continuing existence. Furthermore, by succumbing to the temptation to avoid identifying barriers, a team fails to actualize its potential, often with member dissatisfaction resulting.

"The challenge for a team is to find a strategy that removes the barrier with the most positive benefit for a team's performance."

When a team, having resisted the temptation to deny the presence of a barrier, begins to address it, there is a general procedure that can be followed. In following this procedure, it is important to remember that there can be multiple strategies to achieve an objective, in this case to remove a barrier. The challenge for a team is to find a strategy that removes the barrier with the most positive benefit for a team's performance.

Consider again the financial review team described at the outset of this chapter. The team members learned from their supervisor, *after* they submitted their report, that the report didn't outline clear recommendations for improving the financial operations of the area examined. The team did not know that recommendations were expected. They realized that their performance was not as good as they had thought. How can they improve? The method proposed here for removing barriers to high functioning combines brainstorming to develop a comprehensive set of possible solutions, with decision making to select the best solution. A plan for implementing the solution is also needed. This is followed by actual implementation and evaluation of the action to determine whether the desired effect is being achieved. The following describes these steps more fully.

Defining the Problem

When symptoms of a problem are detected and acknowledged, a team's first step is to define the problem. This is not always easy. If a precise definition is not evident, brainstorming to develop a list of possibilities can be useful. This engages all members in the process and draws on their varied perspectives. Once a list of possibilities is developed, the most adequate definition can be selected. Because the formulation of a solution and its implementation requires the active involvement of every team member, it is important for all to "buy into" the problem definition.

"When symptoms of a problem are detected and acknowledged, a team's first step is to define the problem."

An example from athletics is a football team that consistently has its passes intercepted. Is this due to the quarterback's inadequacy, the slowness or lack of agility of the receiver, or the capability of the defense? How the problem is defined determines the solution that will be chosen. A more technical example comes from the corporate research problem-solving session on high-speed machining, described in Chapter 4. The problem concerned the machine tool's impact on the material being machined. Participants viewed the problem as one of "grinding" the material that became deformed by the heat. One participant suggested, however, that the problem could be viewed as a "ballistics" problem in which a projectile hits the material at high speed, deforming the material. This provided a different view of the problem and a different approach to a solution.

Formulating a Solution

Once the team has a workable definition of the problem, a strategy for solving it is needed. Again, brainstorming provides a way to develop a list of possible strategies from among which the most effective solution can be chosen. It sometimes happens in the process of selecting a strategy that the problem definition must be revised. As long as a revision provides a more realistic perspective on the problem, rather than some degree of avoiding the problem, the best possible definition provides the best foundation for developing a solution.

In both the problem definition phase and the solution development phase, team members may think about both the problem and its solution in a more conventional way. Team members' different perspectives can, however, "break the mold." To return to our high-speed machining example, the need was expressed for machine tools that machined in a way that did not deform the material being machined. At the point where many participants had begun to question whether there was a solution, one researcher described machine tools he had developed that met the desired specifications. This led participants to change their perspectives from doubting that a solution could be found to considering ways to test the proposed solution.

Implementing the Solution

"An important feature of any strategy is the specification of a way to evaluate the plan's effectiveness."

Having formulated a solution does not necessarily mean that a single path to implementing the solution is evident. Again, a list of possible implementation strategies can be developed and one chosen that is likely to be most effective. An important feature of any strategy is the specification of a way to evaluate the plan's effectiveness. An example that combines planning and implementing a solution and evaluating the results is provided by our high-speed machining example. Once a perspective on the problem was identified and a broad approach to solving the problem was selected, a series of "experiments" were designed. These enabled the researchers to evaluate several approaches in an effort to identify the most effective implementation strategy.

Carrying Out the Implementation Plan

Once an implementation procedure is undertaken, difficulties can arise. The solution or the way it is implemented may not achieve the desired change. A different approach may be needed. Team members may be resistant to change. Whatever behavioral adjustments are required by the solution may be resisted and the old ways perpetuated. This resistance may originate with one, some, or all team members. Another difficulty is losing sight of the solution's objective. This can occur because in practice the objective, that is, removing the barrier, is not precisely defined. It can also happen because of a resistance to change that is reflected in the team or a subset of team members "going off on a tangent." Each of these threats to effective barrier removal must be resisted.

"Another difficulty is losing sight of the solution's objective."

Evaluating the Result

If evaluation is not included when the solution is designed and implemented, it is important to do so as a follow-up step. The core question is this: Does performance improve? Preferably, the implementation plan includes a set of indicators that suggest whether the solution is achieving the desired improvement. If indicators on which to base a judgment of success or failure are not included, they should be developed.

In summary, when a team's performance is less than desired, a team is confronted with a challenge to its creative thinking and problem solving. How is the problem defined? When this question is answered, the team proceeds into a problem-solving mode of formulating a solution, of developing and carrying out a procedure to implement the solution, and of evaluating its effect. In athletics, alternative "plays" are identified, practiced, used in a game, and evaluated in terms of yards gained or points scored. If these or other indicators are below expectation, adjustments are made. From game to game, videotapes of plays in previous games are studied to identify and define performance problems. These provide the basis for developing a solution by creating new plays or adjusting old ones. Improving team performance involves a similar procedure.

COMMITMENT TO IMPROVEMENT

Commitment to improvement grows out of a team's desire to achieve its goal, out of a desire to know how well the team is progressing toward its goal, and, once the steps to the goal have been completed, out of a desire to know how well the accomplishment fulfills the team's vision for quality. Members' willingness to commit to improvement grows out of a team vision that is clear and engaging. The team sees improvement as a way to fulfill its vision. Improvement is achieved through operations that include evaluation and by recognition of member and team accomplishments when improvement occurs. Member recognition is particularly important for member satisfaction, since recognition acknowledges and makes objective a member's accomplishments in improving performance.

> *"The team sees improvement as a way to fulfill its vision."*

The Challenge Revisited
Team Products

1. Producing its product is a team's primary challenge.

2. Achieving its vision for the product is a closely related, even greater, challenge.

3. Evaluating and improving its product are crucial for a team to achieve its vision.

4. Commitment, persistence, and practice are required for improvement to occur.

5. Producing its product and achieving its vision gives satisfaction to the team's customer and to the team's members.

EXERCISE 12.1 • *Improving Team Performance*

Instructions: The objective of this activity is to help teams to improve their performance. The procedure involves identifying areas of team functioning that can be improved and developing and implementing strategies to accomplish the improvement.

1. Complete an assessment to assist your team in identifying areas of functioning that need improvement. The assessment itself is a relatively simple procedure. However, team members may need to address difficult issues in the interests of finding ways to improve team performance. To begin the assessment, turn to page 251.

2. Select the areas most in need of improvement and develop a team strategy by which to accomplish the improvement.

QUESTIONS FOR REVIEW AND DISCUSSION

1. What is meant by the phrase *a team's product?* What is the primary consideration in judging a product's quality?

2. What is meant by the phrase *a team's customer?* What are the implications of the customer's evaluation of the team's product?

3. What is the role of evaluation in producing a team product? What does a team's evaluation of its product involve? What are the implications for a team of an unrealistic evaluation?

4. What are the primary issues for a team to consider when evaluating its product and performance process? How can these be assessed? Why is the type of assessment important?

5. Why is it assumed that team performance can always be improved? What is the relationship between product improvement and evaluation?

6. What are the steps in the strategy for improvement outlined in this chapter? What is a team leader's role in helping the team to carry out this strategy?

7. Once a problem is identified and defined, what is the process for formulating a solution? When a presumed solution is implemented, why is it important to evaluate the result?

NOTES

1. The emphasis on product improvement is based on the emphasis of the total quality management movement. See M. Walton (1986), *The Deming Management Method,* New York: Perigee Books.

2. J. R. Hackman (Ed.) and associates (1990), *Teams That Work,* San Francisco: Jossey-Bass, provide case studies of teams, including those in business and industry.

3. See S. Jones (1997), Team performance measurement: Theoretical and applied issues, in M. Beyerlein and D. Johnson (Eds.), *Advances in Interdisciplinary Studies of Work Teams,* Vol. 4, London: JAI Press.

The Challenge
Team Development and Learning

Teams are formed to achieve a goal and, once formed, begin to work toward it. In the process, members get to know each other, develop working relationships, and perceive themselves as part of the team. One challenge is to understand how a team develops and learns to produce its product and achieve its vision. This involves learning how to perform relevant tasks, how to interact in ways that support task performance, and how to integrate task performance and social interaction so as to achieve a goal. Understanding these developments enables a team to improve its performance, to support its longer term viability as a performing unit, and to ensure that members experience satisfaction during the process.

chapter 13

Team Development and Learning

Several people who have never met form a team with a goal. Calling them a team does not necessarily mean that they can work together and certainly does not mean that they can be effective. Individuals who have not worked together often do, after a period of time, begin to work together effectively. Others do not. This implies that they undergo some type of transformation. Changes take place in the interactions among members, in their task performance, and in their own and others' views of their team. Understanding this transformation—how and why it occurs—is important for understanding how and why some teams achieve their goals and fulfill their visions while others do not.

One conception of this transformation is that it occurs in stages. If some or all of these stages are completed, a prescribed level of functioning is reached. This conception implies several important questions: What are the stages? What is their order? Must the stages be in a fixed order? Are the stages universal; that is, do all teams develop through the same stages to achieve high performance? What other conceptions are there of how teams change over time? How valid are these? Let's look at these stages in detail.

STAGES OF TEAM DEVELOPMENT

There were several early views of how teams develop from aggregates of individuals to organized, goal-directed groups or teams. One conceptualization[1] proposed that team functioning develops in three stages. This theory hypothesized that teams change in their interactions from an emphasis on problems of *orientation* (clarifying relevant facts) to problems of *evaluation* (developing criteria by which to judge facts), to problems of *control* (pressuring for team decisions and joint action). A less patterned perspective[2] emphasizes how team members struggle with two questions: (1) To what degree are members to be emotionally involved with the team and with each other? (2) Who is to have control of the team's activities? A team's development reflects how these questions are answered. The answer to the first question is for each member to respond along a dimension of *involved or aloof*. The answer to the second question is for each member to respond along a dimension of *in control or not*. After a few team meetings, members arrive at answers to these questions. However, across teams patterns of members' answers can take a variety of forms. Some members are involved, others less so; some are more in control than others.

> *"Who is to have control of the team's activities?"*

Another view[3] assumes that every action has both a work and an emotional dimension. Work is analyzed on four levels. The first level concerns personal goals and their fulfillment. The second involves routine group work. The third is active problem solving. The fourth level concerns creative, integrative problem solving. The emotional dimension, related to the work, involves different "moods" that characterize members' responses to other members. In a "fight" mood, a member (or members) expresses and elicits from others hostile feelings. In a "flight" mood, a member evades or ignores issues that need to be addressed. In a "pairing" mood, members carry on personal conversations, often with the implicit acceptance of other team members. In a "dependent" mood, members, rather than addressing problems and barriers facing their team, look to someone else to solve or remove them.

> *"In a 'flight' mood, a member evades or ignores issues that need to be addressed."*

Each of these perspectives identifies issues that confront team members. How they are addressed reflects on how a team will perform. Whether these responses, considered generally, represent stages of performance is doubtful.

Possibly, the best known characterization of team development originally posited four stages.[4] These stages were identified through analysis of reports about several types of groups: therapy groups, human relations training groups, and natural groups. The author noted, however, that groups from industrial settings were not included.[5] The four stages are formative, negotiative, norm setting, and performance. A fifth stage, termination, was added later to designate the point at which the group's task is complete and the team is restructured or disbanded.[6] Within each stage are two orientations. One is members' orientation to the task. The other is members' orientation to other members. These orientations correspond roughly to the technical and group maintenance orientations discussed elsewhere in this book.

This five-stage conceptualization is frequently applied to team development. It assumes that individuals who have not worked together begin to work as a team and develop by stages until the team disbands. At the **formative stage,** sometimes referred to as *forming,* members orient to the task by identifying relevant parameters and determining how the team's experience will be used to accomplish the task. Members also decide the type of information needed to perform the task and how to obtain it. At this stage, members orient to other members by testing and by dependence to discover what behaviors others will or will not accept. Members may also look to a powerful team member or to existing norms in a dependent way, seeking guidance and support in the new and unstructured situation. This is a process of "scoping out" the situation (task and people).

At the **negotiative stage,** sometimes referred to as *storming,* members develop an emotional response to the task. They consider and often resist demands of the task. There is often a discrepancy between each member's personal orientation and that demanded by the task. For example, a member prefers to work individually, but the task requires coordination among members. At this stage, members' orientation to other members can involve interpersonal conflict. Team members can become hostile toward one another as a way to maintain their individuality and to resist the formation of a team social structure. Tension exists between individuality and interdependence.

At the **norm-setting stage,** sometimes referred to as *norming,* a more open exchange of task-relevant information and interpretations is found. Information is acted on in order to arrive at alternative interpretations. At this stage, orientation to other members begins to develop some sense of cohesion. Members accept the team and the idiosyncrasies of fellow members. The team becomes an entity by virtue of members' acceptance of each other, by their desire to maintain and perpetuate the team, and by the establishment of norms generated to ensure the team's existence. Harmony becomes important.

> *"Members accept the team and the idiosyncrasies of fellow members."*

Stage four involves **performance,** sometimes referred to as *performing.* Members orient to the task and suggest task-related solutions. Constructive attempts are made to complete goal-oriented tasks. In the first three stages, a correspondence between the team's social structure and task performance was lacking. At this stage, the emphasis is on constructive action, and the two realms come together so that energy previously invested in establishing a social structure can be directed to performing tasks. At this stage, members focus on task-related roles. The team, which became an entity in the preceding stage, can now become a problem-solving entity. Members now adopt and perform roles that enhance the team's task performance. Role structure is not an issue but an instrument that can now be directed at the task.

Stage five concerns **termination** of the team, referred to as *terminating.* There can be several reasons for termination. For instance, the task is completed, the team disbands or is disbanded even though the task is not complete, or the team's membership is restructured. This stage is significant because task performance is evaluated from the perspective of the team's work being over and because team members must address the separations that results from

"Members orient to other members in preparation for separation and the anticipated dissolution of the team."

termination. At this stage members arrange to end task activities. Members orient to other members in preparation for separation and the anticipated dissolution of the team. When teams function effectively and provide satisfaction, this stage assumes greater prominence, since termination will involve a sense of loss for team members. Members may even ask to continue relationships among team members.

One commentator notes that the perspectives described here (and similar ones not described) address four fundamental problems or needs: to develop a consensus on underlying values and goals, to have or develop resources to attain the goals, to develop norms to guide goal-directed behaviors and cohesiveness to support norms, and to undertake effective task performance as a team. When a team must address full-fledged problems, unlike the partial problems on which many studies of team development are based, the range of issues teams must address is broader, as described in Table 13.1.[7]

"teams were found to form, at the very beginning of their activities, a somewhat arbitrary framework about the situation and how the team should behave"

In contrast to teams developing through a series of stages, one researcher reports finding no universal sequence of activities and no steady developmental progression. Rather, teams were found to form, at the very beginning of their activities, a somewhat arbitrary framework about the situation and how the team should behave. These frameworks persist until almost halfway through the total time allotted for a team's project. At this point there is a transition from approaches and behaviors used previously to new ones more suited to making progress toward the team's goal and completing the activity. From this perspective teams confront four challenges: (1) to develop a prescribed product at some specified level of quality (2) with the mutual support of team members (3) in accord with available resources and according to specified requirements (4) in a specified time frame. Teams differ greatly in how they deal with the first of these challenges. At the *midpoint transition*, when members confront the fourth challenge, they proceed to fit "an indeterminate amount of work into a fixed amount of time."[8]

TABLE 13.1
Task Performance Processes, Interpersonal Processes, and Stages of Team Development

	Stage			
	I	II	III	IV
Task	Generate plans and ideas	Choose (correct or preferred) alternatives	Resolve conflicts of viewpoints and interests	Perform action tasks
Interpersonal	Generate values and goals	Agree on values and goals	Develop norms, allocate roles	Establish and maintain cohesion

SIGNIFICANCE OF THE STAGE PERSPECTIVE FOR TEAM PERFORMANCE

An emphasis on stages underscores how good teamwork develops rather than exists from the outset. Most of the research on team formation implies that teams progress through each stage, although some teams can presumably become fixed in a stage and not be able to progress further. For example, members of a new team can look to their leader for ideas and direction, and if the leader continues to accept such dependency, rather than facilitating members' taking responsibility, members can remain dependent. Likewise, it may be possible for a team to progress to effective performance, then allow interpersonal conflict to arise, and regress to an earlier stage.

There are other possible exceptions to the progression. For example, when potential team members are sufficiently well trained (e.g., the military or flight crews), stages of the progression are passed over to go directly to the performing stage.[9] Another possible exception occurs when pressure to perform is high, either due to an important deadline or to emergency conditions. In either case, the progression may not be followed. One author commented on the presumed progression through the stages as follows: "These models are grounded in the paradigm of development as an inevitable, hierarchical progression; a group cannot get to stage four without first going through stages one, two, and three. Development is construed as movement in a forward direction, and every group is expected to follow the same basic path."[10]

Another exception occurs when, within a stage, team members are predominantly oriented in either of two ways: to the task or to interpersonal issues. When a group addresses issues in one orientation, time is taken away from orienting to the other. According to some commentators[11], the two processes are interrelated, but they are to a degree in opposition. For example, concerted attention to the task can lead to socioemotional friction. Being overly attentive to socioemotional issues can detract from task efforts. Inordinate attention to either process leads to system breakdown because of the failure of the other process, that is, either socioemotional disruption of the team or team failure to do the tasks necessary to the team's goals. Thus, a team has a major challenge to maintain a balance between the two sets of issues.

> *"When a group addresses issues in one orientation, time is taken away from orienting to the other."*

WHAT DEVELOPS?

A conceptualization based on stages of team development implies that a team is an organism that develops (or fails to develop) along a preordained path. A problem with such a conceptualization is that the stages are not, in practice, necessarily clearly differentiated nor sequential. A team's development may move back and forth between stages, especially in the early phases. A further difficulty is that there is no indication about how a team moves from one stage to another. There are several additional questions. The developmental stages are described only up to the point of the performing stage. What happens after

*"Social struc-
ture can evolve
in ways that
enhance or
detract from
a team's
effectiveness."*

reaching that stage and before termination? This characterization of stages fails to consider specific throughput issues, such as planning, coordination, or feedback.

From a systems perspective, as a team develops, some features of its functioning may change in one direction while other features change in a different direction. For example, communication can become more or less effective in coordinating activities. Social structure can evolve in ways that enhance or detract from a team's effectiveness. Leadership can develop that either facilitates or doesn't facilitate team performance. Individual satisfaction may or may not be achieved, affecting members' motivation. Evaluation feedback may or may not inform the team about its level of functioning and provide a basis for adjustment. All features must function or change in a positive direction for team performance to improve.

*"Keeping all
parts of the sys-
tem functioning
at a high level
and directed
toward its goal
is a challenge
that must be
addressed by
concerted
effort."*

From this broader system perspective, team functioning is comprised of a complex set of dynamic subsystems. In this view, the team has the ability to monitor its inputs (Does it have appropriate and sufficient resources to carry out its tasks?), to monitor its throughput processes (Does each subprocess function in a way that supports the team's progress toward its goal?), and to monitor outputs (Are the outputs of a number, type, and quality that meet the team's standards?). Each of these questions must be evaluated and answered, and activities aligned in ways that make a team effective. Keeping all parts of the system functioning at a high level and directed toward its goal is a challenge that must be addressed by concerted effort. When viewed in this way, the behavioral adjustments required to meet specific challenges do not seem to be preset. There are multiple paths requiring continuous learning to develop effective performance.

TEAM LEARNING

*"Through
learning, a
team develops
new or
improved
behaviors and
controls its
destiny."*

Learning means changing behavior. For a team oriented to reaching a goal, learning means changing behavior in ways that make that achievement possible. Knowing which behaviors to change and how to change them, however, can be problematic. A team's system, if adequately designed, includes feedback to identify where specific changes are needed. Once the changes are made, the feedback provides information about the effects of the changes. It is team members who must decide what technical or behavioral changes are needed and then make them. Through learning, a team develops new or improved behaviors and controls its destiny.

The team system has inputs, throughput subprocesses, and outputs. For any team, each of these features can be at the level of all the others or be better or worse. For example, considering inputs, what happens if there is a high level of skills but unclear goals? The throughput subprocesses provide further examples. Aspirations (a feature of vision) may be high but communication skills are so poor that the degree of interpersonal coordination needed to achieve the aspirations cannot be attained. Or, goals may be clear but there is little ability or willingness to evaluate the team's performance relative to its goals and, consequently, the team is never quite sure where it is relative to its goal. Processes that are at different levels of development cannot be aligned so they can move in concert. Teams can, however, learn to align all of these features.

Team learning occurs on two levels. One is learning **team alignment.** The other is learning to perform a specific process or combination of processes. Alignment has to do with whether a team, functioning as a whole, works with the same purpose or at cross purposes. A relatively unaligned team wastes energy. A team that becomes more aligned, however, develops a communality of direction and individual energies "harmonize," resulting in less wasted energy. In fact, a synergy may develop through a communality of purpose, a shared vision, and an understanding of ways to complement each other's efforts. "Individuals do not sacrifice their personal interests to the larger team vision; rather the shared vision becomes an extension of their personal visions. In fact, alignment is the necessary condition before empowering the individual willpower of the whole team. Empowering the individuals where there is a relatively low level of alignment worsens the chaos and makes managing the team even more difficult."[12]

Team learning at this level is the process of aligning and developing the capacity to create the results team members truly desire. Two capabilities are at the core of team learning. One is the importance of *thinking insightfully about complex issues.* Each team member must be committed to addressing important issues that affect the team's functioning. The second capability is *innovative, coordinated action.* Each team member must be conscious of other team members so that each can be counted on to act in ways that complement one another's actions. Developing the ability to address complex issues and to take innovative, coordinated action are at the heart of team learning. This "discipline" of team learning by which these capabilities are developed requires mastering the skills of constructive dialogue and discussion, dealing creatively with the forces that oppose productive dialogue and discussion, and practicing this discipline.

> *"Developing the ability to address complex issues and to take innovative, coordinated action are at the heart of team learning."*

A third capability is *fostering learning in other teams* through modeling the practices and skills of team learning. This benefits the organization of which the team is a part by proliferating the learning model. It benefits the team's own learning by helping to develop an organizational environment conducive to team learning. It also benefits the team by reinforcing its own team learning.

Dialogue and Discussion

Collaborative learning means that collectively team members can be more insightful and productive than they can be individually. Collaborative learning is accomplished through **dialogue,** a practice with roots in ancient Greek society. When different parties in a discussion advocate for different positions, they generally assume that the best alternatives are already apparent (sometimes a valid assumption). Dialogue seeks new, more effective alternatives than team members already envision.[13]

Dialogue aims to identify views that are different from any already advocated by a team's members. That this can be accomplished is based on several assumptions. One is that there is a real world, a system that works in a specific manner, if one can only learn what that reality is. A further assumption is that each individual has his own model of how the world works based on a set of personal assumptions about how the world works. Positions an individual advocates in discussion and his behaviors reflect his model of how the world works. If the assumptions implicit in an individual's worldview can be brought to light, others' views about those assumptions can be obtained. To collectively examine each other's assumptions can result in adjustment of the assumptions to more closely accord with the way the real world "works." This in turn can result in changing behaviors based on the original assumptions.

> *"Dialogue aims to identify views that are different from any already advocated by a team's members."*

In dialogue, team members explore complex, difficult issues initially from members' different points of view. Personal assumptions are to be communicated freely. By seeking to look at an issue from the perspective of another, team members begin to see the issue from perspectives other than their own, yet not fully the perspective of the other team member. The result is exploration of people's thoughts and experience in ways that can move beyond individual views. Among members there develops a pool of (relatively) common meaning that is capable of constant development and change. In dialogue, people become observers of their own thinking.[14]

> *"This creates a positive, supportive context and offsets the sense of vulnerability that accompanies dialogue."*

There are three basic conditions for dialogue.[15] First, team members must *suspend their assumptions*. This means becoming aware of their assumptions and holding them up for examination. This does not mean throwing them out, suppressing them, or avoiding them. Suspending assumptions cannot be done if members are defending their opinions, or if they are unaware of their assumptions or are unaware that their views are based on assumptions rather than being incontrovertible facts. Second, dialogue can occur only when members *see each other as colleagues,* that is, as individuals in a mutual quest for deeper insight and clarity. This creates a positive, supportive context and offsets the sense of vulnerability that accompanies dialogue. Treating each other as colleagues acknowledges the risk in holding assumptions in suspension and creates a safe context in which to face that risk. Third, *a facilitator is needed* to help members maintain ownership of the process and outcomes, to keep the dialogue moving, and to influence the flow of development simply through their participating in the process.

In a **discussion,** different views are presented and defended. A discussion provides an analysis of the situation. In dialogue, different views are presented in the interests of discovering a new view. In a discussion, decisions are made. In a dialogue, complex issues are explored. When a team must reach agreement and make decisions, discussion is needed. Discussions converge; dialogues diverge. Dialogue seeks new courses of action. A learning team masters movement back and forth between discussion and dialogue.

A unique relationship develops among team members who enter a dialogue regularly. They develop trust that will carry over to discussions. They develop a better understanding of each other's point of view. They further experience how layers of understanding emerge by holding a point of view "gently." When it is appropriate to defend a position, they do it more gracefully and with less rigidity, that is, without putting winning as the first priority.[16]

> *"A unique relationship develops among team members who enter a dialogue regularly."*

Part of the vision afforded by dialogue is the search for a "larger pool of meaning." It is accessible only to those who develop it. This idea appeals to those who cultivate the subtler aspects of collective inquiry and **consensus building.** There are two types of consensus. One type seeks the common view in multiple individual views. It builds consensus by discovering parts of views shared by all or by most group members. The other type of consensus seeks a picture larger than any one person's point of view. By looking across each person's view, one may see a new view that might not have been seen by any one person alone. This latter is the goal of dialogue.

Conflict and Defensive Routines

High-performing teams experience **conflict.** Conflict can arise over various issues. For example, the visioning process involves the gradual emergence of a shared vision from different personal visions. As this process proceeds, individuals can experience conflict among differing views. Even when people share a vision, they may have different ideas about how to achieve the vision. In the process of carrying out the agreed-on strategy, one or more members can feel that they have not been given the recognition they need or deserve.[17] On high-performing teams, such conflict is expressed and addressed by the principles of conflict resolution (see Chapter 5) and the source of the conflict removed.

Teams that perform at a mediocre or low level are often characterized by one of two conditions surrounding conflict. Either there is, on the surface, the appearance of no conflict or there is rigid polarization. On teams that appear to be running smoothly, members believe they must suppress their conflicting views in order to protect the team's functioning. Each member fears that if she expresses what she thinks or feels the team will be torn apart by irreconcilable differences. By contrast, polarized teams are those where members speak out. Everyone knows the position of everyone else on the team. Differences are pronounced. When conflicts are unexpressed or when conflicting positions are expressed and rigidly held, team performance will be mediocre or poor. In either case, the conflict needs to be addressed. Finding

> *"Each member fears that if she expresses what she thinks or feels the team will be torn apart by irreconcilable differences."*

a view that transcends existing views among team members is important for improved performance.

Teams made up of capable members might also be unable to function effectively depending on how conflict and the defensiveness that invariably surrounds conflict are addressed. Defensiveness is manifest in **defensive routines,** that is, habits individuals use to protect themselves from the embarrassment and the threat that comes from exposing their thinking.[18]

"Defensive routines form a protective shell around our deepest assumptions, defending us against pain, but keeping us from learning about the causes of the pain."

Defensive routines form a protective shell around our deepest assumptions, defending us against pain, but keeping us from learning about the causes of the pain. According to this view, the source of a defensive routine is not a belief in our views or desire to preserve interpersonal relations, as a person might tell him- or herself, but fear of exposing the thinking that lies behind the views. For most persons, the perceived threat of exposing their thinking starts early in childhood. It is often reinforced in school and further reinforced in work. The most effective defensive routines are those we resist seeing. If expressed as a conscious strategy, the defensiveness is obvious, although the defensive individual will almost certainly disavow it. That it remains hidden to the individual keeps it operative.

Defensive routines are a response to a problem. The more effective defensive routines are, the more effectively they cover up the underlying problems, the less effectively the problems are faced, and the worse the problems tend to become. The paradox is that "when defensive routines succeed in preventing immediate pain they also prevent us from learning how to reduce what causes the pain in the first place."[19]

"Defensive routines block the flow of energy in a team that otherwise would progress toward its common vision."

Defensive routines block the flow of energy in a team that otherwise would progress toward its common vision. To the members of a team caught in their defensive routines, they feel very much like barriers that must be both defended and worked around. This requires energy, often considerable energy, that otherwise could be used by a team to pursue its vision.

Defensive routines are difficult to change. They arise from an individual's perception of a threat and are sustained by the generally held view that defensiveness is not good. This in turn is linked to the view of many team members that good teamwork means avoiding conflict by remaining "mannerly," regardless of the cost to team members and to the team. By remaining closed to discussion, defensive routines retain their power.

Several strategies can be used to change defensive routines. One is to establish the norm that team members can discuss each other's strengths and weaknesses. Discussing both strengths and weaknesses is important for reducing the threat posed by looking at weaknesses. As a norm, it makes every team member subject to the same rules.

Another strategy is for the team's leaders to discuss their own feelings of threat posed by a particular issue. This can reduce the feelings of threat for others and aid discussion.[20] Defensive routines usually take more than one person to be effective. The person perceiving it is in some way part of it. Rather than confront the other person, the person who perceives a defensive strategy working can say, "I feel somewhat threatened by this proposal (strategy, etc.). Why is it I feel that way?" This paves the way for others to acknowledge their feelings of threat and to explore reasons for the feeling. A major barrier is crossed. The defensive strategy is open to discussion.

A third strategy for reducing defensive routines is to strengthen the fundamental solution. For those committed to learning, sensing that one or more defensive routines are at work is a signal that learning is not occurring. Defensive routines may also be related to especially difficult, important issues. The more important the issue, the stronger the defensiveness. When these issues are addressed squarely, team members develop a better understanding of each other and a barrier to learning is removed.

> *"The more important the issue, the stronger the defensiveness."*

When team members learn to use their defensive routines as guides rather than let them be barriers to learning and high performance, they gain the experience that there are many aspects of their reality that they have the power to change. It is not the absence of defensiveness that characterizes learning teams but the way defensiveness is faced. A team committed to learning must be committed to telling the truth about what is going on within the team. To see reality more clearly, we must see clearly our strategies for obscuring reality.[21]

Practice

Team learning is a team skill. Teams learn how to learn together. Team skills are more challenging to develop than individual skills. Learning teams need "practice fields" (ways to practice together) so that they can practice their learning skills. The almost total absence of meaningful practice (or rehearsal) available to teams is probably the predominant factor that keeps most teams from being effective learning units. Team learning requires regular practice. Practice is essentially experimentation with freedom from repercussions for missteps. In such situations, the pace of action can be increased or slowed. Situations can be varied. No move is irreversible. Actions can be repeated in variations. Complexity can be simplified by addressing subunits.

> *"Team skills are more challenging to develop than individual skills."*

There are two types of practice fields, practicing dialogue and environments in which team functioning can be simulated. **Dialogue sessions** allow a team to practice dialogue and develop the skills dialogue demands. The basic conditions for such a session are (1) having all members of a team together; (2) explaining the ground rules of dialogue; (3) enforcing the rules in the sense that whenever any member is unable to "suspend" his or her assumptions, the team acknowledges that it is now *discussing*, not dialoguing; and (4) encouraging team members to raise the most difficult, subtle, and conflict-laden issues essential to the team's work. Such sessions are practice because they are designed to foster team skills.

Simulated environments are another context for practice. Here teams learn by confronting the dynamics of complex problems. Team members can experiment with different solutions to complex problems. Simulations are contexts for relevant "play"[22]. The issues and dynamics of complex situations can be explored through trying out new strategies and policies and seeing what happens. In simulated environments, teams can explore diverse issues. These experiments build on and incorporate insights about system structures, team learning, and working with mental models.

The Challenge Revisited
Team Development and Learning

1. A challenge for a team is to address the tension between reaching its goal, that is, getting done, and achieving its vision, that is, getting better.

2. A team's vision of high performance encompasses its expectations for and the significance of reaching its goal and producing its product.

3. Identifying and removing barriers to high performance are essential if a team is to achieve its vision.

4. Removing barriers requires a team to develop its collective skills, to learn to align its activities, and to remove whatever hinders alignment.

5. Members' disparate assumptions about performance can prevent alignment and defensive routines can prevent addressing the assumptions.

6. Dialogue enables team members to view barriers from new perspectives and to develop and practice strategies to remove barriers.

EXERCISE 13.1 • *Towering Vision*[23]

Instructions: Your team has been commissioned to demonstrate to a group of corporate executives how high-performance teams function. They desire to see a demonstration of effective teamwork. To perform this demonstration, your team is to design and build a tower-like structure with materials that are provided, and only those that are provided.

- The structure must be self-standing on the floor, with nothing propping it up, such as a string tied to furniture.

- Completed structures will be judged on four characteristics: (1) quality of concept, (2) creativity of design, (3) structural stability, and (4) height.

Each team must decide which one characteristic or combination of characteristics to emphasize.

Begin assembling your tower, according to each of the following timed steps. Teams must proceed to the next step when the time limit is reached. Use only material from this list:

- Newspaper
- String
- Scissors
- Notepaper

1. Think about structure and develop preliminary sketch (5 minutes).

2. Discuss design ideas and arrive at an integrated design that represents the team (15 minutes).

3. Construct your tower (25 minutes).

4. Put finishing touches on your construction and develop a marketing "pitch" to induce judges to vote for your tower (10 minutes).

5. Conduct presentation of structure.

After the presentation each team casts one vote for the structure that best meets the stated criteria. A team may not vote for its own tower.

EXERCISE 13.2 • *Barriers to Performance*

1. Identify two barriers to high performance encountered in performing the Towering Vision exercise. Follow the procedures for dialogue described in this chapter. (Be sure to appoint a discussion facilitator.)

2. Conduct further dialogue to identify ways to resolve each of the barriers. Use the five-step problem-solving process (described in chapter 12) for implementing and examining the effectiveness of the strategy chosen to improve your team's performance.

3. Prepare a short report of the process and the results of your team's deliberations.

QUESTIONS FOR REVIEW AND DISCUSSION

1. What does the term *stage* mean when used to describe a team's development process? Is the term appropriate for describing a team's development? Explain.

2. Four characterizations of team development are described in this chapter:

   a. Three stages: orientation, evaluation, and control.

   b. Answering two questions: how emotionally involved are members and who controls team activities?

   c. Four levels of two dimensions: work and emotion.

   d. Four (later five) stages of team development.

   What are the strengths and inadequacies of each characterization?

3. One different perspective on team development proposes four challenges that teams must address. What are the challenges? Why does the way a team addresses these challenges not represent stages?

4. Viewed from a systems perspective, how does team performance develop? To what extent do the system subprocesses address the same questions addressed by the stages or the challenges conceptualization?

5. What does the phrase "team learning" mean? How does it differ from individual learning? What are the two levels of team learning? What are

the two capabilities at the core of team learning? Why can this type of learning be more insightful and productive than individual learning?

6. How do dialogue and discussion differ? What is the objective of dialogue? What is the process by which dialogue is conducted? Why is a facilitator important for dialogue to occur? How does a team know when dialogue has occurred?

7. What are defensive routines? How is conflict (or potential conflict) related to defensive routines? What is the purpose of a defensive routine? What are the consequences of defensive routines? What are the strategies for changing defensive routines? How can a defensive routine be used as a guide to addressing difficult issues?

NOTES

1. R. F. Bales & F. L. Strodbeck (1951), Phases in group problem solving, *Journal of Abnormal and Social Psychology,* 46, 485–495.

2. W. G. Bennis & H. A . Shephard (1956), A theory of group development, *Human Relations,* 9, 415–457.

3. W. R. Bion (1961), *Experiences in Groups,* London: Tavistock/Routledge.

4. B. W. Tuchman (1965), Developmental sequence in small groups, *Psychological Bulletin,* 63, 384–399.

5. An addition to this latter group is provided by the work of J. R. Hackman (Ed.) (1990), *Groups that Work (And Some that Don't),* San Francisco: Jossey-Bass.

6. L. J. Braaten (1974–1975), Developmental phases of encounter groups and related intensive groups: A critical review of models and a new proposal, *Interpersonal Development,* 5, 112–129; also B. W. Tuchman & M. A. C. Jensen (1977), Stages of small-group development revisited, *Groups & Organization Studies,* 2, 419–427.

7. J. E. McGrath (1984), *Groups: Interaction and Performance,* Englewood Cliffs, NJ: Prentice Hall, pp. 160–161.

8. C. J. C. Gersick (1990), The students, in Hackman, op. cit., pp. 89–111.

9. S. G. Cohen & D. R. Denison (1990), Flight attendant teams, in Hackman, op. cit., pp. 382–397.

10. Gersick, in Hackman, op. cit., p. 100.

11. McGrath, op. cit., p.160–161.

12. This section on team learning is summarized from a chapter of the same name in P. M. Senge (1990), *The Fifth Discipline,* New York: Doubleday, pp. 233–269. The quotation is from pages 234–235.

13. Senge, op. cit., p. 239.

14. Senge, op. cit., p. 241.

15. Senge, op. cit., p. 248.

16. Senge, op. cit., p. 248.

17. Senge, op. cit., p. 249.

18. Senge, op. cit., pp. 249ff, reflects on the views of C. Argyris regarding defensive routines.

19. Senge, op. cit., p. 254; see also C. Argyris (1985), *Strategy, Change, and Defensive Routines*, Boston: Pitman.

20. Senge, op. cit., p. 255.

21. Senge, op. cit., p. 257.

22. Senge, op. cit., p. 259.

23. "Towering Vision," in S. Kaagan (1999), *Leadership Games*, Thousand Oaks, CA: Sage, pp. 56ff. Used by permission.

The Challenge
Effective Team Performance

An effective team produces a product that meets or exceeds its customer's expectations. An effective team establishes and works toward a significant vision for its product. An effective team uses a strategy that enables it to produce its product efficiently and to manage its resources and throughput processes in a manner that facilitates that goal attainment. As a team proceeds, it learns to improve its performance, to maintain its viability as a performing unit, and to ensure that its members experience satisfaction while doing so. At the heart of a team's effectiveness are its decision-making and problem-solving abilities. This means that it develops its plan, performs tasks, coordinates its activities, establishes an efficient social structure, and gathers and uses feedback to guide and improve its performance.

chapter 14

Effective Team Performance

PERSPECTIVES ON TEAM EFFECTIVENESS

A team's effectiveness can be viewed from several perspectives. Customers use or apply a team's product and want the product on time and in a quantity and of a quality specified. A team's members want their team to perform well and they want to experience satisfaction in the process. Other teams in the same organization, joined in a process with the team, want the team to support their performance. A team's suppliers, that is, those who provide the materials a team uses to reach its goal, want the team's performance to reflect positively on what is supplied. All are among those considered **stakeholders,** that is, those for whom a team's effectiveness has implications.

The Customer and Team Effectiveness

Customer refers broadly to those who use and evaluate a team's product. Consider the following example. In a visit to a resort hotel that was housing several hundred guests, the staff's teamwork was obvious. Staff related to each other smoothly, assisted each other without hesitation, and appeared to enjoy their work. On the second evening of the visit, a freezing rain began early and around 9 P.M. the electric power went off for a short time, then returned. Guests learned that falling trees had broken the power lines and an emergency generator was operating. Later in the evening and through the night, tree limbs and whole trees could be heard splintering and falling under the weight of the ice. By morning, many downed trees and limbs blocked the two-mile access road to the hotel. Several hours would be required to reopen it. Meanwhile, staff working in the hotel the previous evening could not leave, and those seeking to come to work the next morning could not. In the morning, guests found staff, obviously tired from having worked late the night before, beginning early and working with a fraction of the normal number. Food was prepared and service provided. Notable were a gift shop supervisor who was seating guests in the dining room and a headwaiter making omelets for guests who wished them. Staff members were cheerful and maintained a high level of service. This team's effectiveness extended to serving customers well under emergency conditions .[1]

> *"Staff related to each other smoothly, assisted each other without hesitation, and appeared to enjoy their work."*

Team Members' Perspective on Effectiveness

Team members tend to focus on how well their team is functioning, that is, how well task performance and interactions with other team members are proceeding. The immediacy of these processes for team members, often unknown to the team's customer, can distract team members from focusing on achieving the team's goal, that is, producing a product that meets the customer's standards.

This concern for internal functioning is exemplified by students' characterizations of the *most effective* and the *least effective* teams they experienced. Most frequently cited regarding effective teams was members' willingness to work as a team to achieve a goal. Also noted were good communication; members knowing and doing their part; members having a shared goal and vision; members having the diverse experience, skills, and ideas needed to achieve the goal; members' willingness to sacrifice individual recognition; having an effective leader; and having fun. Characteristics of the *least effective* teams were member apathy, that is, missing meetings, being too busy doing other things, being unprepared, indicators of an attitude that "others will do the work," goals being out of focus, or members differing on what the goal was. Also noted were all members wanting to be the leader or no one wanting to lead and members being poor communicators, closed to each others' ideas, having different priorities, lacking trust, or simply being unhappy.[2]

Models of Team Effectiveness

Both the customers' focus on a team's product and team members' focus on team functioning are important for understanding team effectiveness. A challenge is to join the two perspectives. Social scientists, seeking a more comprehensive perspective, have focused on two questions: (1) What is effective performance? and (2) What behaviors or conditions give rise to effective performance? One author noted with reference to these questions, "...practice has greatly outstripped theory"[3]. This is to say, the ability to measure performance is much better than the ability to predict it. Several models have proposed answers to these questions.

> "The goal model specifies that an effective team will achieve its goal and the goal(s) of the organization of which it is a part."

The **goal model** specifies that an effective team will achieve its goal and the goal(s) of the organization of which it is a part. This model assumes that for every team there is a readily identifiable set of outputs that can be agreed on and measured. Outputs include units produced, quality, sales, and customers served, among others. Effectiveness is reflected in the rate of progress toward the goal[4] and producing the agreed-on output.[5]

The **natural systems model** questions the assumption that every team has a readily agreed-on, consistent goal by noting the possibility of conflicting goals. This model assumes that a team is an open system with the primary goal of survival. Rendering a desirable output (product) is central to that survival. For example, a team whose mandate is to produce a superior product and also keep costs to a minimum may find these goals in conflict. It may need to decide which goal has priority, then problem solve to achieve the other goal as much as possible. Effective teams must manage such conflicts to survive. This requires a team to stay in touch with key features of its functioning, primarily group maintenance processes, to develop and maintain its problem-solving skills.[6]

> "Rendering a desirable output (product) is central to that survival."

The **multiple constituents model,** unlike both the goal model and the natural systems model, does not assume a single view of team effectiveness. Rather, a team orients to the expectations of multiple stakeholders, that is, those who stand to gain or lose depending on a team's level of effectiveness. Different constituencies—a team's customer, other teams that work with a team, a team's supplier, a team's manager, among others—may use somewhat different measures of effectiveness.[7]

> "Effective teams must manage such conflicts to survive."

These models are complementary.[8] Each offers a different view of effectiveness. The **normative model,** developed more recently, combines features of the preceding models and defines three effectiveness criteria: (1) that *output* meet or exceed a customer's standards, (2) that the *social processes* required to carry out the work maintain or enhance members' ability to work together on subsequent tasks, and (3) that the *group's experience* satisfies (rather than frustrates) members' needs.[9]

A subsequent model[10] focused on *team performance measurement,* noting the range of operational definitions of performance in general and goal achievement in particular. This model includes a team's organizational culture and customer needs as the context for understanding performance measurement. Also included in the model are an organization's goals, strategic plans, and mission. Once these are understood, an appropriate organizational effectiveness model can be specified. This model also includes two additional issues. Benchmarking involves comparing a team's performance to the performance of other comparable teams, either within the organization or in other organizations. Constraints or barriers to effectiveness are also considered, assuming that, once identified, they can be reduced or removed to improve effectiveness.

EFFECTIVE TEAM PERFORMANCE: A REVISED MODEL

The preceding discussion has identified a variety of considerations relevant to understanding a team's performance effectiveness. The following model builds on the models just described. The organizing framework is the systems process: input, throughput, and output. In the model *inputs* involve the direction and support provided by the organizational context, the design of the team as a performing unit, and the characteristics of team members. *Throughput processes* involve the way a team organizes its throughput subprocesses, the strategy it uses to perform the subprocesses, the team's degree of collective efficacy in pursuing its goal, the comparative information (benchmarks) a team gathers about other relevant teams' performance, and the barriers a team encounters and reduces or removes in the process. *Outputs* involve the status of a team's product, the degree of improvement in a team's performance, the viability of the team as a performing unit, and the satisfactions experienced by its members. Figure 14.1 depicts this model and the following discussion elaborates its elements.[11]

Inputs

A team's **organizational context** specifies for a team a significant, challenging goal and the expectations for its achievement. A supportive organizational context provides several resources to aid a team in pursuit of its goal. One is an

FIGURE 14.1
Model of Team Effectiveness

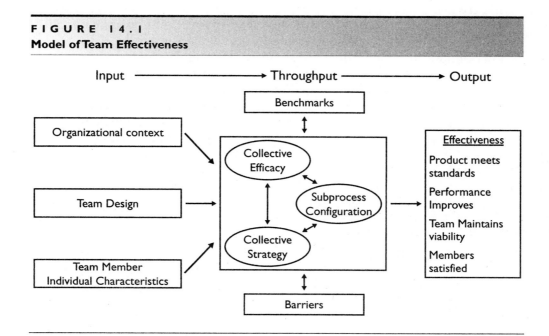

educational system that delivers relevant educational resources in a way that meets a team's needs. Another is an information system that enables a team to plan, evaluate, and execute a goal-appropriate performance strategy. Information is needed about task requirements and constraints, about available material resources, about how the product will be used, and about the standards to be used to evaluate it. Another is *material resources* sufficient for accomplishing goal-related tasks well and on time. Finally, a *reward system* is needed that complements the motivating qualities of the task, that rewards team performance, and that recognizes excellent individual performance.

> *"A team's membership should be sufficiently large and their skills sufficiently diverse to provide the team with the task and interpersonal skills needed to reach its goal."*

A team's design as a performing unit should promote effective task behavior and minimize the likelihood of encountering built-in obstacles to high performance. Two **team design** features make the work meaningful. A **task structure** is needed that engages a relatively high skill level, that has as a whole a visible outcome with significant consequences, that gives members sufficient autonomy to feel ownership of the task, and that provides regular, trustworthy feedback about the quality and quantity of the work. **Group composition** concerns the size of the team and the amount of knowledge and skills members have. A team's membership should be sufficiently large and their skills sufficiently diverse to provide the team with the task and interpersonal skills needed to reach its goal.

Team member characteristics concern the individual skills, behavior styles, and attitudes that either enable or limit each member's working with other members as an effective performing unit.

Throughput Process

At the core of a team's throughput process, as depicted in Figure 14.2, is the interrelation of its throughput subprocesses, its strategy, and its sense of collective efficacy. These interacting features demonstrate how a team does its "work" and have important implications for performance effectiveness.

A team's **performance subprocesses,** discussed individually in Chapters 5 through 11, are the components used to design the path to its goal. A challenge for a team is to configure these subprocesses in a manner that enables it to achieve its goal, that is, to produce the specified product in an efficient, timely,

> *"An effective team configures its subprocesses both to reach its goal and to address these difficulties."*

and qualitatively acceptable manner. Further challenges are to have the chosen configuration facilitate the other characteristics of an effective team, its ability to improve its performance, its developing and learning as a team, and its providing satisfaction to its members. These challenges are often daunting. A specific goal may be difficult to achieve and the environment in which the goal is to be reached not wholly supportive. An effective team configures its subprocesses both to reach its goal and to address these difficulties. How well each subprocess functions individually and in concert with other subprocesses affects both a team's progress toward its goal and the status of its product when its goal is reached. The following paragraphs summarize key features of the subprocesses.

F I G U R E   1 4 . 2
Core Features of Throughput Process

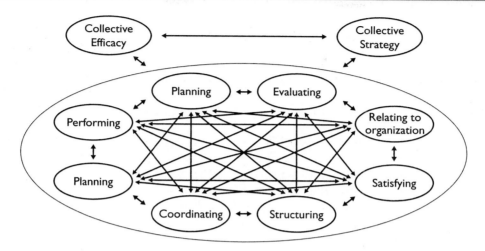

Subprocess configuration

Planning enables a team to lay out a path to its goal and enables members to reach agreement about the path. The plan defines each step, specifies the relationships between steps, and establishes a time line for accomplishing the steps. For each step, a team's plan specifies the tasks to be performed, the role of leadership, how activities are to be coordinated and interactions structured, and how the process will be evaluated. If barriers are anticipated, how these will be addressed is specified.

Performing is what a team does to carry out its plan. There is generally room to improve a plan, since even the best plan may not specify everything about a step. This will create the need for team problem solving to find improvements. A combination of realistic appraisal of previous performance, agile revision of its current plan, and practice to improve performance can have a significant impact on the quality of team performance.

Leading facilitates a team's progress by maintaining a focus on the goal, by helping members to identify appropriate tasks and roles, by encouraging member participation, by maintaining a flow of useful feedback, by recognizing member contributions, and by sharing team recognition with all members. A leader encourages members' sense of interdependence and fosters members' satisfaction and involvement.

Coordinating facilitates a team's progress by synchronizing members' task performance and interactions. Coordination requires planning, effective communication, practice, and continuous evaluation. It is enhanced by members' cooperation and by collaborative learning.

Structuring is used by a team to manage its more repetitive processes. Norms or mutual expectations regulate and control members' behavior. Structure also involves members assuming roles, such as leader. Communication networks are structures that

"A leader encourages members' sense of interdependence and fosters members' satisfaction and involvement."

reflect the frequency with which members communicate with each other. Members establish structures and come to feel comfortable with them. Replacing existing structures with new, more efficient ones can create discomfort and require effort and practice.

Satisfying members' interests and motivation encourages involvement. Members find satisfaction by contributing their capabilities to the team's progress, by feeling "heard" by other members, and by having their contribution recognized. Lacking these opportunities, members feel excluded, devalued, and hurt. As a result, motivation declines and involvement disappears. A team's leader must ensure that each member contributes and that significant contributions are recognized.

> *"Information reflective of collective performance is also important to support interdependence."*

Evaluating provides information about a team's level of performance and its progress toward its goal. Team members need such information, although gathering it can be time-consuming. Clear, objective, reliable information is crucial for identifying barriers to high performance. Information reflective of collective performance is also important to support interdependence.

A team's execution of its **collective strategy** involves three features that determine the effectiveness of the strategy. One is the *appropriateness of the strategy*. Are the subprocesses combined, coordinated, and as a whole implemented in a way that enables a team to efficiently reach its goal? Another is the *amount of knowledge and skill* members have available to execute the strategy. Do members have the requisite expertise and are they using their knowledge, skill, and effort efficiently? Finally, there is the *level of collective effort* members exert to implement the strategy. Is the team working hard enough to accomplish the prescribed steps required to achieve the team's goal, well and on time?

A sense of **collective efficacy** results from team members pursuing a mutual goal by coordinating activities smoothly, interacting cooperatively, and performing tasks successfully. This experience increases members' confidence that their team can address the demands and opportunities of a performance situation. *Member effort* is supported by minimizing coordination and motivation losses and by experiencing shared commitment to the team and its work. *Knowledge and skill* are supported by the mutuality of members' contributions and by the experience of collective learning. The *performance strategy* is supported by innovative strategic plans and minimal slippage in strategy implementation.

Some commentators on team functioning assume that a team can not only avoid "process losses"[12], but achieve a level of performance that exceeds the aggregate of individual performances. This *synergistic effect* is assumed to be a group-level phenomenon that emerges from member interactions and affects how well a team is able to meet the demands and take advantage of the opportunities in the performance situation.[13] This effect enables members to find innovative ways to reduce inefficient use of member resources and to interact in ways that create new internal resources, that is, resources not previously available for the team's work. "Commitment to a team sometimes can result in high effort on the group task even when the objective performance conditions are highly unfavorable (e.g., a team that develops a 'can do' attitude and comes to view each new adversity as yet another challenge to be met)."[14]

This "can do" attitude is best described as *collective efficacy* .[15] Collective efficacy is

> . . . a group's shared belief in its conjoint capabilities to organize and execute the courses of action required to produce given levels of attainments. The collective belief centers in the group's operative capabilities. Group functioning is the product of interactive and coordinative dynamics of its members. Interactive dynamics create an emergent property that is more than the sum of the individual attributes. . . . A host of factors contribute to the interactive effects. Some of these factors are a mix of knowledge and competencies in the group, how the group is structured and its activities coordinated, how well it is led, the strategies it adopts, and whether members interact with one another in mutually facilitory or undermining ways. The same participants can achieve different results depending on how well their particular skills and efforts are coordinated and guided. A group's capability to perform as a whole can vary widely under different blends of interactive dynamics. Therefore, perceived collective efficacy is an emergent group-level attribute rather than simply the sum of the members' perceived personal efficacies.[16]

Constraints to Effective Teamwork

Teams encounter barriers or constraints to progress toward their goals or to performance improvement. A **theory of constraints**[17] assumes a performance process that occurs in consecutive, interdependent stages. The end of each stage produces an output for use in the next stage. One author notes, "Due to the linkages of interdependency and variability, a constraint will delay throughputs throughout the system"[18]. For example, consider a five-member manufacturing team that produces electronic devices. Each member in succession inserts a different component into a frame. Any member who is slower than others is a constraint. Removing the constraint means identifying the reason for the slower pace and reducing or eliminating it.

An effective team proceeds as expeditiously as possible along the most direct path to its goal. A variety of potential barriers may limit progress. Constraint theory specifies the need to identify constraints to progress, select the one or two that are most limiting, and seek to reduce or remove them. The following are examples of barriers.[19]

Communication difficulties often underlie unclear expectations by those whose role it is to formulate them, an equivocal strategy for tracking accomplishments or nonaccomplishment of the expectations, or a leader who does not provide information needed to perform the expected activities in a timely manner.

"Teams encounter barriers or constraints to progress toward their goals or to performance improvement."

"An effective team proceeds as expeditiously as possible along the most direct path to its goal."

Unproductive team meetings often arise from failing to decide what a meeting is intended to achieve and to plan the meeting carefully. Using team meetings to settle disputes or to resolve crises can be helpful, but if the time is used only for such matters, little time will be left to plan strategy and to identify ways to improve team functioning.

Failure to understand interrelationships means that members do not understand how their own performance affects the performance of other team members, of the team as a whole, and of the overall organization. Stressing the concept of "customer" is a way to get team members to broaden their views from considering only their own tasks to understanding how their tasks link to the tasks of others.

Unclear vision contrasts with a vision that is clear, forward looking, realistic in a business sense, and in which rewards are shared with team members as progress is made toward achieving the vision. A clear vision gives meaning and significance to a team's goal and its achievement.

> *"Making progress toward a goal and improving in the process means change."*

Aversion to change works in opposition to most team functioning. Making progress toward a goal and improving in the process means change. Members and whole teams can resist change, fearing things will get "out of control." One reason companies encourage teamwork is to provide teams a sense of control over their own work. A sense of control also arises from a team's having the required capabilities and from the sense that it can use the capabilities effectively, that is, it has a sense of collective efficacy.

Failure to gain commitment arises from several sources. *Inequitable treatment of workers,* in which a team and its leaders set expectations and then do not enforce those expectations, undercuts members' motivation. Members who simply "don't care," who miss meetings, who are unprepared, or who fail to perform agreed-on tasks, and who are not sanctioned, generate resentment in other members. Members who feel responsible and take up the slack resent having to do so. An *inequitable reward and recognition system* can also detract from commitment. The most effective system is likely to be a combination of team rewards and individual recognition. *Peer pressure* can exert influence to resist improvement. When some members are committed to their own individual goals, they can pressure other members to moderate their efforts to avoid creating higher expectations for their performance. At the root of such resistance is distrust and fear of exploitation.

> *"Leadership inadequacies occur when the leader's role is unclear, especially when a team is new."*

Leadership inadequacies occur when the leader's role is unclear, especially when a team is new. Questions may arise about whether leadership is one person's responsibility or a shared or rotated responsibility and about how much responsibility a leader should have. There are other questions: Do leaders give orders, suggest, facilitate, or coach? How should a leader be chosen: by vote, by volunteering, or by being appointed? What is the team leader's role in setting team direction? What is the team leader's role in team meetings? When is leadership training appropriate? These are issues that a team needs to consider and arrive at conclusions acceptable to all members.

Benchmarking

Benchmarking in business most frequently involves comparing a particular set of practices in one company with similar practices in another company. For a team, it can mean much the same. For example, a business unit that responds to customer complaints compares (benchmarks) its practices with those in a similar business unit from another company. Such comparisons are important because of the information they provide about both process and outcome.

Benchmarking can also be used to set performance standards.[20] It involves an organizational subunit seeking to identify *best practices* and then comparing its own practice to them. Such comparisons can focus on a range of activities from how the activity is performed to how the activity is measured. "The best case determinations emerge naturally from benchmarking the best teams. Based just on their own experiences, teams may not know how well they can do. . . . Benchmarking . . . broadens the team's perspective beyond its boundaries and challenges the team to push its own limits"[21].

For a team, there are other, not so obvious, sources of comparison. An important one is members' experience with previous team activities. A member who has had a positive experience brings a different perspective and set of standards to the team's activities than a member who has had a negative experience. These experiences need to be shared by team members and their implications for the team's performance discussed.

Underlying benchmarking is a "social comparison process" that underscores the importance of clear evaluation information.[22] This perspective proposes that in the absence of objective, reliable information about the status of one's thoughts and actions, a person will seek comparable information from other persons in an effort to clarify that status. For example, a student who receives a test score of 35 but does not know the maximum, possible score, will seek to compare his or her score with others to determine the "meaning" of the score. When the status of one's performance is unclear, the need to clarify can be a powerful stimulus to seeking relevant information. This applies to teams as well, and benchmarking is one way to provide such information.

"When the status of one's performance is unclear, the need to clarify can be a powerful stimulus to seeking relevant information."

The need for comparative information can vary. For example, a team with a deadline for delivering its report at 3 P.M. on Friday has little ambiguity about whether it meets that expectation. The same team, having the vision that its report will have a significant impact on practice in its organization and in the industry generally, may find it very difficult to determine if the vision is fulfilled. If the team knows nothing about practice in the rest of the industry, the relevance of its report to other companies' practice will be unclear. Clarification can be achieved by gathering comparative information.

"Clarification can be achieved by gathering comparative information."

Such comparative information can be complex. The information for which comparison may be needed can be diverse and relevant sources varied. For example, comparative information includes how goals are reached, how plans are made, how communication occurs, how tasks are performed, how members' activities are coordinated, how activities are structured and evaluated, and how satisfactions are experienced. Obtaining relevant information can be a challenge.

ACHIEVING EFFECTIVE PERFORMANCE

Achieving high performance is a process that can be distinguished from producing a product, but the two processes are related. Just as there are multiple paths by which a team can achieve its goal, there are also multiple paths by which a team can achieve effective performance. Finding the latter path is as much a problem to be solved by a team as is identifying and taking the steps to its goal. The duality of these processes is evident when a team first tries to reach its goal and learns about itself as a performing group. Without that first experience (and sometimes more than one), a team will not have a "feel" for what it means to produce a product. Once this develops, how to improve its production process can be addressed with its prior experience as the point of reference.

In planning and implementing its plan to achieve its goal, a team is undertaking a group problem-solving task. In seeking to improve its performance, a team is undertaking another, possibly more complex, group problem-solving task. In this process, a team must examine the features of its team system and decide which ones, if changed, could improve its performance. Unless a team has (or develops) a systematic way to evaluate the different features of its system, the process will be rather hit or miss and fail to focus on the most strategic points for or barriers to improvement.

"These interrelated processes require of team members an underlying trust in each other and a willingness to be open and nondefensive in discussing ways to improve team performance."

These interrelated processes require of team members an underlying trust in each other and a willingness to be open and nondefensive in discussing ways to improve team performance. One barrier, discussed in depth by Argyris,[23] occurs when some or even all of a team's members are unwilling to voice their self-censored thoughts about reasons for their team's inadequate functioning. These must be voiced—whether about the process or about other team members—in as constructive a manner as possible. One way to do this is to propose observations about team inadequacies or about barriers to improved performance as "hypotheses" to be specified and tested by gathering and evaluating relevant information. This is a form of hypothesis testing that a team must practice to become comfortable with and effective in using.

The Challenge Revisited
Effective Team Performance

1. An effective team must meet or exceed its customer's expectations for product standards, timeliness, and resource use.

2. The quality of a team's performance determines the quality of its product.

3. To improve its performance, a team must overcome barriers such as communication difficulties, aversion to change, lack of commitment, leadership inadequacies, and distrust.

4. Effective performance enables a team to achieve its goal. It requires planning, members' willingness to be open about team inadequacies, trust, practice, commitment, and perseverance.

5. The challenge for a team is to organize its performance in a manner that enables it to become effective in pursuing its goal and achieving its vision.

EXERCISE 14.1 • *Team Performance*

1. As a team, develop a list of the most important things learned about team performance.

2. Develop and present a skit depicting one or more things learned.

QUESTIONS FOR REVIEW AND DISCUSSION

1. Why is it important for a team to determine the criteria its customer will use to evaluate its product? Why do criteria differ from customer to customer?

2. Why do team members tend to focus primarily on team functioning? What is the advantage of this for a team? The disadvantages? How can the disadvantages be overcome?

3. The different models of team effectiveness described in the text are the goal model, the natural systems model, the multiple constituents model, and the normative model. What are the similarities and differences among these models?

4. In the performance measurement model, what are the dimensions to be measured? What is the significance of each dimension for a team's effectiveness?

5. In the revised model, what are the three types of inputs? What comprises each type? What is the significance of each type for team effectiveness?

6. What are the core features of the throughput process? What is the significance of each for team effectiveness?

7. What comprises the configuration of throughput subprocesses? How is a team's path to its goal defined by the specific way a team configures these subprocesses?

8. What comprises a team's collective strategy? What is its significance for team effectiveness?

9. What is meant by the phrase *a team's collective efficacy*? What is its significance for a team's effectiveness?

10. What is meant by the term *benchmarking*? What process underlies benchmarking and gives it significance for a team's effectiveness?

NOTES

1. Observed by the author at Mohonk Mountain Resort, New York, November 2002.

2. Summary of responses of Lehigh University students in answer to the question of effective and ineffective teams.

3. S. Jones (1997), Team performance measurement: Theoretical and applied issues, in M. Beyerlein and D. Johnson (Eds.), *Advances in Interdisciplinary Studies of Work Teams*, Vol. 4, London: JAI Press, p. 116.

4. R. L. Kahn (1977), Organizational effectiveness: An overview, in P. S. Goodman, J. M. Pennings, & Associates (Eds.), *New Perspectives on Organizational Effectiveness*, San Francisco: Jossey-Bass, pp. 13–55.

5. Jones, op. cit.

6. See J. P. Campbell (1977), On the nature of organizational effectiveness, in Goodman, et al., op. cit.; also Jones, op. cit.

7. Jones, op. cit.

8. S. E. Seashore (1983), A framework for an integrated model of organizational effectiveness, in K. S. Cameron & D. A. Whetton (Eds.), *Organizational Effectiveness: A Comparison of Multiple Models*, New York: Academic Press, pp. 55–70.

9. J. R. Hackman (1987), The design of work teams, in J. W. Lorsch (Ed.), *Handbook of Organizational Behavior*, Englewood Cliffs, NJ: Prentice Hall, pp. 315–342.

10. Jones, op. cit., p. 127.

11. Elements of this model are based on models described in Hackman, op. cit., and Jones, op.cit.

12. I. Steiner (1972), *Group Process and Productivity*, New York: Academic Press.

13. Hackman, op. cit.

14. Hackman, op. cit., p. 326.

15. A. Bandura (1997), *Self-efficacy: The Exercise of Control,* New York: Freeman; and A. Bandura (2000), The exercise of human agency through collective efficacy, *Current Directions in Psychological Science,* 9, 75–78.

16. Bandura, op. cit., pp. 477–478.

17. E. M. Goldratt (1986), *The Goal,* Croton-on-Hudson, NY: North River Press.

18. Jones, op. cit., p. 128.

19. To answer this question, a series of interviews was conducted in companies using team-based management. Questions concerned how well teams were functioning and the barriers to their effective functioning. Employees ranging from plant managers to hourly assembly-line workers were asked the questions. Responses varied. They could, however, be grouped in a limited set of broad categories. The interviews were conducted in 1996 and 1997.

20. A description of the results of benchmarking visits by teams is given in R. S. Wellins, W. C. Byham, & G. R. Dixon (1994), *Inside Teams: How 20 World-Class Organizations Are Winning through Teamwork,* San Francisco: Jossey-Bass.

21. Jones. op. cit., pp. 127–128.

22. See L. Festinger (1954), A theory of social comparison processes, *Human Relations,* 7, 117–140; and W. Stroebe, M. Diehl, & G. Abakoumkin (1996), Social compensation and the Kohler effect: Toward a theoretical explanation of motivation gains in group productivity, in E. Witte & J. H. Davis (Eds.), *Understanding Group Behavior,* Vol. 2, Mahwah, NJ: Erlbaum, pp. 37–65.

23. C. Argyris (1993), *Knowledge for Action: A Guide to Overcoming Barriers to Organizational Change,* San Francisco: Jossey-Bass.

Concluding Remarks

section four

Successful teamwork, as described in the preceding chapters, is not an accidental phenomenon for which no guidelines are available. Rather, it consists of a set of attitudes and actions that, when performed in a coordinated manner, enables a team to achieve its goal. An inexperienced team may include some members who have the necessary attitudes and some members who can perform only some of the actions. Ideally, all must share the same attitudes, especially commitment and a willingness to get involved and to work to achieve the team's goal. As a new team becomes more experienced, its members begin to understand how the different actions are relevant to successful goal-directed performance. They can also identify actions that do not contribute to the team's progress. Experience can also enable members to recognize those actions that all members must be able to perform and those that can be performed by subsets of members.

This book began with an overview of team functioning and proceeded to examine the different features of that functioning: the resources and expectations that are inputs; the subprocesses that comprise the throughput process by which a team proceeds toward its goal; and the results of achieving the goal, that is, the team's product and what the team learns in the process. The preceding chapter on team effectiveness presented a model of how these features interrelate to achieve effective goal-oriented performance.

The effectiveness model may seem rather abstract to a new team confronted with an unfamiliar goal and unfamiliar teammates. In such a situation, a team may flounder until members become sufficiently comfortable with each other and are able to focus on their team's goal. For the inexperienced team, performance often involves becoming acquainted with fellow members, figuring out what the team will do, and pondering what satisfactions will be experienced. Eventually, often because a deadline looms, the team begins to organize itself by assigning and undertaking tasks and seeking to achieve the prescribed goal in the requisite time.

With more experience, a team will learn that a certain set of attitudes and actions is reflected in the effectiveness model that team members or the team as a whole must perform to move effectively toward its goal. These "operating principles" underlie effective teamwork. All are necessary at some point in a team's progress toward its goal. The lack of an important attitude or action at a critical point in a team's functioning can have serious, negative consequences for a team's performance.

A set of important attitudes and actions are outlined next. For each one described, its implementation means the addition of a dimension of strength, and its absence means the weakening of the team's effectiveness.

AT THE OUTSET (INPUT)

Commitment to work with other team members to achieve the team's goal and trusting other members to do the same. A team's effectiveness is based on each member's commitment to perform as a team. This means that each member contributes his or her relevant capabilities to the team and expects the same of other members. One member's lack of commitment can negatively affect the commitment of others and jeopardize a successful outcome.

Ability and willingness to discuss difficult topics related to team performance. Discussing team performance issues is central to effective teamwork. Such discussion is required for identifying member styles, for planning and coordinating team tasks and member interactions, for performing tasks, and for identifying and removing performance barriers. Such discussions can be challenging, but they make it possible for a team to find the most efficient strategy for reaching its goal. Failure to participate fully in team discussions denies the team access to crucial resources.

Ability to establish and maintain interdependence among team members and their activities. Interdependence requires members to depend on each other and to see results as team accomplishments, not as individual accomplishments. As a result, members become aware that what affects one member affects every member. Although some may be uncomfortable with interdependency, it is the key advantage that team performance has over individual performance.

Ability to develop and maintain focus on a clear, mutually agreed-on goal. Team members must examine the nature of the team goal and persevere in their discussions until a clear, mutually agreed-on goal is defined. Failure to do so can result in misdirection, wasted resources, and team member dissatisfaction. Similarly, if a team loses sight of its goal as it proceeds, it can fail.

Ability to identify the skills needed to achieve the team's goal and to determine who among the members possesses each skill. Discussions about what skills are needed to reach the team's goal and who among the team's members has relevant skills can be difficult, especially if some members are hesitant to speak or are unrealistic about their capabilities. Failure to correctly identify relevant capabilities, to appropriately match those capabilities with tasks, or to identify capabilities requiring development or practice can result in wasted effort.

Ability to identify one's own and others' behavior styles and to coordinate them to benefit team performance. Team members' behavior styles influence how tasks are performed and how members interact. Failure of the team to acknowledge that each member has a behavior style and that these unique styles must be coordinated or synchronized, can lead to conflicts that may undermine team performance.

AS THE TEAM WORKS (THROUGHPUT PROCESS)

Ability to use the planning process to design an efficient, mutually agreed-on path to the team's goal. This is strategy development. Teams are often tempted to begin performing tasks before undertaking careful planning of the path to be taken to reach their goals. Planning enables a team to examine alternative paths and to select the best one. It also enables all members to understand, to participate in selecting, and to agree on the path the team will follow. Failure to plan can result in missteps, wasted effort, and often failure.

Ability to select a team leader best suited to facilitate the team's goal achievement process. Selecting an effective team leader requires that a team discuss the qualities it needs in its leader and which member has those qualities. Some teams resist choosing a leader. Inexperienced teams, especially, need someone to focus and facilitate team activities. Without a leader, a team's activities can become disorganized and misdirected.

Ability to design team tasks that contribute maximally to achieving the team's goal. Team tasks can be designed in a variety of ways. In selecting tasks and deciding how to perform them, it is important for team members to understand the restraints that varying types of tasks impose on members and how to optimize the performance of chosen tasks. Failure to consider this issue can result in unexpected task constraints.

Ability to coordinate members' activities and to encourage cooperative interactions that support goal achievement. For interdependence to enhance team performance, team member activities must be carefully coordinated or, if they are incompatible, at least synchronized. An atmosphere of cooperation can assist the coordination process. Failure to appropriately coordinate member activities can result in some activities interfering with others and, hence, reducing a team's efficiency.

Ability to identify and put in place different features of social structure that enhance member interactions and improve performance. Important features of social structure include group norms or standards of behavior, roles or responsibilities accepted by members, and communication networks among members. Social structure can enhance performance if its features are well chosen. If they are inappropriate, they can diminish performance efficiency.

Ability to support other members' experiencing satisfaction from task performance and from social interactions. Satisfaction from participation in team activities is crucial for maintaining member commitment and involvement. Each team member has a responsibility for every other member's experiencing satisfaction. When one or more members fail to experience satisfaction, the team must solve that problem. Lacking satisfaction, members lose interest and performance deteriorates.

Ability to recognize and praise the contributions of other team members and to share with them credit for team accomplishments. A major contributor to team member satisfaction is members' acknowledging each other's contributions and accomplishments. Team members depend on the recognition and respect of their teammates. An important factor in member satisfaction and team cohesion is lost when those who know members' contributions best fail to recognize those contributions.

Ability to work with other team members to develop and maintain positive relationships with the team's organizational environment. A team is dependent on its organizational environment for support and continuity. Team members must be mindful of the importance of this relationship to their team's success and must address constructively issues that arise between the team and features of its environment. Failure to address problematic team–environment issues can jeopardize the environment's support for the team's needs.

Ability as a team to generate and utilize evaluation feedback required in guiding team performance. A team needs feedback about the direction and quality of its performance and about coordination of its activities. Feedback helps to maintain members' involvement and enables them to correct misdirection or to address barriers to improving performance. Feedback enables a team to improve the quality of its product. Without adequate feedback, a team can lose its way and its members can lose interest. Consequently, the team fails to reach its goal or does so at a low level of quality.

WHEN THE GOAL IS REACHED (OUTPUTS)

Ability to reach its goal, that is, to produce a product at a desired level of quality. A team produces a product to deliver to its customer. Its customer's satisfaction with the product results in rewards to the team that can affect the continuation of the team as a performing unit. Failing either to deliver its product or to achieve the expected level of quality can result in denial of rewards and even termination of the team.

Ability to develop and learn to perform as a unit. A team must develop as a team both during the process of reaching its goal and, if required, in the process of repeatedly reaching its goal. Development and learning are required for a team to improve its performance and its product. A team that does not develop and learn as a problem-solving, goal-achieving unit will find that its performance deteriorates. When this happens, the team will be viewed unfavorably by its organizational environment.

OVERALL PERFORMANCE (SYSTEM MAINTENANCE)

Ability to coordinate effectively and to perform the set of actions required to achieve its goal. The preceding list outlines actions necessary for a team to perform effectively. These must be coordinated into a team strategy. A team's members, assisted by the leader, must carry out the strategy. Not coordinating these actions appropriately can result in lost effort and reduced effectiveness, if not failure.

In contrast to an inexperienced team, a more experienced, successful team understands the routine of teamwork and the principles and actions involved. At the outset, such a team examines its goal and the resources available to it, selects a leader, initiates a planning process, and, when planning is completed to the satisfaction of all team members, proceeds along the team's chosen path to its goal, making sure that its activities are optimally coordinated and encouraging members to act interdependently. As barriers to progress arise, the team goes into a problem-solving mode to remove them and then continues along the chosen path. When one or more members make notable contributions, other members congratulate them. Along the way, the team monitors feedback from indicators previously put in place to verify that the team is moving in the desired direction and is performing at the desired level of quality. Eventually, the team reaches its goal, delivers its product to its customer, and reviews how well it has done and what the team can do to improve.

The difference between an experienced and an inexperienced team is obviously *experience*. Experience, as described in this book, involves learning how an effective team system works and what the principles are that enable such a system to work effectively. Next, it involves a certain amount of experimentation on a particular goal-achievement problem to fine-tune coordination among team members and their activities. Finally, it involves practice and a commitment to improvement to achieve and maintain a level of effectiveness that is often referred to as *high performance*.

Good luck! "Becoming a team" can be an interesting and satisfying journey!

Appendix 1

—Assessments and Exercise Documents—

This appendix contains assessments and other documents that you will need to complete selected end-of-chapter exercises.

Determining Your Social Style

Individual Feedback Notes

Bewise College Briefing and Data Sheets

Bewise College Candidate Summary Sheet

Improving Team Performance

DETERMINING YOUR SOCIAL STYLE[1]

Directions: Check the word or phrase in each set that is most like you, then turn the page to score your responses.

1.___Competitive	1.___Tries new ideas	1.___Willpower	1.___Daring
2.___Joyful	2.___Optimistic	2.___Open-minded	2.___Expressive
3.___Considerate	3.___Wants to please	3.___Cheerful	3.___Satisfied
4.___Harmonious	4.___Respectful	4.___Obliging	4.___Diplomatic
1.___Powerful	1.___Restless	1.___Unconquerable	1.___Self-reliant
2.___Good mixer	2.___Popular	2.___Playful	2.___Fun-loving
3.___Easy on others	3.___Neighborly	3.___Obedient	3.___Patient
4.___Organized	4.___Abides by rules	4.___Fussy	4.___Soft-spoken
1.___Bold	1.___Outspoken	1.___Brave	1.___Nervy
2.___Charming	2.___Companionable	2.___Inspiring	2.___Jovial
3.___Loyal	3.___Restrained	3.___Submissive	3.___Even-tempered
4.___Easily led	4.___Accurate	4.___Timid	4.___Precise
1.___Stubborn	1.___Decisive	1.___Positive	1.___Takes risks
2.___Attractive	2.___Talkative	2.___Trusting	2.___Warm
3.___Sweet	3.___Controlled	3.___Contented	3.___Willing to help
4.___Avoids	4.___Conventional	4.___Peaceful	4.___Not extreme
1.___Argumentative	1.___Original	1.___Determined	1.___Persistent
2.___Light-hearted	2.___Persuasive	2.___Convincing	2.___Lively
3.___Nonchalant	3.___Gentle	3.___Good-natured	3.___Generous
4.___Adaptable	4.___Humble	4.___Cautious	4.___Well-disciplined
1.___Forceful	1.___Assertive	1.___Aggressive	1.___Eager
2.___Admirable	2.___Confident	2.___Life-of-the-party	2.___High-spirited
3.___Kind	3.___Sympathetic	3.___Easily fooled	3.___Willing
4.___Non-resisting	4.___Tolerant	4.___Uncertain	4.___Agreeable

SCORING YOUR SOCIAL STYLE

1. Count the number of ones (1s) marked. Write that number in the space provided in the Tally Box labeled "Total 1s." Do the same with the numbers two (2), three (3), and four (4). The number of your responses should add up to 24.

2. On the first scale, draw a line through the number on the bar graph that corresponds with your total number of "ones." This marks the end line for your bar graph.

3. Beginning at the left end, shade in the space on the bar up to your end line.

4. Do the same for the second, third, and fourth bars.

5. The longest bar is your predominant style. The second longest bar is your backup style.

Tally Box		Scale			
Scale	Total 1s				
1		0 1 2 | 3 4 5 6	7 8 9 10 11	12 14 16 18	
2		0 1 2 | 3 4 5	6 7 8 9 10	11 12 14 16	
3		0 1 | 2 3 4	5 6 7 8 9	10 12 14 16	
4		0 1 | 2 3 4	5 6 7 8	9 10 12 14	
	_____ Total (equals 24)				

6. After you have completed the scoring of your assessment, review the descriptors associated with each style, provided on the next page. Also listed are companion sets of high wants for each style. Are you a **driver,** an **expressive,** an **amiable,** or an **analytical?**

(1)	(2)	(3)	(4)
Driver	**Expressive**	**Amiable**	**Analytical**
action oriented	verbal	patient	diplomatic
decisive	motivating	loyal	accurate
a problem	enthusiastic	sympathetic	conscientious
direct	gregarious	a team person	a fact finder
assertive	convincing	relaxed	systematic
demanding	emotional	mature	logical
a risk taker	impulsive	organized	conventional
forceful	generous	questioning	analytical
adventuresome	influential	supportive	sensitive
competitive	charming	stable	controlled
self-reliant	confident	considerate	orderly
independent	inspiring	empathetic	precise
determined	dramatic	persevering	disciplined
an agitator	optimistic	trusting	deliberate
results oriented	animated	congenial	cautious

High Wants

challenges	social recognition	guarantees	high standards
authority	freedom from details	security	details
freedom from controls	to be with people	appreciation	perfection
options	provide service	quality control	traditional
	group activities	specialization	procedures

INDIVIDUAL FEEDBACK NOTES

Team Member Name: _____

Boat Parts Assigned to Team Member:

_____, _____, _____

_____, _____, _____

_____, _____, _____

I wish you would **start** _____

_____

_____

_____

_____

I wish you would **stop** _____

_____

_____

_____

_____

I wish you would **continue** _____

_____

_____

_____

_____

One thing I really **value** about you is _____

_____

_____

_____

_____

INDIVIDUAL FEEDBACK NOTES

Team Member Name: _____

Boat Parts Assigned to Team Member:

_____, _____, _____

_____, _____, _____

_____, _____, _____

I wish you would **start** _____

_____

_____

_____

_____

I wish you would **stop** _____

_____

_____

_____

_____

I wish you would **continue** _____

_____

_____

_____

_____

One thing I really **value** about you is _____

_____

_____

_____

_____

INDIVIDUAL FEEDBACK NOTES

Team Member Name: _____

Boat Parts Assigned to Team Member:

_____, _____, _____

_____, _____, _____

_____, _____, _____

I wish you would **start** _____

_____

_____

_____

_____

I wish you would **stop** _____

_____

_____

_____

_____

I wish you would **continue** _____

_____

_____

_____

_____

One thing I really **value** about you is _____

_____

_____

_____

_____

INDIVIDUAL FEEDBACK NOTES

Team Member Name: _____

Boat Parts Assigned to Team Member:

_____, _____, _____

_____, _____, _____

_____, _____, _____

I wish you would **start** _____

_____

_____

_____

_____

I wish you would **stop** _____

_____

_____

_____

_____

I wish you would **continue** _____

_____

_____

_____

_____

One thing I really **value** about you is _____

_____

_____

_____

_____

INDIVIDUAL FEEDBACK NOTES

Team Member Name: _____

Boat Parts Assigned to Team Member:

_____, _____, _____

_____, _____, _____

_____, _____, _____

I wish you would **start** _____

_____

_____

_____

_____

I wish you would **stop** _____

_____

_____

_____

_____

I wish you would **continue** _____

_____

_____

_____

_____

One thing I really **value** about you is _____

_____

_____

_____

_____

INDIVIDUAL FEEDBACK NOTES

Team Member Name: _____

Boat Parts Assigned to Team Member:

_____, _____, _____

_____, _____, _____

_____, _____, _____

I wish you would **start** _____

_____

_____

_____

_____

I wish you would **stop** _____

_____

_____

_____

_____

I wish you would **continue** _____

_____

_____

_____

_____

One thing I really **value** about you is _____

_____

_____

_____

_____

BEWISE COLLEGE[2]

Briefing and Data Sheet I

- This is the first meeting of your team to select a Bewise president.
- As a representative of one of the five subgroups: college board members, alumni, administrators, faculty, and students of the Bewise community, you have certain data given below.
- Assume that there is one solution.
- There must be substantial agreement among your team that the problem has been solved.
- You are to work on the problem as a team.

Data

Your team is a committee consisting of college board members, alumni, administrators, faculty, and students of Bewise College. Your committee has been authorized by the Board of Regents to select a new president for the college from among a list of candidates. Each of the represented groups has its own list of requirements for the new president. Insofar as possible, your committee is pledged to select a candidate who meets these requirements.

Bewise College was established in 1969. It is located in the heart of an industrial city with a population of about 100,000. In addition to a standard liberal arts curriculum, Bewise College students can receive college credit for work and learning experiences outside the college. There is only one other college in the same city, which is the smallest college in the state, and, until 1984, all students attending it were African-American.

The new president faces a series of challenges. The board of trustees wants a president who can raise money to support the college. The college is now in a desperate financial position—it has been losing money for the past two years. It may have to close if it cannot balance its budget. The college administrators want a president with administrative experience. The college is making budget cuts that will require a strong and experienced administrator to orchestrate.

BEWISE COLLEGE

Briefing and Data Sheet II

- This is the first meeting of your team to select a Bewise president.
- As a representative of one of the five subgroups: college board members, alumni, administrators, faculty, and students of the Bewise community, you have certain data given below.
- Assume that there is one solution.
- There must be substantial agreement among your team that the problem has been solved.
- You are to work on the problem as a team.

Data

Your team is a committee consisting of college board members, alumni, administrators, faculty, and students of Bewise College. Your committee has been authorized by the Board of Regents to select a new president for the college from among a list of candidates. Each of the represented groups has its own list of requirements for the new president. Insofar as possible, your committee is pledged to select a candidate who meets these requirements.

Bewise College was established in 1969. It is located in the heart of an industrial city with a population of about 100,000. In addition to a standard liberal arts curriculum, Bewise College students can receive college credit for work and learning experiences outside the college. Within the state, only Brown College, Samuels College, and Holubec College are larger, which makes Bewise one of the largest colleges in the state. Samuels College is attended primarily by students from wealthy families. Andrews is the smallest college in the state.

The new president faces a series of challenges. The board of trustees wants a president who can be effective in public relations, creating a positive image of the college within the community, state, and nation. Public relations primarily depend on the president's ability to make powerful public speeches to a wide variety of groups and organizations. The college administrators want an experienced administrator as president. They are very concerned about hiring a president who will not be a competent administrator. The college is launching a comprehensive assessment of the faculty's teaching performance. Administrative experience is needed to manage such a program.

BEWISE COLLEGE

Briefing and Data Sheet III

- This is the first meeting of your team to select a Bewise president.
- As a representative of one of the five subgroups: college board members, alumni, administrators, faculty, and students of the Bewise community, you have certain data given below.
- Assume that there is one solution.
- There must be substantial agreement among your team that the problem has been solved.
- You are to work on the problem as a team.

Data

Your team is a committee consisting of college board members, alumni, administrators, faculty, and students of Bewise College. Your committee has been authorized by the Board of Regents to select a new president for the college from among a list of candidates. Each of the represented groups has its own list of requirements for the new president. Insofar as possible, your committee is pledged to select a candidate who meets these requirements.

Bewise College was established in 1969. It is located in the heart of an industrial city with a population of about 100,000. In addition to a standard liberal arts curriculum, Bewise College students can receive college credit for work and learning experiences outside the college. The students attending Bewise are primarily minority group members, working-class and lower-income students, the elderly, and dropouts from other colleges and universities.

The new president faces a series of challenges. The faculty wants a president who has teaching experience, because they believe it will make the president sympathetic to the problems of the faculty. In addition, they see the need for a president who comes from a background that would provide insights into the types of students attending Bewise College. They, therefore, want a president with an education degree who can judge the teaching ability of faculty and insist on improvements.

BEWISE COLLEGE

Briefing and Data Sheet IV

- This is the first meeting of your team to select a Bewise president.

- As a representative of one of the five subgroups: college board members, alumni, administrators, faculty, and students of the Bewise community, you have certain data given below.

- Assume that there is one solution.

- There must be substantial agreement among your team that the problem has been solved.

- You are to work on the problem as a team.

Data

Your team is a committee consisting of college board members, alumni, administrators, faculty, and students of Bewise College. Your committee has been authorized by the Board of Regents to select a new president for the college from among a list of candidates. Each of the represented groups has its own list of requirements for the new president. Insofar as possible, your committee is pledged to select a candidate who meets these requirements.

Bewise College was established in 1969. It is located in the heart of an industrial city with a population of about 100,000. In addition to a standard liberal arts curriculum, Bewise College students can receive college credit for work and learning experiences outside the college. The faculty consists primarily of young, and dedicated, but inexperienced instructors. Because universities are always larger than colleges, Bewise is smaller than the nearby State University, but is growing rapidly.

The new president faces a series of challenges. Faculty members are upset with the difficulty of teaching students at Bewise College and are dissatisfied with their unresponsiveness. They, therefore, want a president who has experience in working with the types of students who attend Bewise College. The students have stated that the only qualification they will recognize as valid for judging faculty teaching ability is a president with a degree in education. Students also see the necessity of having a president who comes from a background that would provide insights into the types of students attending Bewise College.

BEWISE COLLEGE

Briefing and Data Sheet V

- This is the first meeting of your team to select a Bewise president.
- As a representative of one of the five subgroups: college board members, alumni, administrators, faculty, and students of the Bewise community, you have certain data given below.
- Assume that there is one solution.
- There must be substantial agreement among your team that the problem has been solved.
- You are to work on the problem as a team.

Data

Your team is a committee consisting of college board members, alumni, administrators, faculty, and students of Bewise College. Your committee has been authorized by the Board of Regents to select a new president for the college from among a list of candidates. Each of the represented groups has its own list of requirements for the new president. Insofar as possible, your committee is pledged to select a candidate who meets these requirements.

Bewise College was established in 1969. It is located in the heart of an industrial city with a population of about 100,000. In addition to a standard liberal arts curriculum, Bewise College students can receive college credit for work and learning experiences outside the college. Since its founding, Bewise has recruited an increasingly diverse student body.

The new president faces a series of challenges. The college administration is very much afraid of a president who will not be a competent administrator. Students are dissatisfied with faculty teaching, and faculty members are dissatisfied with student unresponsiveness to their teaching. Alumni, who are very dedicated to the college, want to contribute to Bewise but do not like high-pressure fund-raising appeals. Alumni want an effective fund-raiser who does not use high-pressure techniques.

Bewise College Candidate Summary Sheet

Name: David Wolcott

Education: Graduated from Andrews College in liberal arts in 1982; master of education in English from Winfield University in 1984; doctorate in political science from Winfield University in 1993.

Employment: Instructor in English at Winfield University, 1984–1988; taught political science at James University, 1988–1997; representative in state legislature, 1990–1992; chairman of the department of political science at James University, 1995–1999; dean of students at James University, 1999 to the present.

Other: Is well known for his scholarship and intelligence.

Name: Roger Thornton

Education: Graduated from Samuels College in science in 1975; master of education in chemistry from Smith University in 1982; doctorate in administration from Smith University in 1986.

Employment: High school chemistry teacher, 1982–1989; high school principal, 1989–1996; school superintendent, 1996 to the present.

Other: Very innovative and efficient administrator; very successful political speaker (the superintendent of schools is elected in his district); his father is vice president of a large bank.

Name: Edythe Constable

Education: Graduated from Brown College with a degree in liberal arts in 1985; master's in accounting from Smith University in 1990; doctorate in administration from Smith University in 1998.

Employment: Insurance agent, 1985–1990; certified public accountant, 1990–1998; vice president of finance, Williams College, 1998 to the present.

Other: Taught accounting in night school for eight years; volunteer director of a community center in a lower-class neighborhood for four years; was highly successful in raising money for the community center; has a competing job offer from a public relations firm for which she has worked part time for two years.

Name: Frank Pierce

Education: Graduated from Smith University with a degree in industrial arts in 1988; master of education in mathematics from Smith University in 1991; doctorate in administration from State University in 1997.

Employment: Neighborhood worker, 1988–1991; coordinator of parent–volunteer program for school system, 1991–1995; assistant superintendent for community relations, 1995 to the present.

Other: Has written training program for industrial education.

Name: Helen Johnson

Education: Graduated from Brown College with a degree in social studies education in 1986; master of education in social studies from Brown College in 1990.

Employment: Taught basic academic skills in a neighborhood center run by the school system, 1986–1990; chairperson of the student teaching program, Smith University, 1990–1994; dean of students, Smith University, 1996–2000; vice president for community relations and scholarship fund development, Smith University, 2000 to the present; frequently asked to give speeches about Smith University throughout the state.

Other: Grew up in one of the worst slums in the state; has written one book and several scholarly articles. Given award for fund-raising effectiveness. She is especially skillful using soft-sell fund-raising tactics.

Name: Keith Clement

Education: Graduated with a degree in biology education from Mulholland College in 1987; master in administration from Mulholland College in 1989.

Employment: Biology teacher in high school, 1986–1992; consultant in fund-raising, public relations firm, 1992 to the present.

Other: Is recognized as one of the leading fund-raisers in the state; entertaining speaker; has written a book on teaching working-class students; extensive volunteer work in adult education.

BEWISE COLLEGE PROBLEM: SOLUTION

Name	Background	Education Degree(s)	Teaching	Public Relations	Fund-Raising	Administration
David Wolcott*	Ethnic	Master's	13 years	None	None	8 years
Roger Thornton	Upper-class family	Master's	7 years	9 years, politics	None	16 years
Edythe Constable	Community center director	Master's	8 years	2 years	4 years	7 years
Frank Pierce	Neighborhood center worker, community relations	BA, Master's	None	14 years	None	14 years
Helen Johnson**	Childhood in low income neighborhood	BA, Master's	4 years	5 years	2 years, soft-sell tactics	15 years
Keith Clement	Volunteer work, author of book	BA	5 years	13 years	10 years	None

* Andrews College is the smallest college in the state and had a completely black student body in 1982.

** All candidates but Helen Johnson are disqualified because, as this table indicates, they lack one of the qualifications outlined in the data sheets.

Table of Contents

General Instructions:

Step 1. Complete the team assessment questionnaire, beginning on the next page, following the instructions on the questionnaire. Please respond to all questions.

Step 2. Review responses under each of the questionnaire's nine areas and follow the instructions on the Member Rankings form.

Step 3. When each team member has completed the Member Rankings form, the team as a whole is to discuss each member's rankings and develop a team ranking on the Team Rankings form.

TEAM FUNCTIONING AND PERFORMANCE ASSESSMENT

Instructions: The statements that follow are designed to help your team evaluate specific sub-areas of team functioning that contribute to overall team performance. This assessment is intended to provide you and your fellow team members an opportunity, both individually and as a team, to identify areas that need to be improved. This, in turn, can enable your team to develop a strategy for improvement. It is important for your responses to be as objective and realistic as possible.

The statements are grouped according to subareas of team functioning. The subareas are labeled in **bold type.** Under each label is a set of statements that describe the subarea in more detail.

Responses to these statements are to be simply "true" or "false." Circle the response **T** if the statement is true or mostly true as it applies to you, your team's members, or to your team as a whole. Circle the response **F** if the statement is false or mostly false as it applies to your team, its members, or to you. It is important that you give as objective and realistic responses as you can. Only then will the information be useful to your team as a basis for improvement. Work as rapidly as possible. Your first response is likely to be the more accurate. Please do not skip any items.

TEAM FUNCTIONING AND PERFORMANCE ASSESSMENT

Clarity of Path to Goal

T F 1. Our team is clear about the steps required to achieve our goal.

T F 2. Our team plans inadequately before beginning tasks to achieve our goal.

T F 3. Our team members cooperate on tasks required to reach our goal.

T F 4. Members seek feedback about our team progress toward our goal.

T F 5. Team members often help each other to reach our team's goal.

T F 6. Our team often begins tasks before members are clear about their parts.

T F 7. Some members are not committed to working to achieve our team's goal.

T F 8. Some of our team members are willing to let others perform their tasks.

T F 9. Our team coordinates members' activities in ways that help to achieve our goal.

T F 10. Recognition of member contributions is important to our team's activities.

T F 11. Poor communication is a barrier to our team's achieving its goal.

T F 12. Our team members disagree about the steps required to achieve our goal.

Involvement and Commitment

T F 13. Each member completes his or her responsibilities.

T F 14. Some members do not follow our team's values and operating principles.

T F 15. Team responsibilities are not shared equally by the team's members.

T F 16. Each member of our team is comfortable taking the lead.

T F 17. Each member of our team is committed to achieving the team's goal.

T F 18. Some members of our team lack good problem-solving skills.

T F 19. Each member feels responsible for improving team performance.

T F 20. My team members take their responsibilities seriously.

T F 21. Once our team reaches a decision all members feel responsible for implementing it.

T F 22. Our members fully cooperate in all team activities.

T F 23. Some members do not take their team responsibilities seriously enough.

Efficiency of Functioning

T F 24. Our team is organized to work effectively.

T F 25. My team does not have a clear picture of what it wants to become.

T F 26. Our team sets high aspirations for its performance.

T F 27. Our team meetings are inefficient.

T F 28. My team members are clear about their responsibilities.

T F 29. I feel frustrated by our team's activities.

T F 30. Our team plans well before acting.

T F 31. My team uses the most efficient procedures for getting its work done.

T F 32. Team meetings are productive.

T F 33. Our team carefully considers the skills needed before beginning a task.

T F 34. Members are concerned for our team to become more efficient.

Coordination and Cooperation

T F 35. Team members assist each other's efforts to reach the team's goal.

T F 36. Team members seldom seek to improve coordination of their activities.

T F 37. Our team members work together well.

T F 38. Our team is more concerned with satisfying members' goals than pursuing the team's goal.

T F 39. Our team members help each other learn better ways to perform our tasks.

T F 40. Team members act in ways that assist each other's actions.

T F 41. Members trust each other to do whatever promotes our team's goal achievement.

T F 42. Our team is not realistic when evaluating our performance.

T F 43. Our team's products are completed on time.

T F 44. Our team works together creatively to achieve the team's goal.

T F 45. Coordination among our team's members is poor.

Seeking and Using Feedback

T F 46. Members use evaluative feedback to decide how to improve our team's performance.

T F 47. Our team has little interest in learning how well we are performing.

T F 48. Our team seeks feedback about how well members coordinate their activities.

T F 49. My team seeks to improve the information it gathers about our team's functioning.

T F 50. Team members have little desire to evaluate their own performance.

T F 51. Our team has established rules for interaction that make us more efficient.

T F 52. Other team members seldom offer thoughtful feedback about my performance.

T F 53. Our team seeks feedback from our customer about the quality of our product.

T F 54. Our team has little need for information about our team's performance.

T F 55. Our team members desire information about the quality of our team's product.

T F 56. The feedback our team receives about its performance is not very helpful.

Barriers to Goal Achievement

T F 57. Our team can identify problems in its functioning but avoids addressing solutions.

T F 58. Our team understands that achieving high performance requires all members to contribute.

T F 59. Our team ignores conflict between team members.

T F 60. Our team does not discuss the lack of cooperation among our members.

T F 61. There are difficult problems for our team that we do not discuss.

T F 62. Our team has open discussion of members' ideas and feelings.

T F 63. Members of our team agree without considering alternatives.

T F 64. Our team is willing to address difficult decisions.

T F 65. Our team enjoys removing barriers to our team's achieving high performance.

T F 66. Our team understands that all members must work together to achieve high performance.

T F 67. Our team resolves problems that prevent our team from performing well.

Leading Team Activities

T F 68. Our team leader involves members in decision making.

T F 69. Our leader helps the team to confront performance problems.

T F 70. Our leader does not give team members recognition for their contributions.

T F 71. Our team leader helps members clarify expectations for their performance.

T F 72. Our leader shares with team members any recognition that is received.

T F 73. Our team leader does not run effective meetings.

T F 74. Our team leader helps members to coordinate their activities.

T F 75. Our team leader helps our team plan before it acts.

T F 76. Members are comfortable discussing team problems with our team leader.

T F 77. Our team leader is uncomfortable with open discussion of team problems.

T F 78. Our team has no designated leader.

Learning to Improve the Product

T F 79. Our team is gradually learning to improve our product.

T F 80. Our team's evaluation of our product is not very useful.

T F 81. Any problems with our team's product are our responsibility.

T F 82. Our team is learning how to function at an improved level of performance.

T F 83. Our team is not concerned with improving the quality of our product.

T F 84. Our team makes too many mistakes when producing our product.

T F 85. The results of our team's activities are of questionable quality.

T F 86. Our team's product is of high quality.

T F 87. Our team has learned little about how to improve the quality of our product.

T F 88. Our team feels responsible for inadequacies in our product.

T F 89. I can see how my work contributes to our team's completed product.

Recognizing and Rewarding High Performance

T F 90. I am proud of my contributions to my team's performance.

T F 91. I receive little recognition for my contributions to our team's performance.

T F 92. Most of what I do as a team member seems useless or trivial.

T F 93. I can see how my work contributes to our team's completed product.

T F 94. I often have trouble figuring out whether I am doing well or poorly.

T F 95. Our team encourages contributions from members who do not participate.

T F 96. Some members are good at helping to resolve conflicts among team members.

T F   97. I receive personal recognition when my work contributes to my team's high performance.

T F   98. My team readily recognizes member contributions to our team's high performance.

T F   99. Recognition of member accomplishments is a regular part of my team's activities.

T F 100. My contributions to our team's achievements are not acknowledged by other members.

MEMBER RANKINGS

Instructions: Each *member* should consider each area addressed in the preceding assessment and decide which areas are in need of improvement.

Step A.   Listed below are the nine areas assessed in the preceding assessment. Review your responses and rank order the areas in terms of your judgment about the area's need for improvement. Mark the area most in need of improvement a "1," the next most with a "2," and so forth until you have rank ordered all nine areas.

Topic	Ranking
Clarity of path to goal	_____
Involvement and commitment	_____
Efficiency of functioning	_____
Coordination and cooperation	_____
Seeking and using feedback	_____
Barriers to goal achievement	_____
Leading team activities	_____
Learning to improve the product	_____
Recognizing and rewarding high performance	_____

Step B.   Select the two areas most in need of improvement and specify (a) what about each area needs improvement and (b) how the needed improvement can be achieved.

Area Most in Need of Improvement: _____

_____

_____

What about this area needs improving?_____

_____

How can improvement best be achieved?_____

_____

_____

Area Next Most in Need of Improvement: _____

_____

_____

What about this area needs improving?_____

_____

How can improvement best be achieved?_____

_____

_____

TEAM RANKINGS

Instructions: The *team* should consider each member's rankings and strategies for improvement and develop a team consensus on both.

Step A. Review each team member's rankings, then rank the areas according to the *team's* consensus judgment about each area's need for improvement. Mark the area most in need of improvement a "1," the next most a "2," and so forth through all nine areas.

Topic	Ranking
Clarity of path to goal	_____
Involvement and commitment	_____
Efficiency of functioning	_____
Coordination and cooperation	_____
Seeking and using feedback	_____
Barriers to goal achievement	_____
Leading team activities	_____
Learning to improve the product	_____
Recognizing and rewarding high performance	_____

Step B. Select the two areas most in need of improvement and specify (a) what about the area most needs improvement and (b) how the needed improvement can be achieved.

Area Most in Need of Improvement: _____

_____

_____

What about this area needs improving?_____

_____

_____

How can improvement best be achieved?_____

_____

_____

Area Next Most in Need of Improvement: _____

_____

_____

What about this area needs improving?_____

_____

_____

How can improvement best be achieved?_____

_____

_____

Step C: Team Plan for Improvement.
What is your team's plan for implementing these improvements?_____

_____

_____

NOTES

1. Adapted from measure of social style provided to author by A. K. Prichard, Boeing Commercial Aircraft, Technical Fellow. The four types that result from this assessment procedure are described in H. Robbins and H. Finley (1995), *Why Teams Don't Work,* Princeton, NJ: Peterson's/Pacesetter Books, pp. 53–59.

2. Adapted from D. Johnson and F. Johnson (1987), *Joining Together: Group Theory and Group Skills,* 3e, Boston, MA: Allyn and Bacon/Pearson Education, pp. 182–188. Adapted by permission of the publisher.

Appendix 2

References

Aiken, M., & J. Hage (1968). Organizational independence and intra-organizational structure, *American Sociological Review,* 33, 912–930.

Argyle, M. (1969). *Social Interaction,* Chicago: Aldine.

Argyris, C. (1982). *Reasoning, Learning, and Action: Individual & Organizational,* San Francisco: Jossey Bass.

Argyris, C. (1993). *Knowledge for Action: A Guide to Overcoming Barriers to Organizational Change,* San Francisco: Jossey Bass.

Armstrong, S., & J. Preola (2001). Individual differences in cognitive style and their effects on task and social orientation of self-managed teams, *Small Group Research,* 32, 383–312.

Arrow, H., J. McGrath, & J. Berdahl (2000). *Small Groups as Complex Systems,* Thousand Oaks, CA: Sage.

Bales, R. (1950). *Interaction Process Analysis,* Reading, MA: Addison-Wesley.

Bales, R., & F. L. Strodbeck (1951). Phases in group problem solving, *Journal of Abnormal and Social Psychology,* 46, 485–495.

Bandura, A. (1997). *Self-Efficacy: The Exercise of Control,* New York: Freeman.

Bandura, A. (2000). The exercise of human agency through collective efficacy, *Current Directions in Psychological Science,* 9, 75–78.

Barnlund, D. (1959). A comparative study of individual, majority, and group judgment, *Journal of Abnormal and Social Psychology,* 58, 55–60.

Beauchamp, M., & S. R. Bray (2001). Role ambiguity and role conflict within interdependent teams, *Small Group Research,* 32, 133–157.

Belasco, J., & R. Steyer (1993). *The Flight of the Buffalo,* New York: Warner Books.

Bennis, W., & B. Nanus (1985). *Leaders: The Strategies for Taking Charge,* New York: Harper & Row.

Bennis, W., & H. A. Shephard (1956). A theory of group development, *Human Relations,* 9, 415–457.

Bettenhausen, K., & J. Murnighan (1985). The emergence of norms in competitive decision-making groups, *Administrative Science Quarterly,* 30, 350–372.

Bion, W. (1961). *Experiences in Groups,* London: Tavistock/Routledge.

Blanchard, K. (1985). *SLII: A Situational Approach to Managing People,* Escondido, CA: Blanchard Training and Development.

Braaten, L. (1974–75). Developmental phases of encounter groups and related intensive groups: A critical review of models and a new proposal, *Interpersonal Development,* 5, 112–129.

Brehmer, B. (1976). Social judgment theory and the analysis of interpersonal conflict, *Psychological Bulletin,* 83, 985–1003.

Brett, J., & S. Goldberg (1983). Wildcat strikes in the bituminous coal mining industry, *Industrial and Labor Relations Review,* 32, 467–483.

Brett, J., & J. Rognes (1986). Intergroup relations in organizations, in P. S. Goodman and Associates (Eds.), *Designing Effective Work Groups,* San Francisco: Jossey Bass, pp. 202–236.

Brewer, M. (1979). In-group bias in the minimal inter-group situation: A cognitive-motivational analysis, *Psychological Bulletin,* 86, 307–324.

Brown, T., & C. Miller (2000). Communication networks in task performing groups, *Small Group Research,* 31, 131–157.

Campbell, J. (1977). On the nature of organizational effectiveness, in P. S. Goodman, J. M. Pennings, & Associates (Eds.), *New Perspectives on Organizational Effectiveness,* San Francisco: Jossey Bass, pp. 13–55.

Campion, M., E. Papper, & G. Medsker (1996), Relations between work team characteristics and effectiveness: A replication and extension, *Personnel Psychology,* 49, 429–452.

Cannon-Bowers, J., R. Oser, & D. L. Flanagan (1992). Work teams in industry: A selected review and proposed framework, in R. W. Swezey & E. Salas (Eds.), *Teams: Their Training and Performance,* Norwood, NJ: Ablex, pp. 355–377.

Cannon-Bowers, J., E. Salas, & C. Converse (1993). Shared mental models in expert team decision-making, in N. J. Castellan (Ed.), *Individual and Group Decision-Making,* Mahwah, NJ: Erlbaum, pp. 221–246.

Carless, S., & C. DePaola (2000). The measurement of cohesion in work teams, *Small Group Research,* 31, 71–88.

Carnevale, P. (1986). Strategic choices by third parties: A theory of dispute resolution, in R. J. Lewicki, B. H. Sheppard, and M. H. Bazerman (Eds.), *Research on Negotiations in Organizations,* Greenwich, CT: JAI Press.

Cartwright, D., & A. Zander (1960). Individual motives and group goals: Introduction, in D. Cartwright & A. Zander (Eds.), *Group Dynamics: Research and Theory,* Evanston, IL: Row Peterson, pp. 345–369.

Chemers, M. (2000). Leadership research and theory: A functional integration, *Group Dynamics,* 4, 27–43.

Choi, J. (2002). External activities and team effectiveness: Review and theoretical development, *Small Group Research,* 33, 181–208.

Cohen, S. (1994). Designing effective self-managing work teams, in H. M. Beyerlein & D. A. Johnson (Eds.), *Advances in Interdisciplinary Studies of Work Teams: Theories of Self-Managed Work Teams,* London: JAI, 67–102.

Cohen, S., & D. R. Denison (1990). Flight attendant teams, in J. R. Hackman (Ed.), *Groups that Work (and Those that Don't).* San Francisco: Sage, pp. 382–397.

Cohen, S., R. Mermelstein, T. Kamarck, & H. M. Hoberman (1985). Measuring functional components of social support, in I. G. Sarason &

B. R. Sarason (Eds.), *Social Support: Theory, Research and Applications,* The Hague, The Netherlands: Martimes Nijhoof, pp. 73–94.

Collins, J., & J. Porras (1994). *Built to Last: Successful Habits of Visionary Companies,* New York: Harper Business.

Colman, M., & A. V. Carron (2001). The nature of norms in individual sports teams, *Small Group Research,* 32, 206–222.

Connolly, C. (1996). Communication: Getting to the heart of the matter, *Management Development Review,* 9, 37–40.

Crano, W. (2000). Milestones in the psychological analysis of social influence, *Group Dynamics: Theory, Research and Practice,* 4, 68–80.

Deutsch, M. (1949). A theory of cooperation and competition, *Human Relations,* 2, 129–152.

Deutsch, M. (1975). Equity, equality, and need: What determines which value will be used as a basis of distributive justice? *Journal of Social Issues,* 31, 137–149.

Deutsch, M. (1979). Education and distributive justice: Some reflections on grading systems, *American Psychologist,* 34, 391–401.

Diehl, H., & W. Stroeba (1991). Productivity loss in idea-generating groups, *Journal of Personality and Social Psychology,* 61, 392–403.

Diesing, P. (1962). *Reason in Society,* Urbana: University of Illinois Press.

Dion, K. (2000). Group cohesion: From "field of forces" to multidimensional construct, *Group Dynamics,* 4, 7–26.

Driskell, J., & E. Salas (1992). Can you study real teams in contrived settings? The value of small group research in understanding teams, in R. Swezy & E. Salas (Eds.), *Teams, Their Training and Performance,* Norwood, NJ: Ablex, pp. 117–119.

Eisenstat R. (1990). Fairfield Coordinating Group, in R. Hackman (Ed.), *Teams That Work (And Those That Don't),* San Francisco: Jossey Bass, pp.19–35.

Emerson, R.(1962). Power dependence relations, *American Sociological Review,* 27, 31–41.

Erikson, E. (1950). *Childhood and Society,* New York: Norton.

Festinger, L. (1954). A theory of social comparison processes, *Human Relations,* 7, 117–140.

Fiedler, F. (1967). *A Theory of Leadership Effectiveness,* New York: McGraw-Hill.

Fisher, R., & W. Ury (1981). *Getting to Yes,* New York: Penguin.

Fishman, C. (1996, April/May). Whole Foods Is All Teams, *Fast Company,* pp. 103ff.

Foels, R., J. Driskell, B. Mullen, & E. Salas (2000). The effects of democratic leadership on group member satisfaction, *Small Group Research*, 31, 676–701.

Gammage, K., A. Carron, & P. Estabrooks (2001). Team cohesion and individual productivity, *Small Group Research*, 32, 3–18.

Gersick, C. (1990). The bankers, in J. R. Hackman (Ed.), *Groups that Work (and Those that Don't)*. San Francisco: Sage, pp.112–125.

Gersick, C. (1990). The students, in J. R. Hackman (Ed.), *Groups that Work (and Those that Don't)*. San Francisco: Sage, pp. 89–111.

Gigone, D., & R. Hastie (1993). The common knowledge effect: Information sharing and group judgment, *Journal of Personality and Social Psychology*, 65, 959–974.

Gladstein, D. (1984). Groups in context: A model of task group effectiveness, *Administrative Science Quarterly*, 29, 499–517.

Glass, D., & J. Singer (1972). *Urban Stress*, New York: Academic Press.

Goldratt, E. (1986). *The Goal*, Croton-on-Hudson, NY: North River Press.

Goleman, D. (1997). *Emotional Intelligence*, New York: Bantam Books

Gresor, C., & R. Drazin (1997). Equifinality: Functional equivalents in organizational design, *Academy of Management Review*, 22, 403–428.

Hackman, J. (1983). Group influences on individuals, in M. Dunnett (Ed). *Handbook of Industrial and Organizational Psychology*, New York: Wiley, pp. 1455–1525.

Hackman, J. (1987). The design of work teams, in J. W. Lorsch (Ed.), *Handbook of Organizational Behavior*, Englewood Cliffs, NJ: Prentice Hall, pp. 315–342.

Hackman, J. R. (1990). *Groups that Work (and Those that Don't): Creating a Foundation for Effective Teamwork*, San Francisco: Jossey Bass.

Hage, J. (1983). Communication and coordination, in S. M. Shortell & A. K. Kalunzy (Eds.), *Health Care Management*, New York: Wiley.

Hammer, M.& J. Champy (1993). *Re-Engineering the Corporation*, New York: Harper Collins.

Hare, P. (1992). *Groups, Teams, and Social Interactions: Theories and Applications*, New York: Praeger.

Herrenkohl, R., G. T. Judson, & J. A. Heffner (1999). Defining and measuring employee empowerment, *The Journal of Applied Behavioral Science*, 35, 373–389.

Hershey, P., & K. Blanchard (1988). *Management of Organizational Behavior: Utilizing Human Resources*, Englewood Cliffs, NJ: Prentice Hall.

Hoerr, J., M. Pollock, & D. Whiteside (1986, September). Management discovers the human side of automation, *Business Week*, pp. 70–76.

Hogan, R., G. Curphy, & J. Hogan (1994). What we know about leadership, *American Psychologist*, 49, 493–504.

Homans, G. (1958). Group factors in worker productivity in E. Maccoby, T. Newcomb, & E. Hartley (Eds.), *Readings in Social Psychology*, New York: Holt, Rinehart and Winston, pp. 583–595.

Homans, G. (1961). *Social Behavior: Its Elementary Forms*, New York: Harcourt Brace.

House, J. (1981). *Work, Stress and Social Support*, Reading, MA: Addison-Wesley.

Iaffaldano, M., & P. M. Muchinsky (1985). Job satisfaction and job performance: A meta-analysis. *Psychological Bulletin*, 97(2), 251–273.

Jackson, S., & M. N. Ruderman (Eds.), (1995). *Diversity in Work Teams: Research Paradigm for a Changing Workplace*, Washington, D.C.: American Psychological Association.

Johnson, D. (1986). *Reaching Out*, 3rd ed., Englewood Cliffs, NJ: Prentice Hall.

Johnson, D. W., & F. P. Johnson (1987). *Joining Together: Group Theory and Group Skills*, Englewood Cliffs, NJ: Prentice Hall.

Johnson, D., & R. Johnson (1974). Instructional goal structures: Cooperative competitive, and individualistic? *Review of Educational Research*, 49, 51–70.

Johnson, D., & R. Johnson (1981). Effects of cooperative, competitive and individualistic goal achievement: A meta-analysis, *Psychological Bulletin*, 89, 47–72.

Johnson, D., & R. Johnson (1989). *Cooperation and Competition: Theory and Research*, Edina, MN: Interaction Book Company.

Jones, S. (1997). Team performance measurement: Theoretical and applied issues, in M. Beyerlein & D. Johnson (Eds.), *Advances in Interdisciplinary Studies of Work Teams*, Vol. 4, London: JAI Press, pp. 115–139.

Jordan, P., & A. Troth (2002). Emotional intelligence and conflict resolution: Implications for human resource development, in *Advances in Developing Human Resources*, Vol. 4, 62–79.

Kaagan, S. (1999). *Leadership Games*, Thousand Oaks, CA: Sage.

Kahn, R. (1977). Organizational effectiveness: An overview, in P.S. Goodman, J. M. Pennings, & Associates (Eds.), *New Perspectives on Organizational Effectiveness*, San Francisco: Jossey Bass, pp. 13–55.

Kanigel, R. (1997). *The One Best Way: Frederick Winslow Taylor and the Enigma of Efficiency*, New York: Viking.

Katz, D., & R. Kahn (1966). *The Social Psychology of Organizations*, New York: Wiley.

Keirsey, D., & M. Bates (1984). *Please Understand Me: Character and Temperament Types*, Del Mar, CA: Gnosology Books.

Ketchum, L., & E. Trist (1992). *All Teams Are Not Created Equal: How Employee Empowerment Really Works*, Newbury Park, CA: Sage.

Klein, J. (1994). Maintaining expertise in multi-skilled teams. In M. M. Beyerlein & D. A. Johnson (Eds.), *Advances in Interdisciplinary Studies of Work Teams: Theories of Self-Managed Work Teams*, London: JAI Press, pp. 145–166.

Komorita, S., & C. Parks (1994). *Social Dilemmas*, Madison, WI: Brown & Benchmarks.

Krakauer, J. (1997). *Into Thin Air: A Personal Account of the Mount Everest Disaster*, New York: Villard.

Lanzetta, J., & T. B. Roby (1956). Effects of work-group structure and certain task variables on group performance. *Journal of Abnormal and Social Psychology*, 53, 307–314.

Latane, B., K. Williams, & S. Harkins (1979). Many hands make light the work: The causes and consequences of social loafing, *Journal of Personality and Social Psychology*, 37, 822–832.

Lawler, E., S. Mohrman, & G. Ledford (1995). *Creating High Performance Organizations: Practices and Results of Employee Involvement and Total Quality Management in Fortune 1000 Companies.* San Francisco: Jossey Bass.

Lawrence, P., & J. Lorsch (1967). *Organization and Environment*, Boston: Graduate School of Business Administration, Harvard University.

Leavitt, H. (1951). Some effects of certain communication patterns on group performance. *Journal of Abnormal and Social Psychology*, 46, 38–50.

Leonard, H., & A. Freedman (2000). From scientific management through fun and games to high-performing teams: A historical perspective on consulting in team-based organization, *Consulting Psychology Journal*, 52, 3–19.

Lewin, K., R. Lippitt, & R. White (1939). Patterns of aggressive behavior in experimentally created social climates, *Journal of Social Psychology*, 10, 271–299.

Lightall, F. F. (1991, February). Launching the space shuttle *Challenger*: Disciplinary deficiencies in the analyses of engineering data, *IEEE Transactions on Engineering Management*, 38, 63–74.

Likert, R. (1961). *New Patterns of Management*, New York: McGraw-Hill.

Maclean, J. N. (1999). *Fire on the Mountain*, New York: William Morrow.

March, J., & H. A. Simon (1958). *Organizations*, New York: Wiley.

Maslow, A. (1970). *Motivation and Personality*, 2nd ed., New York: Harper & Row.

Mathieu, J., T. S. Heffner, G. Goodwin, E. Salas, & J. Cannon-Bowers (2000). The influence of shared mental models on team process and performance, *Journal of Applied Psychology*, 85, 275–283.

McCann, J., & J. Galbraith (1981). Interdepartmental relations, in P. C. Nystrom & W. H. Starbuck (Eds.), *Handbook of Organizational Design,* New York: Oxford University Press.

McGrath, J. (1984). *Groups: Interaction and Performance,* Englewood Cliffs, NJ: Prentice Hall.

Messick, D., & W. Liebrand (1995). Individual heuristics and the dynamics of cooperation in large groups, *Psychological Review,* 102, 131–145.

Morgan, B., & D. Lassiter (1992). Team composition and staffing, in R. W. Swezey & E. Salas (Eds.), *Teams: Their Training and Performance,* Norwood, NJ: Ablex, pp. 75–100.

Murray, H. (1938). *Explorations in Personality,* New York: Oxford University Press.

Myers, D., & H. Lamn (1976). The group polarizing phenomenon, *Psychological Bulletin,* 83, pp. 602–627.

Nichols, M. (1995). *The Lost Art of Listening,* New York: Guilford Press.

Northouse, P. (2001). *Leadership: Theory and Practice,* 2nd ed., Thousand Oaks, CA: Sage.

Paulus, P., T. Larey, & M. Dzindolet (2001). Creativity in groups and teams, in M. E. Turner (Ed). *Groups at Work,* Mahwah, NJ: Erlbaum, pp. 319–338.

Penner, L., & J. P. Crayer (1992). The weakest link: The performance of individual team members, in R. W. Swezey & E. Salas (Eds.), *Teams: Their Training and Performance,* Norwood, NJ: Ablex, pp. 57–73.

Peterson, E., & L. Thompson (1997). Negotiation teamwork: The impact of information distribution and accountability on performance depends on the relationship among team members, *Organizational Behavior and Human Decision Processes,* 72, 364–383.

Prince, C., T. Chidester, C. Bowers, & J. Cannon-Bowers (1992). Aircrew coordination: Achieving teamwork in the cockpit, in R. Swezey & E. Salas (Eds.), *Teams: Their Training and Performance,* Norwood, NJ: Ablex, pp. 340–342.

Nutt, R. C. (1984). *Planning Methods for Health and Related Organizations,* New York: Wiley.

Ray, D., & H. Bronson (1995). *Teaming Up,* New York: McGraw-Hill, pp. 144–145.

Robbins, H., & M. Finley (1995). *Why Teams* Work, Princeton: Peterson's/ Pacesetter Books.

Rychlak, J. (1965). The similarity, compatibility, or incompatibility of needs in interpersonal selection. *Journal of Personality and Social Psychology,* 2, 334–340.

Salas, E., C. Bowers, & E. Edens (2001). *Improving Teamwork in Organizations,* Mahwah, NJ: Erlbaum.

Salas, E., T. Dickinson, S. Converse, & S. Tannenbaum (1992). Toward an understanding of team performance and training, in R. W. Swezey & E. Salas (Eds.), *Teams: Their Training and Performance*, Norwood, NJ: Ablex, pp. 3–29.

Schachter, S. (1951). Deviation, rejection, and communication, *Journal of Abnormal and Social Psychology*, 46, 190–207.

Schachter, S. (1959). *The Psychology of Affiliation*, Stanford, CA: Stanford University Press.

Schwortzman, H. (1989). *Meetings: Gatherings in Organizations and Communities*, New York: Plenum.

Seashore, S. (1983). A framework for an integrated model of organizational effectiveness, in K. S. Cameron & D. A. Whetton (Eds.), *Organizational Effectiveness: A Comparison of Multiple Models*, New York: Academic Press, pp. 55–70.

Senge, P. (1990). *The Fifth Discipline*, New York: Doubleday.

Shapiro, D., R. Drieghe, & J. Brett (1985). Mediator behavior and the outcome of mediation, *Journal of Social Issues*, 41, 101–114.

Shaw, M. (1964). Communication networks, in L. Berkowitz (Ed.), *Advances in Experimental Social Psychology*, Vol. 1, New York: Academic Press, pp. 111–147.

Sheppard, B. (1983). Managers as inquisitors: Some lessons from the law, in M. H. Bazerman & R. J. Lewicki (Eds.), *Negotiating in Organizations*, Beverly Hills, CA: Sage.

Smith, R. & F. L. Smoll (1997). Coaching the coaches: Youth sports as a scientific and applied behavioral setting, *Current Directions in Psychological Science*, 6(1), 16–21.

Steiner, I. (1972). *Group Process and Productivity*, New York: Academic Press.

Steiner, I., & N. A Rajaratnam (1961). A model for the comparison of individual and group performance scores, *Behavioral Science*, 6, 142–148.

Stogdill, R. (1959). *Individual Behavior and Group Achievement*, New York: Oxford University Press.

Stroebe, W., M. Diehl, & G. Abakoumkin (1996). Social compensation and the Kohler effect: Toward a theoretical explanation of motivation gains in group productivity, in E. Witte & J. H. Davis (Eds.), *Understanding Group Behavior*, Vol. 2, Mahwah, NJ: Erlbaum, pp. 37–65.

Suls, J., R. Martin, & L. Wheeler (2002). Social comparison: Why, with whom, and with what effect? *Current Directions in Psychological Science*, 11, 159–163.

Sundstrom, E., M. McIntyre, T. Halfhill, & H. Richards (2000). Work groups: From the Hawthorne studies to work teams of the 1990s and beyond, *Group Dynamics*, 4, 44–67.

Swezey, R., & E. Salas (1992). Guidelines for use in team training development, in R. Swezey & E. Salas (Eds.), *Teams: Their Training and Performance*, Norwood, NJ: Ablex, pp. 219–245.

Taylor, F. W. (1911). *The Principles of Scientific Management*, New York: Harper.

Tesluk, P., J. E. Mathieu, & S. J. Zaccaro (1997). Task and aggregation issues in the analysis and assessment of team performance, in M. T. Brannick, E. Salas, & C. Prince (Eds.), *Team Performance Assessment and Measurement*, Mahwah, NJ: Erlbaum, pp. 197–224.

Thibaut, J., & H. H. Kelly (1959). *The Social Psychology of Groups*, New York: John Wiley.

Thompson, L. (2000). *Making the Team: A Guide for Managers*, Upper Saddle River, NJ: Prentice Hall.

Thompson, L., & C. Fox (2001). Negotiation in and between groups in organizations, in M. E. Turner (Ed.), *Groups at Work*, Mahwah, NJ: Erlbaum, pp. 221–266.

Tisdelle, D., & J. S. St. Lawrence (1986). Interpersonal problem solving competency: Review and critique of the literature, *Clinical Psychology Review*, 6, 337–356.

Trento, J. J. (1987). *Prescription for Disaster*, New York: Crown Press.

Tuchman, B. (1965). Developmental sequence in small groups, *Psychological Bulletin*, 63, 384–399.

Tuchman, B., & M. A. C. Jensen (1977). Stages of small-group development revisited, *Groups & Organization Studies*, 2, 419–427.

Turner, M., & T. Horvitz (2001). The dilemma of threat: Group effectiveness and ineffectiveness under adversity, in M. E. Turner (Ed.), *Groups at Work*, Mahwah, NJ: Erlbaum, pp. 445–470.

Von Cranach, M. (1996). Toward a theory of the acting group, in E. Witte & J. Davis (Eds.), *Understanding Group Behavior*, Vol. 2, Mahwah, NJ: Erlbaum, pp. 147–187.

Wageman, R. (1995). Interdependence and group effectiveness, *Administrative Science Quarterly*, 40, 145–180.

Wageman, R. (2001). The meaning of interdependence, in M. E. Turner (Ed.), *Groups at Work*, Mahwah, NJ: Erlbaum, pp.197–217.

Walton, M. (1986). *The Deming Management Method*, New York: Perigee Books.

Walton, R. (1980). Establishing and maintaining high commitment work systems. In J. R. Kimberly, R. H. Miles, and Associates (Eds.), *The Organizational Life Cycle: Issues in the Creation, Transformation, and Decline of Organizations*. San Francisco: Jossey Bass.

Wellins, R., W. C. Byham, & G. R. Dixon (1994). *Inside Teams: How 20 World-Class Organizations Are Winning Through Teamwork*, San Francisco: Jossey Bass.

Womack, J., D. T. Jones, & D. Roos (1991). *The Machine that Changed the World: The Story of Lean Production*, New York: Harper.

Yeatts, D., & C. Hyten (1998). *High Performing Self-Managed Work Teams*, Thousand Oaks, CA: Sage.

Yost, C., & M. Tucker (2000). Are effective teams more emotionally intelligent? Confirming the importance of effective communication in teams, *Delta Pi Epsilon Journal*, 42, 101–109.

Zajonc, R. (1965, July 16). Social facilitation, *Science*, pp. 269–274.

Zander, A. (1979). The psychology of group process, in M. R. Rosenzweig & L. W. Porter (Eds.), *Annual Review of Psychology*, Vol. 30, Palo Alto, CA: Annual Reviews, pp. 417–451.

Zander, A. (1980). The origins and consequences of group goals, in L. Festinger (Ed.), *Retrospections on Social Psychology*, New York: Oxford University Press, pp. 205–235.

Index